Praise for *Bay of Spi*

"Mowat has a deep understanding of the sea and the natural world. His observations of the outporters are equally perceptive and provide a fascinating window into a little known corner of North America. In this tender elegy to a lost Newfoundland, Mowat shows an amused tolerance for almost everything except the human greed that has inexorably destroyed his adopted home's cultures and environment."　　　　　– *Publishers Weekly*

"Mowat reminisces about his early romance with his wife-to-be, but he's preoccupied with a larger, harder love story – his courtship, adoration and disappointments with Newfoundland at the end of the outpost era."　　　　　– *Canadian Geographic*

"This is a briny maritime tale from head to toe, with Farley and Claire finding any excuse at all to continue exploring. . . . Blessed with an endlessly curious and energetic cast of mind and an outrageously colourful personality, [Mowat] has also been gifted with a perfect life companion and a love that has endured for many decades."
　　　　　– *Quill & Quire*

"Look for Mowat's usual entertaining descriptions of geography, local customs and harrowing, or just plain bumbling, misadventures at sea. It's a fascinating look at the life of a Canadian literary icon."
　　　　　– *Outpost* magazine

"Mowat describes with sailor's envy many enchanting, exhilarating and dangerous journeys in and out of the tiniest outport villages. It is here he is at his best, telling the tales of the local people in their dialect and colour."　　　　　– Halifax *Chronicle-Herald*

FARLEY MOWAT

BAY OF SPIRITS

A LOVE STORY

McCLELLAND & STEWART

Library and Archives Canada Cataloguing in Publication

Mowat, Farley, 1921–
    Bay of spirits : a love story / Farley Mowat.

ISBN 978-0-7710-6538-5 (bound).–ISBN 978-0-7710-6505-7 (pbk.)

    1. Mowat, Farley, 1921– 2. Wheeler, Claire. 3. Newfoundland and
Labrador–Social life and customs. 4. Fishing villages–Newfoundland
and labrador–History–20th century. 5. Harbors–Newfoundland and
Labrador–History–20th century. 6. Burgeo (N.L.)–Biography.
7. Authors, Canadian (English)–20th century–Biography. I. Title.

FC2199.B86Z49 2006   971.8   C2006-902157-0

We acknowledge the financial support of the Government of Canada through
the Book Publishing Industry Development Program and that of the Government
of Ontario through the Ontario Media Development Corporation's Ontario Book
Initiative. We further acknowledge the support of the Canada Council for the
Arts and the Ontario Arts Council for our publishing program.

All photographs © Claire and Farley Mowat
Maps by Visutronx

Typeset in Berkeley Book by M&S, Toronto
Printed and bound in Canada

This book is printed on acid-free paper that is 100% recycled,
ancient-forest friendly (100% post-consumer recycled).

McClelland & Stewart Ltd.
75 Sherbourne Street
Toronto, Ontario
M5A 2P9
www.mcclelland.com

1 2 3 4 5   11 10 09 08 07

A love affair with a special woman and a special world.

Contents

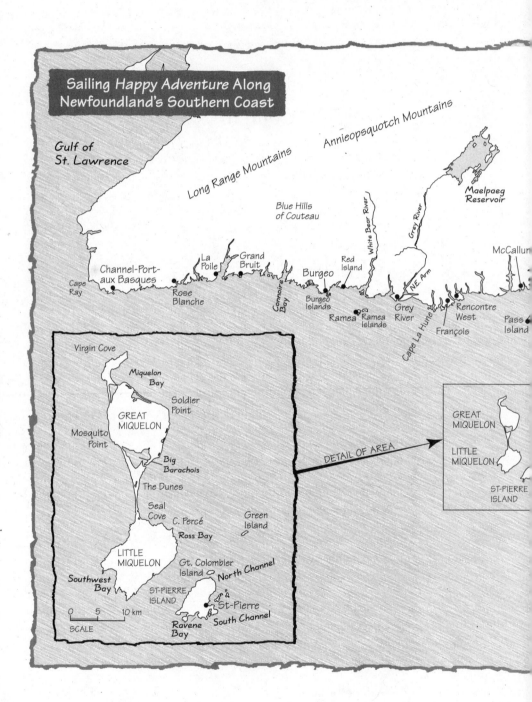

Sailing *Happy Adventure* Along Newfoundland's Southern Coast

Gulf of St. Lawrence

Annieopsquotch Mountains

Long Range Mountains

Maelpaeg Reservoir

Blue Hills of Couteau

White Bear River

Grey River

La Poile

Grand Bruit

Burgeo

Red Island

McCallum

Channel-Port-aux Basques

Cape Ray

Rose Blanche

Connoire Bay

Burgeo Islands

Ramea

Ramea Islands

Grey River

NE Arm

Cape La Hune

François

Rencontre West

Pass Island

Virgin Cove

Miquelon Bay

Soldier Point

GREAT MIQUELON

Mosquito Point

Big Barachois

The Dunes

Seal Cove

C. Percé

Ross Bay

Green Island

LITTLE MIQUELON

Gt. Colombier Island

North Channel

Southwest Bay

ST-PIERRE ISLAND

St-Pierre

Ravene Bay

South Channel

0   5   10 km

SCALE

GREAT MIQUELON

LITTLE MIQUELON

ST-PIERRE ISLAND

DETAIL OF AREA

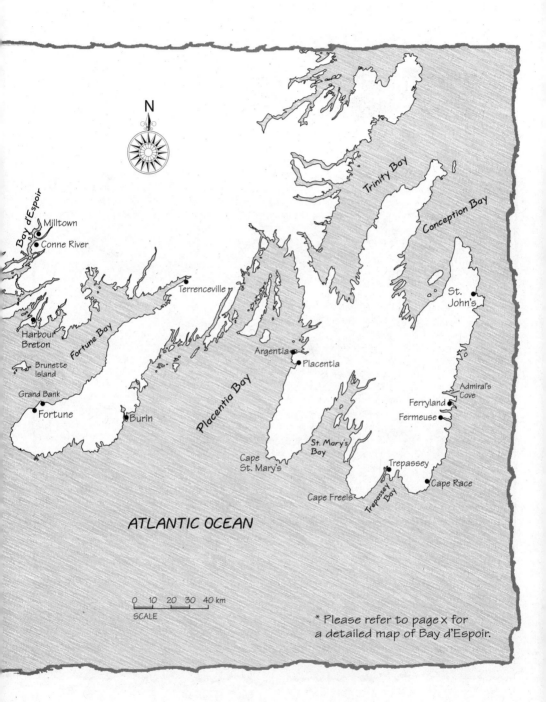

N

Bay d'Espoir
● Milltown
● Conne River

Terrenceville

Harbour
Breton

Fortune Bay

Brunette
Island

Grand Bank
● Fortune

● Burin

Trinity Bay

Conception Bay

St.
John's

Argentia ●
● Placentia

Placentia Bay

Admiral's
Cove
● Ferryland
Fermeuse ●

St. Mary's
Bay

Cape
St. Mary's

● Trepassey
● Cape Race

Cape Freels

Trepassey Bay

ATLANTIC OCEAN

0 10 20 30 40 km
SCALE

* Please refer to page x for
a detailed map of Bay d'Espoir.

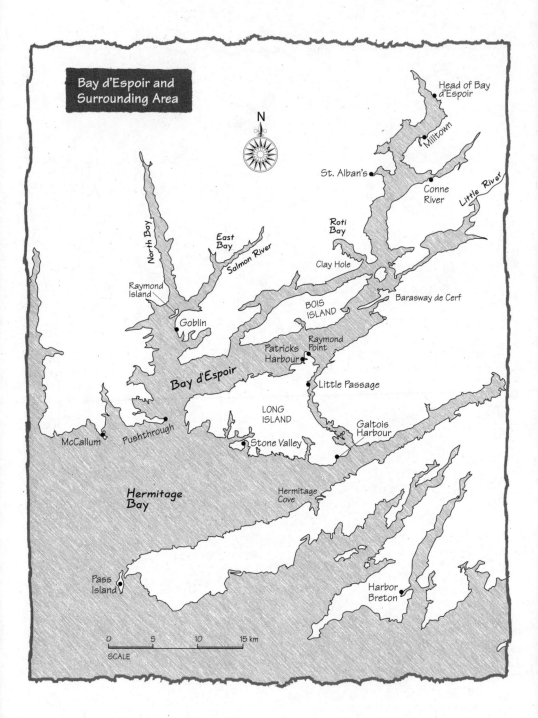

Bay d'Espoir and
Surrounding Area

N

Head of Bay
d'Espoir

Milltown

St. Alban's

Conne
River

Little River

Roti
Bay

North Bay

East
Bay

Salmon River

Clay Hole

Barasway de Cerf

Raymond
Island

BOIS
ISLAND

Goblin

Raymond
Point

Patricks
Harbour

Bay d'Espoir

Little Passage

LONG
ISLAND

McCallum

Pushthrough

Stone Valley

Galtois
Harbour

Hermitage
Bay

Hermitage
Cove

Pass
Island

Harbor
Breton

0   5   10   15 km

SCALE

I am deeply grateful to the many Newfoundlanders who bore with me, gave me access to their lives, and shared what they had with me and mine.

And the same to friend and publisher Susan Renouf, who has been and remains an unfailing source of encouragement and as accomplished and diligent an editor as any writer could hope to find.

Island in the Mist

In the summer of 1954 my father and I sailed his little ketch, *Scotch Bonnet*, down the St. Lawrence River to the sea. When a storm sent us scuttling into Rimouski on the lower river in search of shelter, we moored alongside an ocean-going rescue tug.

It was a safe mooring and a friendly one. The tug's crew consisted mostly of Newfoundlanders – a breed of seamen I had not previously encountered. They invited us aboard their ship, plied us with rum, fed us bowls of a peculiar dish called fish-and-brewis, and, while the storm howled in the rigging aloft, told us stories of their seagoing life.

These tales so enthralled me that I was determined to know them better. When I asked the tug's skipper how best to go about meeting his kind on their home ground (or waters), he advised me to book passage on one of the little freight-and-passenger steamers serving Newfoundland's outport communities.

"She'll give ye the feel of what our old Rock's like. Aye, and the sound of it, and the smell of it too. And if 'twas me I'd carry a bottle or two aboard to ile the whistles of the folk you meets along the way."

Three years passed before I could take his advice. Then, in the late summer of 1957, I flew in to Sydney, Nova Scotia, and took a taxi to North Sydney, a compact little harbour that was home to a busy shipyard where coasting and fishing vessels were built and repaired. On the morning of my arrival a venerable three-masted schooner was cradled on the dry end of the marine railway up which she had been hauled, festooned with weeds, a few days earlier. She was being swarmed by twenty or thirty men armed with caulking irons, long-headed hammers, and great hanks of golden oakum made from teased-out strands of manila rope soaked in Stockholm tar. The caulkers were crawling all over her, busily driving bales of oakum into her gaping seams to keep her afloat for a few more years. The sound they made was like a confabulation of giant woodpeckers. It was a sound that had not changed much since Nelson's time. It rang down the centuries as I carried my gear up the gangplank of the ferry that would carry me across the Cabot Strait to that great island known to its people as the Rock.

Newfoundland is of the sea. A mighty granite stopper thrust into the mouth of the Gulf of St. Lawrence, its coasts present more than five thousand miles of rocky headlands, bays, capes, and fiords to the sweep of the Atlantic. Everywhere hidden reefs, which are called, with dreadful explicitness, sunkers, wait to rip open the bellies of unwary vessels.

Fifty thousand years ago this great Rock was mastered by a tyranny of ice that stripped it of soil and vegetation and carried the detritus eastward to form the Grand Banks. The ice grinding relentlessly across the southern coast slashed a series of particularly deep fiords through the granite sea cliffs. Every few miles there was such an opening – sometimes a narrow knife wound, sometimes wide enough to admit a dozen ships sailing abreast.

After the departure of the ice, the high plateau of the interior was able to support only the most tenacious life. It was a world notably inhospitable to people of European origin. The first such interlopers to reach southern Newfoundland, perhaps as early as six centuries ago, were, however, men of the sea, not of the land. They were fishers in pursuit of cod for food, of walrus for ivory, of whales for oil, with little or no interest in the interior. They found the brooding granite barrier of the south coast adequate for their needs. It contained countless nooks and crannies well suited to shelter their boats, fishing stages, and houses, so there they planted themselves, always within sailing or rowing distance of the enormously rich coastal fishing grounds.

When Newfoundland joined Canada in 1949, more than eighty such "outports" dotted the Sou'west Coast, the name bestowed on the wall of cliffs and fiords stretching from Port aux Basques in Newfoundland's southwestern corner to the bottom end of Fortune Bay, more than two hundred miles to the eastward. Although some had as few as a dozen inhabitants, others held a hundred or more. Each was a little world of its own, living by and on the sea. First used as summer fishing stations by itinerant Basque, Portuguese, French, and English fishermen, they gradually acquired permanent residents by attracting runaways, castaways, and fugitives from the law and from the poverty of their European homelands. The names of these little lodgings of humanity, with their hodgepodge of linguistic origins much corrupted through the centuries, suggest their origins. Some that were still extant when I first visited the Sou'west Coast included Fox Roost (Fosse Rouge), Isle aux Morts, Rose Blanche (Roche Blanc), Harbour le Cou, Gallyboy, Grand Bruit, Ramea, Burgeo, La Hune, Cul de Sac, Rencontre, Dragon, Mosquito, Pushthrough, Goblin,

Lobscouse Cove, Mose Ambrose, Belleoram, Femme, and Fortune.

By 1957 only thirty-eight of the original eighty still existed. The rest had fallen victim to the post-Confederation craze for centralization. Pressure brought to bear by the Newfoundland and federal governments had already resulted in the death of more than half of the island's outport communities whose inhabitants had been encouraged, bribed, or threatened into abandoning their age-old homes and ways of life in order to move to larger centres, mostly in the interior, where they were supposed to become productive citizens of the modern industrialized world.

A fleet of small passenger and freighter steamers operated by the maritime branch of Canadian National Railways continued to provide a lifeline for the remaining outporters on the Sou'west Coast, which was without either roads or airports. The coastal steamers numbered half a dozen, including the *Baccalieu*, which I was to join at Port aux Basques.

Baccalieu was unquestionably the doyenne of the fleet. Built in Paisley, Scotland, in 1939, she was two hundred feet long and displaced fourteen hundred tons. She came from a long line of little steamers that had been working the coasts of the British Isles for a century and more. She was a lady, with a handsome cruiser stern; elegant, flaring bows; and a funnel raked just enough to give her a dashing look. She had been sailed out to Canada in 1940 and had been working the Newfoundland coasts ever since.

Every Friday she or one of her sister steamers would depart from Argentia in Placentia Bay, upbound (westbound) for Port aux Basques, where she would meet the ferry sailing across Cabot Strait to Canada. Every Saturday she, or a sister, would depart from Port aux Basques bound "down" the coast to Argentia. The direct distance between the two ports was less than three hundred miles, but the actual course, following the deeply indented coastline and in and out of the remaining outports, was at least three times that.

Tough and enduring little ships, small and nimble, the coast steamers were thoroughbreds. Their upper-deck accommodations were fitted in teak and mahogany instead of chrome and plastic. The dining and passenger saloons displayed stained glass windows and Victorian lamps. Meals were gargantuan, if heavy on such things as fish-and-brewis, fried cod, boiled haddock, salt beef, and cabbage. They were served on real china accompanied by Sheffield ware and sterling silver sugar bowls and cream jugs.

The steamers had class, but were wonderfully democratic. Passengers could wander almost anywhere they pleased and quickly established a first-name relationship with the crew.

Not only were these steam-powered (though oil-fired) little ships the chief means of getting to and from the outer world and of keeping the outports supplied with almost all the imported goods required, they also served as bank and post office; brought itinerant dentists and optometrists to the coast; and functioned as local buses, carrying people back and forth between neighbouring outports.

It was not surprising that they were held in high regard. When the steamer sounded her whistle as she approached an outport, the people of the place would flock to meet her, whether by day or by night, in fair weather or foul. Her arrival was always a celebration. The local wharf (if there was one) would sprout a mushroom growth of men, women, children, and the big black dogs that were symbolic of the coast. Shouts of "Steamer's in!" would echo through the village. Once more the world had come to the outport's door.

The steamer would moor alongside or, if there was no wharf, anchor in the stream surrounded by a flock of skiffs and dories. Her hatches would come off; cargo booms would get to work; and out of her holds would come all the things the outport people were unable to make or raise themselves: crates of hens, barrels of molasses, bundles of milled lumber, stoves, mail-order furniture, and a thousand other things.

An Anglican minister who used the steamers to visit his outlying parishes described them to me this way.

"They were like floating cornucopias. Almost anything a person could ever need would come out of their holds. They were also like spaceships from distant planets, bringing visitors from away who could tell us what it was like out there. They took our people out to hospital; and young folk out to school and, later, to see if they could find a place for themselves outside. But the biggest thing they did was keep us together. Sooner or later you'd meet everyone along the coast, either aboard the steamers or on the wharfs waiting for them. I can't think what we'd have done without them."

The steamers not only served the material and emotional needs of the far-flung outports, they also provided a medical lifeline. Almost no steamer ever completed a voyage without having to sprint ahead or double back at least once to pick up an emergency patient and carry him or her to the nearest doctor, or to within reach of a hospital at Cornerbrook or St. John's.

There was generally at least one pregnant woman aboard. Liza Parsons, *Baccalieu's* matronly stewardess, could not remember the number of times she had been a midwife. She became so expert and so renowned that hospital-bound pregnant women would deliberately take passage at the last possible moment in hopes of being able to give birth aboard under Liza's practised hands.

Such was the nature of the creature that lay awaiting me at dockside when I disembarked at Port aux Basques. Already laden to her marks, the SS *Baccalieu* was noisily blowing off surplus steam, which veiled her black hull and white-painted upperworks.

She was not going to be crowded on this trip. Instead of her usual complement of a hundred or so passengers, she was carrying only seventy-five. Her blushing young purser, who was new to his

Farley and Claire in the bows of the Baccalieu.

job, gave me cabin B on the upper deck. It was a wonder of Victorian elegance gone a little shoddy: creaky wicker chairs, worn Persian carpet, etched glass in the alleyway door, and an enormous English "water closet" almost big enough to serve as a sitz bath.

I had barely taken all this in when the ship's whistle let out a throaty roar and *Baccalieu* began to throb with the slow revolution of her great propeller shaft. I rushed on deck to find we were underway; but there was little to see. Night had fallen and the weather was chill and "thick-a-fog," as a passing deckhand unnecessarily noted. Never mind. I retreated to the snug warmth of my cabin for a good night's sleep.

It was not to be. At 11:30 p.m. a deckhand knocked hard upon my door to tell me the captain wanted me on the bridge.

Half expecting we would be taking to the lifeboats, I flung on my clothing, hurried across the bridge deck, and entered the wheelhouse – the holy of holies on any ship. A squat figure took shape in the darkness within and introduced himself.

"Ernie Riggs, skipper of this one. Heard you've been in the salvage boats out of Halifax. Thought you might like to help us take this old she-cunt into Rose Blanche . . . if we can *get* in. Nasty little place. Tight as a crab's arsehole."

I did not know if the captain was serious or not. There was certainly nothing I could do to help. The night was black as death and the fog almost too thick to breathe. Pretending I wasn't there, I backed into a corner and watched and listened as Skipper Riggs and the helmsman took *Baccalieu* through a maze of reefs into an unseen and unseeable little harbour, then laid her alongside a wooden wharf that I never even saw until the lines went ashore and the fog-diffused glow from a lamp on the shore told me we were there.

I remained on the bridge most of the rest of that black night so as not to miss the succeeding episodes of *Riggs Dares All* – a harrowing life-and-death adventure in real time.

Coming in to La Poille two hours later, Riggs could not have been able to see much farther than the nose on his face. Furthermore, *Baccalieu's* searchlight was out of order and her old-fashioned radar useless at close quarters. None of this seemed to concern Riggs as he paced rapidly back and forth, muttering to himself:

"Oh you she-cunt! Where's she going? Narrow place this . . . very narrow place. *Fucking* narrow place. Can't turn her here. Oh hell, s'pose I got to try."

Then, as the end of a dock miraculously appeared about ten feet off our bows: "Never goin' to make it. Lard *Jesus*, not going to make it!"

When people on the dock began yelling that we were going to make a hole in their island, Riggs stepped out on the bridge wing and shouted back:

"What're you silly fuckers worryin' about? We're right as houses! Finest kind!"

With which he pulled the engine telegraph to FULL ASTERN, and *Baccalieu* kissed the dock.

An hour later we continued on our way and, with the coming of a pallid dawn, Riggs turned the bridge over to the second mate and took me with him down to the saloon for breakfast.

"You'll do, Little Man," he said over his fourth mug of tea. "Long as you knows enough to keep your mouth shut when you're ignorant, you're welcome aboard of this one."

Through our subsequent friendship he continued to call me Little Man, and to treat me with the affectionate impatience he might have shown a slightly backward son. I learned a lot about Newfoundland and Newfoundlanders from Skipper Riggs.

A ruddy-faced, burly lump of a man, Riggs had been born in the small settlement of Burin on the shores of Placentia Bay. He was as much a child of the sea as of the land. At the age of eight he had gone to the Grand Banks aboard a fishing schooner owned by an uncle. By the time he was twelve he had a berth as fo'c'sle hand, and at fifteen was fishing down the Labrador. At twenty he got his mate's papers and signed on aboard an English tramp freighter to spend the next several years travelling the world and, incidentally, picking up some of the worst of the argot used by British seamen. In 1936 he became the freighter's Master. In 1943 she was sunk under him by a German U-boat. After the war, so he told me, he decided to "settle down, so I married a maid from Fortune and, I supposes you could say, married the *Baccalieu* as well."

His was hardly a settled life. He had managed to get home for Christmas only once since 1946. His working schedule consisted of two months aboard his ship, followed by a month ashore. When he got home he was often unable to sleep, only able to doze with one ear cocked for trouble. He seldom slept while on board because the ship ran day and night and he was usually on the bridge, and always on call.

Although he could, and did, gorgeously curse the world around him, and everything in it including his beloved *Baccalieu*, he never seemed to have a hard word for any of his crew, though he had no patience with shore-side management.

"I got to keep the old bitch going come hell or high water, into and out of places a duck would leave alone. Places there ain't even room to change your mind, and do it any time, day or night, in any kind of weather. They's got to be accidents, and there is. And when some damn fool thing goes wrong, the skipper gets suspension, whether he be at fault or no. But we don't do it for they office fuckers in St. John's. We works for the people on the coast. The thanks we gits comes from them. I believe there's nothing on God's earth they wouldn't do for we. Or we for they."

He told me *Baccalieu* had not been dry-docked for a year and her bottom was so foul with marine growth that "the silly old bitch won't steer anyways at all. Radar's no good and the chief keeps the engine going with curses and prayers. Needs a rest, the old she-cunt do, and so do I."

I had come on this voyage to see Newfoundland, but was not seeing much of it except for the insides of the *Baccalieu*. I wrote in my journal:

> *The fog is impenetrable. It defies the laws of probability that Riggs can take this vessel in and out of places a seal would have trouble navigating on a sunny day. . . . We came into Grand Bruit (the name means Big Noise) at 0700 hours and never saw a bloody thing. A dory came out of the murk and took off a woman passenger bound for some place called Otter Point; then we were away again. . . . Burgeo was next. According to the chart it has about 100 islands and three thousand reefs. The* Baccalieu *went through the middle of them like shit through a goose and I never saw a thing except some blacker shadows*

in the darkness. He did it by the horn! He blew the damn thing every few seconds, and said he could tell where we were by the sound echoing off the rocks! So help me God, that's what he said.

Our next port of call was Ramea, a cluster of small islands some fifteen miles offshore and outside the barricade of fog that sealed off the mainland coast. Ramea gave me my first real look at an outport – thirty or forty wooden houses clinging to treeless lumps of water-rounded rock. The houses were a sight to behold, painted in patterns and colours more spectacular than any rainbow. Purple, yellow, magenta, orange, and scarlet seemed to be the favourite hues, but some were like layer cakes, horizontally banded by two or three blazing colours. Riggs explained: "Afore we joined up to Canada no person spent money on paint for houses. Boats, certainly, but houses would be a waste. Then come the Canadian family allowances, pension and welfare cheques flying around like snow. And a crowd of paint salesmen from up-along who turned that money into paint. That's why, Little Man, the outports looks like bowls of jelly beans."

The fog closed in around us as we approached an unseen granite wall a few miles farther down the coast. The chart showed it to be not quite an impervious obstacle. Somewhere ahead was a narrow slit, behind which was said to lie the settlement of Grey River. There was no foghorn or anything else to guide us to it, but we had Skipper Riggs.

Baccalieu went charging in, horn bellowing every few seconds. Neither Riggs nor the lookout could have seen a thing except swirling fog. The murk became even darker.

"Got to be right here," Riggs remarked conversationally. "You, Little Man, step out on the wing of the bridge. Stretch your hand out with a match into it. If it strikes and lights, let me know right quick."

I was not amused. In truth, I was seriously apprehensive.

"Port a leetle," said Riggs almost dreamily.

"Port it is, sorr," repeated the helmsman.

"Steady as she goes."

"Steady, sorr."

With never a glimpse of the land, and running close to full speed in order to counter the outgoing tidal current, *Baccalieu* went through the unseen eye of the needle, a cleft in the face of the mountain not much wider than she was long.

Then Riggs turned to me with a slow smile.

"I believes we's made it."

Squeezed into a narrow crotch between barren, rocky hills, Grey River was tiny. Its two or three dozen houses and a small church with a tarpaper roof clinging to the slopes seemed very brave in their multicoloured paint.

The current was too strong to allow Riggs to take us alongside the tiny wharf so we offloaded two passengers and twenty or so

Unloading freight at Grey River.

packages into an open boat. Then the skipper rang for full ahead and soon we were back in the void of fog.

At supper that evening I sat beside the chief engineer, a sour sort of fellow – or so I thought until I voiced a minor complaint about the captain's perverse sense of humour, and the chief told me a little story.

Some years earlier the *Baccalieu* had been threading her way through a notorious maze of sunkers, reefs, and half-awash rocks on the Labrador coast when a woman passenger "from away" nervously asked Riggs if he knew where all the hidden dangers lay. The answer was pure Riggs.

"No, ma'am. I'm afeared as I don't." Long pause. Then, "But I hopes I knows where they ain't."

With night upon us I thought the skipper might take it easy. Not he. Moodily remarking that we were behind schedule (the steamers were *always* behind schedule) and ignoring the stygian darkness and dripping fog that enveloped us, he ran *Baccalieu* along the coast at full revolutions before hauling her into a little hole-in-the-wall called Cape la Hune.

The engine stopped and we drifted in an invisible world, our whistle blaring throatily like a matronly monster calling her brood. Three dories emerged out of the murk and came alongside. Freight was unloaded and a few passengers exchanged. Then everything vanished again and *Baccalieu* felt her way back out to sea.

I was sorry not to have seen La Hune. One of our stewards, who came from there, told me it consisted of ten houses clinging to a rocky spur jutting into the sea from the foot of towering cliffs. He said soil was so scarce that, in order to bury the dead, it had to be brought in by the dory-load and even that was sometimes washed away again by the next sou'west gale.

Baccalieu drove on through the night to another slit in the cliffs. This one was called Francois on the chart but known to everyone on the coast as Fransway. A small lighthouse clung to the rocks above the narrow entrance. Fortunately it had a diaphone – a foghorn – for we never saw the light at all. Riggs steered straight for the sound of the horn, then, at the last possible moment, told the helmsman to haul to starboard, and we slithered through a twisty gut of a channel into a rock-girt basin a quarter mile across that closely resembled the crater of an extinct volcano. The fog was thinner here, and the shape of the basin was eerily defined by the dim, yellow glow of oil lamps in the windows of a semicircle of unseen houses.

"I don't suppose," Riggs said gloomily, "we can lay alongside the fucking little wharf," and then proceeded to do so, with a flourish.

The wharf, which was hardly longer than a good-sized dory, was jam-packed with people and black dogs, all of them evidently glad to see us. People swarmed aboard for a gam while the dogs headed for the galley looking for bones. The wharfinger (the man in charge of the wharf) told me that, four days earlier, the downbound steamer had gone past Fransway without coming in.

"That hang-ashore she got for a skipper be afraid to stick his nose in here for fear he'd bust it on the rocks. But Skipper Riggs now, *that* man'd sail the *Baccalieu* where Jonah went."

The first mate assured me we would remain at the wharf for the rest of the night so I went gratefully to bed. He must have forgotten to tell Riggs, who at midnight ordered *Baccalieu* to sea again.

The next port should have been Rencontre West, a notoriously difficult place to enter even in daylight and clear weather. We were spared the attempt. Somewhere off a massive and unseen headland known as Iron Skull, our lookout spotted a spark of light in the murk ahead. This proved to be a gasoline lantern lashed to the mast of a dory. *Baccalieu* slowed and stopped. The dory came alongside, and we were hailed by someone wanting to know if Mrs. Fudge and her baby were aboard. They were. Would they get off? They would.

The companionway was lowered, and as *Baccalieu* rolled ponderously in the swell, the intrepid Mrs. Fudge and her baby were transferred into the dory.

This was a hairy business. The steward literally tossed the baby to a doryman, who caught it on the fly. The woman had to jump for it as *Baccalieu* rose and fell, a dark abyss gaping between ship and dory. The dory cast off, and as it vanished our propeller began to turn and we pulled away from this unmarked bus station in the sea.

Richards Harbour was another "rats' burrow in the rocks," as our first mate called it. We came to it at dawn, and the fog lifted as we entered a small and almost perfectly round harbour encompassed by low hills glowing red in the early light. Two schooners and a flock of dories and trap boats swung at moorings. The harbour was ringed with spidery constructs made of spruce poles, called "stages" – small wharves with little sheds on their seaward ends where fish were cut and gutted and fishing gear stored and repaired.

The houses clustered close to the landwash and to one another on steeply sloping ground, looking as if they had dug in their heels to prevent themselves from slipping into the harbour.

Back at sea, we welcomed a brisk westerly breeze that finally chased away the fog. I spent most of that day running from one wing of the bridge to the other, or climbing up to "monkey island" on top of the wheelhouse in order to miss nothing of the passing show. Newfoundland's great inland plateau remained partially veiled in cloud, but the coast was revealed in all its brutal majesty – a colossal palisade of silvery-grey rock reared against the never-ending assaults of the western ocean.

That evening, at the invitation of the dour and diminutive chief engineer, I went below to admire the great reciprocating steam engine. Built to a design that had not changed significantly in a hundred years, it was a symphony of polished brass and gleaming iron whose many shafts, cams, and arms ran slickly and almost soundlessly in a faint haze of steam. Here was none of the stupefying din produced by the giant diesels that drive more modern vessels. This was the dancing place of shadowy metal djinns performing to the soft fluting of escaping steam, the point and counterpoint of muted brasses, the occasional clash of cymbals, the pulsing rhythm of the mighty shaft revolving in its well-oiled bearings, and the clarion ring of telegraphed orders from the bridge.

The following night *Baccalieu* steamed through the labyrinthine passages of a great fiord that was virtually an inland sea. Called Bay d'Espoir on the charts, but known as Bay Despair, it thrust thirty miles inland and harboured half a dozen little settlements. I saw little of them. Exhausted by sightseeing, I slept my way around Bay Despair and was bitterly regretful when I woke next morning, for I had no way of knowing that I would return to spend some of the happiest times of my life in its web of mystery.

I rolled out of my bunk just as we were emerging from the bay, in time to watch Riggs do his stuff at Gaultois. In order to enter this busy little port, the site of a fish-filleting and -freezing plant, *Baccalieu* had to squeeze through an opening between a mid-channel rock and the mainland cliff with about twenty feet to spare on either side. She then had to turn completely around in her own length and ease into the wharf. Obviously it couldn't be done. But Riggs paced up and down his bridge, muttering about "she-cunts," and did the impossible, tucking the ship into place like a baby into a buggy.

That day we did the rounds of Hermitage Bay (Gaultois, Pink Bottom, Hermitage Cove, Grole) accompanied by a rising nor'easter to make things lively. By the time we reached Pass Island at the mouth of the bay an hour after sunset, the nor'easter had become a gale and there could be no thought – even by Ernie Riggs – of trying to moor to the small and exposed wharf of the small settlement on this pitch-black night filled with sound and fury.

There followed a most harrowing manoeuvre during which Riggs anchored *Baccalieu* as close to shore as he dared, with her bows to the storm and the breakers roaring close under her stern. Wind and tide acting together began to make her drag her anchor, but Riggs held her off the rocks by running the engine half ahead. We were not more than the ship's own length from the breakers.

Meanwhile our little motorboat had been swung out and launched. It immediately developed engine trouble and with great difficulty was *rowed* back to the ship. Then the Pass Islanders tried to come out to us in two dories. Only one was able to make it. There was no possibility of putting any freight aboard it, but we had three women with two small children to go ashore. As they clung to the companion ladder and to three stewards, waiting to jump and scramble into the wildly pitching dory, Riggs paced the bridge, his gaze fixed on the rocks astern. The moment the dory left our side he gave *Baccalieu* full power. The anchor was brought home and we ran for the shelter of Jerseyman Harbour.

Here we found the middle portion of the wharf occupied by a big Royal Canadian Mounted Police patrol vessel. There was so little space remaining that, on his first attempt to dock, Riggs put *Baccalieu*'s bow aground. It was a soft touch, however, and she took no damage. He wiggled her off and tried another shot, laying his ship so close to the police vessel that a colossal crunch seemed certain.

The captain of the patrol boat was on his own bridge and we could see him clenching and unclenching his hands, but he said not a word. Perhaps he did not dare, for it was well known that Skipper Riggs despised the police for their interference with the local "import" trade in rum from the off-lying French islands of St. Pierre and Miquelon. In the event, the two vessels barely touched. The police skipper went silently and, I imagine, thankfully below. Riggs went growling to his cabin for an hour's rest.

He reappeared when we reached Coombs Cove – an exposed little place without a wharf. It was still blowing half a gale and the seas were fierce as we anchored off. Three dories fought their way out to us, and into them we dropped the mail, twenty cases of beer, twenty more of pop, a hot-water boiler, a bed spring, four passengers, and numerous miscellaneous packages. Although practically awash under their loads, the little boats headed resolutely back toward their harbour.

"Takes some awful chances, they fellows," was Riggs's comment as he watched them go. I looked at him long and hard, but said not a word.

Next day found us entering the great bight called Fortune Bay – a world of its own with twenty outports strung along its ragged coast. It brought good fortune to us, for the sky cleared and the wind dropped out.

Instead of slowing down as we approached what Riggs referred to as a "one-dory hole" (it actually boasted a dozen or more), he rang the telegraph for full speed and *Baccalieu* came dashing into Saint-Jacques with a bone in her teeth. In a moment I saw why. There was room for only one vessel of her size at the wharf, and we had arrived just in time to edge out her sister ship *Bar Haven*, bound up the coast.

"I knowed Skipper Ro Penney were making a run for it," our skipper said with a grin. "He left his radio turned on and I could hear him panting, he was that anxious to beat us to the wharf."

A discomfited *Bar Haven* had to stand off and wait for two hours while we unloaded our cargo.

By the following noon we were as far along as Bay L'Argent. While the mate directed the offloading, Skipper Riggs told me the story of how *Bar Haven* had driven ashore here the previous autumn.

"A dirty black night in November, it was. Skipper Ro was inbound for Argentia when there come on a god-almighty westerly gale. We was moored snug in Hermitage Cove to ride it out, but Skipper Ro was caught all-standing. He tried to claw into Bay L'Argent but his radar give out and before he knowed it she run hard onto the Ragged Rocks at the mouth of the harbour.

"About two in the morning the mate wakes me. 'Call from Captain Penney,' he says. So I got on the radio.

"'Come on down here, skipper,' Ro says. ''Cause I'm aground.'

"'Nah, bye, *can't* be!'

"'Yiss, old son, I is, and good and proper. Come right down here.'

"We let go the lines and put out into a howling starm. We give her everything she had. The chief tied down the safety valves and

Baccalieu come out around Pass Island at fourteen and a half knots. With the gale behind us, we come near to flying across Fortune Bay. I don't say the old girl ever went that fast afore or ever will again. When she lifted on the big fellows coming up astern, the screw come right out of water and she shook so bad she like to fall apart.

"We was off Bay L'Argent just at dawn, and there was the *Bar Haven* pounding on the rocks. Her bows was badly holed and she was flooded forward almost to her main deck. Didn't look like she could last much longer. A great big sea was breaking over her stern and high along the cliff to looward of her. No chance to get a boat off of her, or a line ashore, and the wind and sea was shifting northerly lookin' to roll her down.

"Well, there was twenty-five passengers aboard of her, a lot of them women and children. We had to do something. . . .

"I turned *Baccalieu* around, heading into the storm. Dropped my bower anchor, let seven shackles of chain pay out, then brought her up and held her stern-to, as close as ever I dared to the Ragged Rocks.

"She was pitching and rolling something awful, but the mate got on our afterdeck and shot a rocket line onto *Bar Haven*'s afterdeck. Her people hauled over a heavy mooring line. Then we launched our lifeboat, shackled it to the line, and hauled it back and forth between the two vessels, bringing *Bar Haven*'s passengers and the most of her crew aboard of us. Took seven trips, and they were some lively rides! The women was pretty leery about getting into that little boat at all, and just as leery when it come time to scramble up *Baccalieu*'s side.

"The boat brought off one lady in her seventies clinging to the gunwales with my second mate behind her, holding her steady. Afraid he was squeezing her too hard, he eased off – and she went overboard.

"They fished her out pretty quick, and when we hoisted her aboard I poured her a big tumbler of rum. 'Sink it down, my dear,' I tells her.

"'I would, could I hold onto the glass,' says she.

"So I holds it for her and she sinks it down and asks could she have another. We put her to bed then, and she slept for twenty hours.

"What about *Bar Haven*? Well, Little Man, Skipper Ro and his engineer and a couple of others stayed aboard. When the storm died out, the salvage tugs come and hauled her off and patched her up and towed her into St. John's, where she was repaired pretty good. Poor old thing."

Some years later, when he had come to know me well enough, Skipper Riggs added a postscript to this story.

It had to do with an old Mi'kmaq woman from Eskasoni in Cape Breton. Every year for half a century this woman, who seems to have been known to whites only by her first name, Lizbet, made two journeys by steamer along the south coast of Newfoundland, selling handmade wicker baskets in the outports, where they were purchased not because they were needed but because it was believed they brought good luck. *And* that failure to buy one would bring bad luck.

In 1956 Lizbet had stored half of her supply of baskets in Canadian National's freight shed at Port aux Basques, where they were trampled and largely destroyed by a bull that broke out of its shipping pen.

When the CN agent refused to pay damages, Lizbet said to him, "All right. That's all right. You'll pay later." With which she put a curse on the CN coastal boats.

In the next four months four major strandings took place, the last of which was that of the *Bar Haven* at Bay L'Argent. At that point the CN compensated Lizbet for her lost baskets.

Riggs explained that *Baccalieu* had escaped the curse because he always made a point of treating the old woman well.

"Like a queen. Always give her everything she wants, I tells my crew. A *deluxe* cabin if she wants. I tells the cook to feed her up the best he can. Give her the run of the ship. Oh yes, my Little Man, I treats her proper!"

In return Lizbet had assured him nothing bad would ever happen to the *Baccalieu*, and nothing ever had.

Ferryland

Reluctantly, I left the *Baccalieu* at Fortune, the largest settlement in Fortune Bay, in order to spend a few days at St. Peters, as Newfoundlanders called the offshore islands of St. Pierre and Miquelon. I needed some firsthand information about the stranding and subsequent salving there of the British freighter *Fort Boise* – an event that played a role in the book I was currently writing.

The visit was short but seminal since it drew me back to these French islands, where I would meet a woman who would become central in my life.

From St. Pierre I made my way to St. John's, capital city of Newfoundland, where I encountered Harold Horwood, a lean, hawk-nosed, sharply blue-eyed man of my own age. Harold's family had been fishermen, boat builders, and master mariners in Newfoundland for seven or eight generations, but he had broken with that long tradition to become a political activist, a sometime poet and artist, a vitriolic journalist, and the paramount gadfly of Premier Joey Smallwood, the ruler of the island.

Acerbic and iconoclastic, Harold had a low opinion of "Canadians." Almost his first words to me after we met were these: "From Ontario, are you? I suppose you intend to pick my brains then fly away back to Toronto and write a piece about the colourful natives of NewFOUNDland, as you people from away insist on calling us. Well, good luck."

That would have been that, except for a benevolent fate that had put me in possession of a bottle of St. Pierre rum on a day when all the liquor stores in St. John's were closed. By the time the bottle was empty, Harold conceded that I just might be worth knowing. We spent much of the next few days together and, by the time I flew back to Ontario, had become friends. And Harold had invited me to come along with him the following summer in his new Chevrolet on a month-long exploration of Newfoundland.

This adventure took us from one side of the great island to the other; sometimes by car or, when roads ran out, by rail, but nothing brought me closer to understanding the Rock than a prolonged visit to the village of Ferryland on what is called the Southern (but is really the eastern) Shore, some fifty miles to the south of St. John's.

My chief mentors in Ferryland were members of the Morry family, of which Howard Morry was the patriarch. Then in his eighties, Howard could have passed for a man of fifty. Tall and heavy-set, with a rubicund visage, he could almost have been the reincarnation of a west coast of England farmer-fisherman of Drake's time. A widower, he lived in a large and rambling old wooden house with his laconic son Bill, and his voluble daughter-in-law Pat. Pat "took in" occasional visitors (there were no hotels or motels in Ferryland); her men ran a small salt-fish plant. The couple had two vivacious children: Peter, aged ten, and Paula, aged eight.

The Morrys adopted me into their household. Pat fed me gargantuan meals whose principal ingredients came directly from the ocean at our door: cod, flounder, halibut, mackerel, salmon, sea trout, mussels, capelin, and lobster being chief among them. She also provided glimpses into the women's world in an outport.

Howard and Bill inducted me into the complexities of a fishery that had not changed significantly since its establishment on this coast five centuries earlier. They revealed the arcane arts and secrets of making the salt fish that they exported to Mediterranean and Caribbean countries, and they sent me to sea in the big, open skiffs used to tend the cod traps along the ragged coast.

Young Peter and Paula did their part by taking me on long rambles into the country over ancient trails originally made by mysterious "Masterless Men" and to a crumbling stone beacon on a high hill called the Gaze from which through the centuries women had watched for the seaborne return of their men, and boys as young as Peter had stood ready to raise the alarm when the sails of pirates, privateers, or French invaders hove into view.

It was principally Howard who guided me into the heart and soul of Ferryland. He knew its story as far back as oral history went. The well-protected harbour at the foot of low hills fringed by a wide foreshore of grassy meadows had welcomed some of the earliest European visitors to the Americas. Basque whalers and cod fishers probably sheltered in Ferryland's harbour before the end of the fifteenth century. During the first decades of the sixteenth, Bretons and Normans built summer fishing stations along its pebble beaches. It appears on a seventeenth-century French map as Farillon, a corruption of the earlier Portuguese name Farelhão.

The French held Farillon until about 1600, when the English seized it. In 1621 Lord Baltimore chose it as the site of a grand "plantation" he intended to build in the New Founde Lande. However, the lord was hag-ridden by a wife who could not stand Firiland, as it had become, and badgered him into moving south to what would one day become the state of Maryland.

Other overlords took control of the place through the succeeding centuries and sweated its inhabitants, who were of French, West County English, Jersey, and eventually some Irish stock. They formed a tough, stubborn, and enduring amalgam able to survive the harsh rule of British fishing admirals, predatory merchants, and an interminable series of raids by French, New Englanders, and stateless buccaneers.

During the eighteenth century the English fishery that dominated eastern Newfoundland was largely worked by men from the western shires of Britain who had been driven to sea by an economic system that treated them little better than slaves. "Planted" in Newfoundland harbours to fish for absent masters, some fled into the desolate interior and became the Masterless Men: a loose-knit outlaw society, somewhat in the romantic tradition of Robin Hood. The interior of the Avalon Peninsula, with its caribou barrens, rugged hills, and sweeping forests, was their domain. Only the best armed and most able British troops dared enter it. The Masterless Men's chief settlement lay in a valley not five miles as the crow flies from Ferryland, under the loom of a mighty hill called the Butterpot, to whose high crest Howard and Peter took me one summer day.

The Masterless Men were never subjugated. Gradually they melded with coastal fishermen-settlers, and to this day their blood runs strongly in the veins of the people of the Southern Shore.

One day Howard and I rowed out to Bois Island, which guards the mouth of Ferryland harbour. As the name indicates, it was once well wooded, though Bois, together with almost all the coast of Newfoundland, now stands denuded of trees.

Bois Island once boasted a considerable fortress. Howard, who had made himself its guardian, showed me the remains of five

Howard Morry making salt fish.

heavy-gun batteries with their circumvallations. And lying in shoal water at the foot of a cliff were four great, brass cannon that had been dumped there, Howard said, by a Yankee privateer who had tried but failed to carry them off. Recently a new kind of privateer had attempted to remove them using divers and heavy lifting gear. He had been foiled by Howard and two friends armed with swiling (sealing) guns, who had sent the vandal and his crew packing.

Howard inducted me into the ancient modes of the cod fishery, first teaching me how to jig the fish using a double-hooked lead model of a capelin at the end of a hand line as bait. Then he sent me out to the cod traps. At four o'clock one morning I joined the four-man crew of a trap skiff, a broad-beamed open boat twenty feet long powered by a five-horsepower "jump spark" gasoline engine. We puttered out of the harbour in inky darkness accompanied by the muted reverberations of a dozen other "one-lunger" engines pushing unseen boats toward the open sea.

We fished two traps. These were great box-shaped nets as much as fifty feet on a side, with a bottom but no top. A long, vertically suspended head net stretched out from a "door" on one side of the trap to guide passing schools of cod into confinement. The whole complicated affair was moored to the sea floor with enormous wrought-iron anchors salvaged from the wrecks of ancient ships.

The first trap had been set in nine fathoms (fifty-four feet) of water off Bois Island. Our skipper tested it by jigging inside the trap. On the first try he hooked a fine, fat cod and hauled it, shimmering, over the gunwale.

"Good enough!" he said. "We'll haul her, byes!"

It took the best efforts of all five of us manhandling the great mass of twine and ropes to "bag" the trap and haul it to the surface. It contained about a ton of big cod, seething against the mesh. Pitching them aboard with glorified hay forks while the skiff lifted and fell in the ocean surge was an exciting and dangerous business. One young fellow was very nearly hauled overboard when his arm became entangled in a mooring line. He would not have lasted long had it pulled him down for the Labrador current, in whose chill waters we were, was only a few degrees above freezing.

It took an hour to clear this trap and reset it. Then we moved on to the second one but a rising wind and sea prevented us from hauling it. We were thankful to regain the shelter of the harbour, where all hands turned to and forked our fish up onto the stage. Here they were gutted, split, and boned preliminary to being "made" into salt fish. Flattened out like triangular shingles, the split fish were carried to the salt shed, sprinkled with coarse salt, and left to cure. Once the salt had thoroughly penetrated the flesh, the split fish were carried on hand barrows by women and children to spindly outdoor structures constructed of spruce "longers" overlaid with spruce boughs. These were the "flakes" upon which the fish were spread to dry in sun and wind, carefully tended against sun burning or against infestations of maggots. Seen from a distance, the flakes looked as if they were covered with snow.

I spent hours on the stages watching the trap boats come home and yarning with men like Uncle Jim Welch and Uncle John Hawkins – "Uncle" being an honorific title conferred on older outport men.

Jim was eighty-eight, and John was ninety, but, as they assured me, they were "still good fur it." They greeted every arriving boat with kindly but critical comments as to the quality and quantity of fish aboard it – comments the crews accepted good-naturedly, for the old fellows enjoyed the unstinting respect of all hands.

They had surely earned it.

Uncle John had first gone to sea at the age of eight with his father, jigging fish from a dory. He was a late starter. Uncle Jim had begun *his* career at seven as cabin boy aboard his grandfather's small schooner fishing down the Labrador. Salt water was almost their blood. As Howard said of them: "They be as well pickled as the finest Madeira." He was referring not to Madeira wine but to the best grade of salt cod, called Madeira because that was where most of it was sold.

The stories men like these and Howard had to tell were legion.

One I especially liked concerned Albert Billard, from nearby Mobile, who had died only a year previously. Although primarily a fisherman, Billard had also worked a potato patch in which he took much pride. Unfortunately his neighbours' goats were forever getting into Billard's potatoes. The feud between goats and man was already old when, late one summer day as Billard was harvesting his potatoes, back bent and eyes fixed on the stony soil, the stout parish priest, a man famous for his appetite, happened by. Seeing Billard at work, the Father leaned upon his stick and hopefully remarked: "Ah, so ye're diggin' 'em, Billard."

Glancing out from under his bushy eyebrows, Billard failed to see the priest. Instead he found himself looking into the baleful yellow eyes of a nanny goat busily munching one of his spuds.

"*Yiss*, ye *whore!*" Billard shouted furiously. "And if 'tweren't for the likes of you there'd be more for the rest of we!"

Another tale illuminated the indomitable nature of Southern Shore women.

During Howard's childhood a runaway from an English fishing ship – an "Irish youngster," as such men were called – had appeared in Ferryland.

"They was hard times that year and this fellow must have had a fill of it. He had nought but the clothes on his back. Ferryland folk took him in and made him welcome. My old father give him a hand and he worked at the fishing; but he was always, as you might say, looking over his shoulder, afeared he'd be captured.

"He *did* look to his front sometimes, 'cause he fell in love with a maid from Acquaforte called Rose and married she, and began fishing on his own. But his fears never left him and one autumn he took his wife and their two babies and rowed his skiff forty mile down the coast to a spit of a cove no ships and few boats would care to enter. He built a cabin there and went about living far away as he could get from the world.

"It must have been some hard lines for Rose. They had nought but what they made for theyselves. No neighbours to pass the time with, or lend a hand when they was need. Me old mother felt so sorry for that maid she got a crew to make a trip down to the cove they was in to take some clothes to her little boys and herself. Those fellows said it was the roughest place ever they saw. Rose's family was so little used to seeing strangers they hardly had a word to say.

"Once or twice a year the man would row into Ferryland to trade his salt fish for fishing gear, powder and shot, a puncheon of molasses, fat pork, maybe a bit of flour. For the most of it, them people lived like they was the only people in the world. They lived from the sea and off the country, eating fish, caribou, ducks, and the few potatoes they could grow on a patch of moss and dirt scrabbled out among the rocks.

"One February morning the man was struck down. Paralysis, it seemed like. Rose nursed him for two weeks but he got worse. Then she made up her mind to go for help, so she left her boys – they was nine or ten years old by then – to care for their poor father, and set out single-handed to row the skiff forty mile to Ferryland in wicked winter weather with the floe ice not a half a mile offshore.

"Rose'd made about fifteen miles before a nor'east gale blew up and drove the ice in. It nipped the skiff and broke her into match-wood. Rose made her way ashore on foot – copying, we calls it – over the ice pans. Then she clumb the cliffs, waded five brooks that was full of ice, and walked, knee-deep in snow, to Ferryland.

"Her toes and fingers was mostly frozen and for a time she'd lost the power to speak. It were three days before we knew what had happened, and two more afore the nor'easter died down and a westerly blew the ice far enough off shore so's a party of men could make their way to the cove. Rose tried to go along but they made her stop where she was to."

The rescuers were met by two silent boys. The men went up to the little house and found it snug, warm, and tidy. They asked the boys where their father was and the oldest – the ten-year-old – silently led them to a shack some distance from the cabin. Inside was the missing man.

He was strung up to the roof beam by his feet; he had been cleanly bled and gutted.

"You sees how 'twas," Howard told me sombrely. "Them lads never seen a dead *man* before. But they'd seen a good many deer killed, and watched their poor father hang them up and gut them. So, poor lads, they thought that was the way to treat any dead creature, be it man or beast.

"They done the best as they knowed how. . . ."

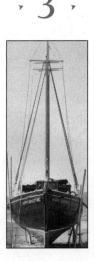

· 3 ·

A Southern Shore Bummer

My Cook's tour with Harold Horwood had given me a kaleidoscopic overview of Newfoundland, and my visits to Ferryland had
provided glimpses into the lives of its people. Wanting to dig
deeper, I pondered a lesson that time spent with the Inuit had
taught me: in order to gain any real insight into the lives of a tribal
people it is necessary to at least try to be one. Although it was
patently too late for me to assume the oilskins, sou'wester, and
persona of a born-and-bred Newfoundland fisherman, I thought I
might at least approach them in a familiar context as a sailor
manning one of their own boats.

One mid-January day in 1960 I drove to Toronto to see Jack
McClelland, head of McClelland & Stewart, the firm that published
my books in Canada. Jack was a close friend so we migrated to a bar
where I unburdened myself of the plan I had been developing.

"I want to go back east, Jack. The salvage book I've written and the trips I've made down there have given me a taste for the place."

"More likely a taste for the local rum."

"That too, of course. But the thing is I'd like to get me a boat, sail right around Newfoundland, then write a book about it."

Jack rose to the lure like a hungry cod to the jigger.

"Hell of a good idea! I've still got a yen for salt water myself, from my navy days. Maybe we could get a boat together. What would it cost?"

"Peanuts, Jack. Newfie's full of little fishing schooners that're being replaced by power boats. They're a bit old and a bit smelly maybe, but dirt cheap. We could fly down; pick up something suitable; have her refitted locally; then this summer cruise around Newfoundland. After that? Well, how does Tahiti sound?"

It all sounded fine to Jack. Since he could not spare the time to go boat-hunting, it was left to me to put the plan into action. In February I flew to St. John's, where Harold Horwood grandly offered to help me find a suitable vessel.

We visited many fishing villages clinging like treacle to the wave-battered cliffs of the Avalon Peninsula and examined a multitude of vessels ranging from small and ancient "bully boats" to a venerable two-hundred-ton, three-masted schooner. Most were no longer seaworthy, but eventually we found a small schooner of a kind known as a Southern Shore bummer hauled out at the little outport of Admiral's Cove, not far from Fermeuse.

She was a rough-looking little thing, measuring thirty feet on deck with a beam of nine feet and a draft of four feet six inches. On close inspection she looked as if she might have been flung together by a band of Neolithic builders equipped with stone tools. Flush-decked, she had three narrow "fishing wells" in each of which a man could stand while jigging for cod. A dark hole aft housed the enormous phallus of the single-cylinder, make-and-break engine that was her chief means of propulsion. Her two masts were hardly more than sticks stayed with lengths of old telephone wire, while her sails – not much bigger than bedsheets – were as sere and patched as Jacob's coat. It did not appear that the two Fennely brothers who owned her relied much on sail.

Her holds and bilges had never been cleaned and were encrusted with a glutinous layer of slime, old blood, and fish scales. This was not because of bad ship-keeping. It was because, as Manuel Fennely explained in the accent prevalent on the Avalon, "de bummers be built of green wood and when dey dries dey opens up. Divil a seam can ye keep tight wit' caulkin'; but dey seals dersels wit' fish gurry, and dat keeps dey tight."

Although her faults (some of them) were apparent, she *was* only five years old and the price – nine hundred dollars – did not seem exorbitant to me. It was, in fact, about twice the going price for her kind, but Harold refrained from telling me this and congratulated me on having struck a shrewd bargain.

Jack's reaction was different. When, a few months later, he beheld her for the first time he stared unbelievingly.

"My God, Farley! Were you out of your mind? Or drunk? Or both? . . . What are you going to call her, supposing she floats at all?"

"*Happy Adventure*," I replied humbly. "Harold suggested it. It's the name of a pirate ship that worked Newfoundland waters a couple of hundred years ago."

"Fucking appropriate!" said Jack succinctly.

Having bought the vessel, I made arrangements with her builder, a skeletal, walleyed fellow named Neddy Coffin who lived in nearby Fermeuse, to restore and refit her as a proper sailing ship with accommodations for a crew of two. Then I flew back to Ontario, satisfied I had acquired the means of entering into the heart and soul of Newfoundland.

I returned to Fermeuse at the end of June to claim my ship. At first I could not find her. Thirty or forty trap boats, skiffs, and dories were slumbering at their moorings in Fermeuse harbour, which was dominated by a fish-filleting plant spouting a plume of oily black smoke from its iron chimney. It was a peaceful scene, typical of most of the hundreds of little outports that still clung to the coasts of the Rock. But where was the green schooner that should have been waiting for her new skipper?

A little boy appeared beside me, as if sprung from the rocks.

"Would you happen to know," I asked, "where the little bummer that used to belong to the Fennelys might be?"

He nodded and led me at a trot between two decayed warehouses to a spindly stage of peeled spruce poles.

Moored to it was a boat. The tide was out and she was aground and lying on her side amid broken bottles, rotting kelp, dead fish, and nameless slimy objects. Her hull had received no attention since I had last seen her, and the remains of her green paint hung from her in scrofulous tatters. Her deck presented a patchwork of gaping holes surrounding a huge, unpainted wooden box that reached from the steering well almost to the base of the bowsprit. It made her look as if she was carrying her own coffin on her back.

She was a spectacle that left me breathless.

"Lard Jasus, sorr!" said my guide with sincere appreciation. "Don't she be a wunnerful quare sight?"

I had given Neddy Coffin detailed instructions for converting the vessel into a small cruising yacht, but my wishes had conflicted with centuries of tradition, which dictated that space allotted to people aboard a boat must be kept to the irreducible minimum so as to leave as much room as possible for fish.

Neddy's attempts to obey my instructions, in opposition to his deep-rooted instincts, had led to no happy compromise. He had begun by ripping off the deck and building a cabin-trunk raised just high enough over the hull to provide a bare five feet of headroom. Then he had further shrunk the available living space by partitioning off the after third to house the monstrous engine, which, in his view, was of greater importance than the crew.

Built in the 1920s at a foundry in Lunenburg, the engine was a monolithic chunk of cast iron weighing five hundred pounds, equipped with a flywheel almost the size of a freight car wheel. To start it you poured half a cup of raw gasoline through a priming cock on the top of the single cylinder then laboriously turned the flywheel by hand until (and if) the engine fired.

Neddy had roughed out the accommodations to include two plank bunks, each sixteen inches wide at the head and twelve at the foot. They were sloped in such a fashion that the occupants' feet would normally rest six inches higher than their heads. What little space remained was mostly occupied by a galley equipped with a two-burner gasoline stove and enough lockers to hold the supplies of hardtack biscuit, salt pork, flour, tea, sugar, and turnips normally carried by fishing vessels of *Happy Adventure*'s ilk. With the exception of a small battery-powered radio and flashlights, she consumed no electricity at all. Her running lights and cabin lights were oil-fuelled. Her pumps and all her gear, including winches, were hand-powered.

Completing the work required to make her more or less seaworthy turned out to be a long and tedious business. It was not until the end of June that we felt ready to embark upon our maiden voyage. Considering what he had endured in preparation for the voyage, Jack demanded that our first port of call be some special place. The choice fell on St. Pierre and Miquelon, which we thought we could reach in three or four days.

Happy Adventure made a brave sight as she ran down Fermeuse harbour toward the open sea. With all sails set she lay over a little and snored sweetly through the water, actually overtaking some powered skiffs bound out to the fishing grounds.

All that morning we sailed south on a broad reach, keeping a two- or three-mile offing from the grim sea cliffs. Then the wind switched into the sou'east to become a dead muzzler right on our bows, bringing with it the threat of fog.

With difficulty we started the engine and by four o'clock Cape Race was looming bleak and barren off to starboard. And there we stuck. The engine thundered and the water boiled under our counter, but a powerful current had us in its grasp and the massive headland of the cape refused to slip past. Off to port an ominous grey curtain of fog was driving in from the Grand Banks. At six-thirty Jack went below to rustle up some food. An instant later his head appeared in the companionway.

"Christ, Farley! The bloody boat is *sinking!*"

I jumped to join him and saw water sluicing across the floor-boards down below. Jack was working the hand pump as if his life depended on it. It dawned on me that his life *did* depend on it, and so did mine.

Then the pump jammed.

It was a foolishly complicated thing whose innards consisted of a mass of springs and valves easily jammed by the bits of flotsam and jetsam floating in the bilges. Jack held a flashlight while I unbolted the pump's faceplate. Instantly all the springs and valves shot out and went ricocheting around the engine room like a flight of manic bees – before falling into the swirling water in the bilges.

Improbable as it may seem we found them all, put back the faceplate, and began to pump. We pumped and we pumped – and the water level rose until it reached the flywheel, which began sending a Niagara of spray onto the red-hot exhaust pipe.

We pumped.

The fog closed in inexorably until the darkness surrounding us became almost absolute. I steered what I hoped was a course for

Trepassey harbour, where we thought we might have a chance of beaching the vessel on a non-lethal shore.

Shortly before midnight I saw a faint, flashing light and headed for it, hoping it marked the harbour entrance. I did not need Jack's warning shout to tell me time was running out. The rising water had reached the carburetor, and the engine had begun to sputter.

It coughed. Stopped. Picked up again. Coughed. And stopped for good. Silently in the black night the little ship lost way. Then her forefoot struck something. She jarred and made a strange sucking sound. She had run ashore!

Trepassey, clinging forlornly to the rocky southeastern snout of Newfoundland, is a windswept, desolate little place whose houses straggle dismally around the edge of its harbour. It is, as they say in other parts of Newfoundland, "where t'fog is made."

I believe it. During the long days we lay there repairing the leak (it was in the propeller shaft) and waiting for better weather, we lived in a world of uncertain shadows where nothing seemed quite real. The fog was almost tangible. After a week of waiting for it to lift, we were desperate enough to depart for St. Pierre, though the murk was still so thick we could hardly see the length of our own vessel.

Just after noon the shadowy shape of a big motor vessel, which had picked us up on her radar, loomed alongside.

"Where you bound, skipper?" someone hailed.

"St. Pierre!"

There was a long, thoughtful silence, then, "Well, bye, I don't say as you're going to make it steering the course you're on. Unless you plans to take her up Branch River and put her on a railroad train. If 'twas me, I'd haul off to port about nine points."

Her diesels roared as she pulled away and quickly disappeared.

I altered course *ten* points, just to be sure. The compass now indicated we were steering for Bermuda, a thousand miles or so to the southwest. I wished fervently we had had our compass adjusted before sailing. As the hours dragged on, we reluctantly admitted to one another that we really did not know where we were.

Jack found this unsettling because in five days he was due back at his Toronto office. Muttering darkly, he went below to try to get a weather forecast on our small radio.

He emerged in a few minutes to say quietly – too quietly: "Farley, you aren't going to want to hear this but they're putting out an all-ships warning. Tropical storm coming up from the south with winds of sixty knots."

We spread our charts out on the wet deck and pored over them for a long time. First Jack would pore, then I would pore. This made us feel better, but was of no practical use. We did not

Jack McClelland lays out a course.

have a clue where we might be. Jack thought it might be best to head southward and try to ride out the coming storm in the open ocean rather than search for some unseen harbour and end up on the roaring rocks. In the end we simply steered straight ahead and hoped for the best.

The fog grew thicker. Somewhere the sun set. We did not bother lighting our oil-burning navigation lights for they would have been invisible from more than a few yards away. We shivered in damp oilskins as we blundered on into the heart of darkness. We told each other this was how mariners of ancient times – the Norse in their longships, the Basques in their cranky vessels, Jacques Cartier in his caravel – must have felt as they ran west into the dark unknown.

When a light breeze began to fill the sails, we shut down the noisy engine and ghosted along, ears straining for any sound. In the small hours of the morning we finally heard, very distant and indistinct off the starboard bow, the faint moan of a diaphone – a foghorn.

Diaphones can be identified one from the other by the patterns of the sounds they make. Thus, one may blow three five-second blasts at three-second intervals, while another blows for ten seconds at half-minute intervals. By timing the distant moans and then consulting the Light and Foghorn List we concluded that the one we were hearing must be on Little Burin Island on the western coast of Placentia Bay. Eureka! We started the engine, pushed it to full speed, and homed in on the horn in hopes of reaching sanctuary in Burin Harbour before the storm broke.

There was a problem. In order to hear the horn we had to stop the engine. It seemed to resent this treatment and became increasingly reluctant to run again. By dawn (indicated by a very slight brightening in the murk around us) the engine was proving almost impossible to restart – and we were close enough to shore to hear the blood-chilling roar of heavy surf bursting on rocks. The next time I stopped the engine, the horn blasted out so close at hand it almost seemed to be at our masthead.

A few days later the keeper of the light on Little Burin Island would tell us: "Heard you fellows out there for hours and hours. Couldn't make out what you was up to. Your engine would run for a bit then shut off and I never knowed was you gone ashore or what. Then, be Jasus, you'd be comin' at me again. The last time I t'ought you was comin' right up the rock and into me front door!"

We never did see Little Burin Island but somehow *Happy Adventure* found her way past it and into Burin Inlet, where we drifted through a grey soup. Somewhere a dog barked and a church bell was ringing. Jack swung the lead from the bows and when he got four fathoms the anchor went over. The heavy chain rattled out and *Happy Adventure* came to rest.

I woke about noon to find the cabin full of sunlight. The fog had gone and the day was brilliant. We were at anchor in the middle of a fleet of trap skiffs and dories. An elderly man wearing his Sunday best was rowing a dory toward us. He paused a few feet away and leaned on his oars.

"Mornin', skipper. Come in through the fog, did ye?"

I admitted that we had.

"Well now. Don't know as ever I see a thicker nor a blacker one. Don't know as I'd a-cared to bring a vessel through it."

We invited him aboard for a drink, after which he carried us ashore for Sunday dinner with his wife and family. Only then did we discover he was the captain of a coastal trading ship and realize how high a compliment he had paid us. He did more. In view of the approaching storm, he insisted on piloting us to a new anchorage at Spoon Cove, the most sheltered nook in Burin Inlet.

Such was our welcome to the Sou'west Coast of Newfoundland.

Jack was unable to enjoy it for long. There was a phone in Burin, with which he foolishly called his office, to be ordered home at once. That afternoon a hired car took him to St. John's, leaving me and *Happy Adventure* to ride out the gale in the snug shelter of Spoon Cove.

Two days later I was joined there by Mike Donovan. Mike, who was currently Newfoundland's director of Library Services, had been one of my lieutenants and closest friends in northwestern Europe during the war. On the pretext of inspecting libraries on the Burin Peninsula (there weren't any), he had now absented himself from St. John's to help me sail *Happy Adventure* on to St. Pierre.

Mike, who described himself as a "long, lean drink of Irish bog water," had a black sense of humour and a talent for getting into and out of difficulties. I welcomed him with open arms, into which he placed six bottles of rum, the bulk of his luggage.

Mike was not what one would call a seasoned mariner. He had lived most of his life in Ontario and had only been to sea as a passenger in troopships crossing the Atlantic. I gave him a crash course. I showed him over the vessel, pointing out and naming everything of importance; then I ran him through such standard procedures as making sail, lowering sail, handling the sheets, steering with a tiller, letting go the anchor, and spinning the flywheel of the engine. He proved adept at all these things and I was much heartened, until I sent him off in our little dinghy to practise rowing and he turned it over on top of himself. When he was hauled, shivering and trembling, onto *Happy Adventure*'s deck, he put on his broadest smile and broadest Irish accent.

"Faith and begorra! And wouldn't that be just the dandy rig for swimmin' in the rain?"

Mike's ignorance of the sea and ships had one advantage: he did not know enough to be nervous. In his eyes *Happy Adventure* was the staunchest little vessel ever launched. He trusted her absolutely, and kept on doing so even when she did her best to disillusion him. Not, mind you, that he failed to take precautions. Before he squeezed into his bunk that first night he hammered a large St. Christopher's medal into the plank above his head.

I am no Roman Catholic but I left the medal there after Mike's eventual departure. *Somebody* must have been keeping an eye on us in the days ahead. Whether it was St. Christopher or the Old Man of the Sea I do not know. It may have taken both of them working as a team to do the job.

Two days after Mike joined the ship, we set sail for St. Pierre, still fifty miles to the westward past the toe of the projecting boot of the Burin Peninsula. In honour of this, Mike's first voyage, I served a special breakfast – boiled rounders with hot pork fat poured over them. A Newfoundland delicacy, rounders are small cod that have been sun-dried "in the round" rather than split. They have a flavour and aroma not unlike old cheese. Mike had never tasted them before, but he was game.

Entering Placentia Bay, *Happy Adventure* began pitching into a big, slow, queasy swell – a legacy of the tropical storm. As she rose and fell Mike turned white, lurched to the rail, and lost his breakfast. When he had finished he announced that he did not really care for rounders – "not twice on the same morning."

The breeze freshened until we were bowling along under full sail. To take Mike's mind off his troubles I gave him the tiller. He had some difficulty at first because, unlike a steering wheel, a tiller requires the steersman to push it in the *opposite* direction to the way he wishes to go. He was beginning to get the hang of this when we passed a pod of pothead (otherwise called pilot) whales: sleek, black beasts as long as a dory. They were pursuing a school of squid with such singleness of purpose that some of them surfaced and blew their fishy breath right alongside, causing Mike to lose his rounders yet again.

In mid-afternoon I slung my binoculars around my neck and climbed to the mainmast crosstree to see if I could spot the distant loom of St. Pierre. Instead, I saw a glistening black object of enormous size close ahead. I took it to be one of the great whales – a finner, or even a blue, the largest creature on earth. However, as we came closer I realized it was not a whale but a basking shark. It was immense. Lazing on the surface with its dorsal fin standing up like a trysail, it appeared quite unconscious of our approach, or at any rate quite unperturbed. Since it was longer than *Happy Adventure*, perhaps it assumed *we* would get out of *its* way.

With a collision looming, I bellowed to Mike.

"Hard a-starboard! Hard over! Quick!"

No blame for what followed should attach to him. He had only just learned that "starboard" meant "right." He had only just learned to steer a boat with a tiller. *Happy Adventure* swung to port. We were travelling at about five knots, which is no great speed, but the shark was very nearly an immovable object. We hit him just behind the dorsal fin. There was a rubbery jolt that almost catapulted me from the crosstree. I don't believe he suffered any serious injury as our cut-water slid up on his slippery back. I don't know about his dignity, but I lost any I possessed as I slid down the mast like a monkey on a greased pole.

It was a wonderful day to be at sea, and the denizens of the ocean seemed to be making the most of it. Skeins of cormorants and gannets threaded the pale blue sky as rafts of eider ducks bobbled out of *Happy Adventure*'s way, casting anxious looks at us over their shoulders. The breeze held steady and *Happy Adventure* practically sailed herself, leaving us to laze about on deck singing Newfoundland songs and toasting the Old Man of the Sea with Mike's rum.

As evening drew on we entered the Passe de Nord-est, leading into St. Pierre's harbour, where we were overtaken by a big seagoing dory under power. Her name, *Oregon*, was writ large on her bow. I recognized her and her owner, bull-voiced Théophile Detcheverry, who, during my visit to St. Pierre in 1957, had taken me to the site of *Fort Boise*'s stranding. I had said then that I would return someday and now here I was in my own boat.

The Angels Sing

Les Isles de St. Pierre et Miquelon are a remarkable anomaly, a tiny piece of France consisting chiefly of three sombre mounds of granite rising out of once fish-filled waters some twelve miles off the south coast of Newfoundland. St. Pierre is a mere four miles long and four wide but, possessed of the archipelago's only deep-water harbour, it became home to the largest settlement.

Three miles to the northwest and separated from St. Pierre by a strait mysteriously called La Baie is Langlade or Petit Miquelon. Farther to the north lies Grand Miquelon. These two are twins linked by a remarkable umbilicus – a seven-mile-long isthmus of sand whose shores boast some of the most spectacular beaches on the northwestern coast of the continent.

The islands were well forested until the arrival of Europeans. Now they are mostly barren, nurturing only scrubby patches of conifers and willows in the most sheltered places. They were denuded (as were the coastal regions of Newfoundland) by far-faring fishers of whales and cod, mostly from the coasts of Portugal and the Bay of Biscay (Bay of the Basques), who as early as the mid-fifteenth century began building their whale-oil tryworks, stages, and fish-drying flakes on the little archipelago.

Few localities in the New World offered better bases for trans-atlantic fishermen. In consequence, Les Isles long remained bones of contention to be fought over, not just by individual squatters but by nations. They changed hands several times but in the end were retained by France as a last fragment of the far-flung lands she had once claimed in North America.

When *Happy Adventure* arrived at St. Pierre, the compact town had nearly three thousand inhabitants. Its crowded houses, narrow lanes, abundance of bistros and cafés, sprawling quays, and a central *place* where old men played the ancient bowling game of *pelota* all gave the impression that this was a part of France that had somehow gone adrift across the foggy waters of the western Atlantic. But although the tricolour flew over it and metropolitan gendarmes patrolled its streets, St. Pierre's inhabitants were of two nations. The majority were descendants of fishermen from ports on the coast of Normandy, but a significant minority were of Basque origin and still used the ancient language of that intractable race which, to this day, has refused to be assimilated by any other.

Théophile Detcheverry was a citizen of France but he was first and foremost a Basque. In his early sixties, solidly built, he had a saturnine, hawk-nosed face and a knowing air. He seemed delighted at my return to what he called, perhaps with some irony, the islands of the blessed. Born of and into the small, almost solidly Basque community that was the only settlement on Miquelon, his allegiance belonged to that mysterious people, not to anything as Johnny-come-lately to history as the French.

Claire and Théophile Detcheverry.

There was more. During the recent war he had actively supported General de Gaulle and the Free French, whereas many St. Pierrais had favoured Marshal Pétain and his collaboration with the Nazis. Théo was also an agnostic with a soft spot for the Baha'i religion whereas most St. Pierrais were at least nominal Roman Catholics. To top it off, he was a fervent socialist in a community dominated by a well entrenched merchant class.

Brimming with primal energy and instinct, Théo vigorously pursued every good-looking woman he encountered. He had fathered four children in wedlock and who knows how many outside of it. Nevertheless, his heart belonged not to a woman but to a boat.

She was his dory, *Oregon*.

Oregon and her sisters were unique to the isles. Twenty-three feet in length, she was almost half as long again as most dories used in the Newfoundland fishery. She was propelled by two pairs of sweeps, a sail of sorts, and a four-horsepower make-and-break engine fitted with a retractable shaft and propeller that could be raised into a housing in her bottom, thus enabling her to be run over shoals. She and her sisters needed no sheltered harbours. They could fish from the "hard" of any sand or gravel beach, where they could be hauled up by wooden windlasses. They had no equal for seaworthiness, regularly venturing out as much as thirty miles to fish the offshore banks. Gull-fashion, they could ride out stormy weather that would send much larger vessels scuttling for shelter.

Théo's dory had been built for him in Miquelon in 1928 and originally christened *Térèse* in memory of his mother. He fished her single-handed until he had saved enough money to marry the girl he wanted. Things went well for the couple until the Great Depression began. Then the market for salt fish collapsed, forcing Théo to mortgage his treasured dory to a St. Pierre merchant.

In the winter of 1932 the American steamer *Oregon*, bound from Montreal to Britain with freight and passengers, diverted to St. Pierre, seeking shelter from a storm that was rapidly developing into a hurricane. By the time the ship had struggled to within sight of the islands, wind and sea were so fierce her captain dared not risk the rock-guarded entrance without a pilot, so he hove to in the maelstrom and radioed for one. By then conditions were so bad the pilots concluded they would be unable to reach her. None would try, but there was one fisherman in St. Pierre who would.

As Théophile Detcheverry recalled his moment of decision: "*Bien*, it was not possible just to let that ship blow down upon the reefs. Perhaps it was also not possible to get aboard her; but me, I believed maybe if I could get out to her I could *lead* her into port like a dog brings a cow into the barn."

A crowd of fellow fishermen helped him launch his dory. Then, when nobody volunteered to accompany him, Théo set off alone. Once in the outer harbour the dory could hardly make headway, pitching so high into the spray-filled air and slamming down so hard against the grey-beard seas that watchers on shore expected to see her break her back. Théo resolutely kept her heading into the breaking seas and, foot by foot, the dory fought her way toward *Oregon*, which by then was labouring so heavily she seemed to be half-submerged as she tried to prevent herself from being driven onto the roaring reefs and islets at the mouth of Passe du Nord-est.

One of the officers clinging to the wing of her bridge spotted the dory when it was only a few hundred feet distant. The cacophony of wind and waves was by then so overwhelming that Théo could not communicate with the ship, except visually. Using one arm to prevent himself being pitched overboard, he waved frantically with the other.

His meaning was unmistakable: FOLLOW ME!

Choosing his moment as the dory sank into the trough between two mighty seas, he slewed her around before she could be caught broadside and capsized. The steamer attempted to do likewise. As the ship came broadside to seas almost as high as her bridge, she rolled so far down Théo thought she would go right over. Somehow she righted herself and slowly followed her barely visible guide between the reefs, into the lee of the land, and so to the safety of an anchorage in the roads of the outer harbour.

Her passengers and crew made much of Théo, collecting a purse of three hundred dollars for him. He used the money to pay off the debt against his dory, to whom he now gave a new name. From now on she would be *Oregon*. When I asked him why he had made the change, he shrugged.

"*Eh bien*, it was *her* save that Yankee ship you know. Me? I was along for the ride."

After helping us moor *Happy Adventure*, Théo took Mike and me to his rambling old house for supper. We were joined there by Martin Dutin, a bouncy municipal *fonctionnaire* from France, now married to Odille, one of Théo's daughters; and by Théo's son

George and his French-born wife. George was the master of a twenty-thousand-ton tanker sailing out of Marseilles, but was home on the islands for a holiday.

The party lasted into the small hours, and Théo became fixated on my little vessel, which, he said, was *un petit fantôme* – a little ghost of the ships his ancestors had sailed in.

"In old times, you understand, Basque ships carried our flag all over the *Atlantique*, whaling, and trading with a hundred countries, and finding the way to strange places. Like those Phoenicians in ancient times we Basques were masters of the northern seas. Then, because there were not so many of us in our little mountain countries by the Bay of Biscay – they are called provinces now – we were driven off the seas by the French and Spaniards, who took our ships, our ports, and our flag, and would have buried us had we not kept our language and our memories alive. These they could not take. What a pleasure it would be to see a ship sailing the seas again with our flag flying at her truck!"

It may have been the passion in his voice, or it may have been the fact that my glass had not been empty since our arrival in St. Pierre. I was in the mood to make grand gestures.

"Théo, I know my boat's just a little bit of a thing but I'd be happy to have her fly your flag."

In an instant he was on his feet, bellowing: "*Nom de nom!* Then we will get her one! *Oui!* We will do more: we Basques of Miquelon, we will adopt your little ship and you and Michel, and make you all Basques!"

Théo's wife, Bernice, promised to make the flag for us. Théo undertook to make a Basque translation of *Happy Adventure* and paint it on her bows and stern. Martin Dutin volunteered to arrange a ceremonial re-christening and blessing of the vessel. Somewhat carried away, George Detcheverry declared his intention of sailing the new Basque flagship back to the homeland.

There remained one small problem. It came to light next morning when I stepped out of my bunk into six inches of icy water. My ship was once again sinking under me.

Helped by the crew of a nearby Spanish dragger, Mike and I pumped like mad and finally got the water level down below the floorboards but it was clear nothing would halt the inflow short of hauling the vessel out and finding and sealing the leak, which, I suspected, had resulted from our collision with the basking shark.

I was ready to run *Happy Adventure* aground on a mud bank at the inner end of the harbour and let the falling tide dry her out, when a red-faced, bald-headed fellow who introduced himself as Paulo Lescoublet, foreman of the St. Pierre Shipyards, offered to haul her out of the water on one of the wheeled cradles of the yard's steam-powered marine railway. An hour later *Happy Adventure* rose dripping from the polluted harbour, like Aphrodite rising from the foam, as Mike poetically put it.

Paulo Lescoublet.

A cursory examination revealed we had not got her out any too soon. Not only was her cutwater cracked but the stop-waters were gone; also an entire plank in her port after-quarter was rotted through. And vibrations from the old bullgine had shaken most of the oakum out of her seams.

Martin Dutin arrived to stare incredulously, shake his head, and passionately urge Paulo to get his shipwrights to work at once because the christening was arranged for Thursday, three days hence. And no, it could not be delayed. A festival to celebrate the rebirth of the Basque mercantile marine had been scheduled and could not be postponed.

It was at this critical juncture that I fell in love.

Cupid was a dog named Blanche who belonged to the shipyard. His name was a puzzlement because Blanche was a very large, coal-black male. According to Théo, who was an expert in such matters, Blanche was a singularly horny male. While inside my vessel painting the cabin, I heard the sounds of a scuffle nearby. I poked my head out the companionway in time to see a lithesome young woman swarming up the ladder that leaned against *Happy Adventure*'s flank. Whining expectantly, Blanche was endeavouring to follow this attractive stranger.

I could see why. As slim and graceful as a ballet dancer (which, I would later learn, was one of her avocations), she appeared to be wearing a gleaming golden helmet (her own smoothly bobbed head of hair) and was as radiantly lovely as any Saxon goddess.

I invited her aboard, while pushing the dog down the ladder.

"That's only Blanche," I reassured my visitor. "He won't bite. He's just, uh . . . being friendly."

"That's nice to know," she said sweetly.

Then she smiled and I was lost.

Claire Angel Wheeler was then twenty-seven. Born in Toronto to a First World War veteran and his English war bride, Claire had lived all her life in that city. A graduate of the Ontario College of Art with an adventurous spirit, she longed to experience something of what lay beyond Toronto's confines. She also wanted to learn colloquial French, so when she heard about a summer school – l'École Orale Française – being started in St. Pierre, she travelled east to enrol in its first session.

On this fine day she had come down to the waterfront to sketch the vessels hauled out at the shipyard. When Blanche spotted Claire, she had sought refuge on top of a pile of lumber. When the indefatigable Blanche pursued her there, she climbed my ladder.

I was in no hurry to see her leave. *Happy Adventure* was due to be launched that afternoon so I invited Miss Wheeler to remain aboard for the occasion. She agreed, perhaps partly because Blanche was still pacing impatiently about at the foot of the ladder.

While waiting for Mike to return from some errand, and for Paulo to fire up the boiler of his winch engine, I showed my guest around my little vessel. Freshly painted inside and out, *Happy Adventure* had never looked (or smelled) better.

Claire examined the two *very* narrow bunks in the forepeak with interest but without comment. Nautical paraphernalia scattered around, including a gleaming brass patent log of early nineteenth-century manufacture designed to be towed astern to measure the speed and distance covered, appealed to the artist in her. A bundle of star flares for use if it became necessary to abandon ship seemed to give her food for thought.

She was intrigued by the little galley, which she said looked as if it belonged in a doll's house with its pint-sized Primus stove, toy-like utensils, and miniature copper kettle. She noted that there was no sink but accepted without comment my explanation that there was no need for one since the ocean was wide, deep, and handy. And she endeared herself to me by *not* asking where the toilet was.

Claire averted her gaze from the monstrous phallus that was the bullgine's single, upright cylinder, but gave a friendly pat to the iron Peanut heating stove, which though just big enough to hold three small lumps of coal was nevertheless capable of keeping *Happy Adventure*'s cabin cosy during the coldest weather.

She also appreciated *Happy Adventure*'s decor. I had received explicit instructions from Théo about the vessel's colour scheme and had obeyed them to the letter.

"You will please to cover up that corpse-green colour of her hull and paint her black above the waterline. Her boot top, she will be white. Her bottom, she will be red. Her deck, she will be dory-buff. Her masts you will scrape, then oil, and you will paint the mast-heads and the crosstrees white. When you have finish, she will not look like something very old and dead pulled out of the sea . . . she will look like a Basque ship should."

I was still explaining *Happy Adventure's* intricacies and mysteries when Mike returned. Shortly thereafter, Paulo blew a great blast on the steam whistle to warn the world that a launch was about to take place. Then the massive wheeled cradle holding *Happy Adventure* went rumbling down the rails, returning her to the sea with a resounding splash.

I started the engine, and we motored over to the government dock to pick up the harbour master, who had undertaken to adjust our compass. Under his instruction and under what I hoped were my guest's admiring eyes, I steered my little vessel on various courses while the harbour master "swung" the compass, adjusting the direction its needle pointed by moving tiny magnets around the circumference of the brass compass housing.

This done, we moored alongside Paulo's old wooden launch and trooped across the *place* to celebrate a day well spent, at the Café l'Éscale.

It had been *singularly* well spent as far as I was concerned. Much later, as I slowly walked Claire back to the house where she was boarding with a St. Pierre family, I sensed this might be the beginning of the happiest adventure of my life.

Happy Adventure began *her* new life as a Basque vessel two days later when Mike and I were wakened not long after dawn by a tentative knocking on the cabin trunk. Sleepily I slid back the hatch to find it was raining, but standing on the wet deck of Paulo's old boat alongside was a bedraggled little group, including a lugubrious Dominican priest and two small boys who I assumed were acolytes. They were accompanied by Théo and George Detcheverry and Martin Dutin.

In the eerie dawn light, they looked not unlike a Dürer print of mourners come to claim a corpse. In truth they were there to bless *Happy Adventure* in her reincarnation, to wash away her Protestant taint and make an honest woman of her.

As they came crowding into the cabin, the Father seemed preoccupied. While the boys intoned a prayer, he uncorked a large bottle of holy water and poised it over our small saloon table. Sniffing softly because he had a cold, he pronounced the blessing. Then, as he uttered the new Basque name of our little vessel, he sneezed. Hugely.

Holy water flew in all directions. The embarrassed Father beat a hasty retreat. Being a good dogan, Mike's sympathy for the priest was deeper than mine.

"Don't snigger, Farley," he said as he mopped holy water off his sleeping bag. "Just *you* try saying the new name of this silly boat and see what happens."

Why don't you, dear reader, try it for yourself?

Itxaxozale Alai, pronounced *Itchatchozale Alai.*

Newfoundlanders have a saying that a voyage badly begun will come to a good conclusion. It was so with this affair. Heedless of the early hour and the drizzling rain, Théo climbed down into our little dinghy and began painting the vessel's new name in gold on both bows and across her stern. Martin shook out the large Basque flag Madame Detcheverry had made for us. It was a gorgeous concoction of silk and satin embroidered with gold thread. Emblazoned on a red background was a green-and-white cross and the crests of the Seven Provinces which had comprised Basque country before the French seized four of them and the Spaniards the other three.

Martin formally opened a squat bottle of a green liquor unfamiliar to me.

"This is Izaro. National drink of the Basques. We will toast *Itxaxozale Alai* in her native drink."

As we did this I ceased to wonder why it had taken the French and the Spanish eight hundred years to overcome the Basques and why they have not yet completely succeeded in doing so.

By eleven o'clock, the hour set for the public celebration, the rain had ceased. A crowd gathered on the wharf and on nearby vessels was in a festive mood. Acting as *chef de protocol*, Martin mounted to the roof of Paulo's launch while a musical group in traditional Basque costume sounded a fanfare. Then Martin called on Madame Detcheverry, godmother to the vessel, to do her duty.

She did it with a will, swinging a ribbon-tethered bottle of Izaro with such vigour it missed its target and soared across our deck to smash with a gratifying explosion against the wharf, while vessels' horns and sirens shrilled from all around the harbour and the hoarse bellow of the shipyard steam engine joined the tribute. As the echoes died away, we all adjourned to l'Éscale to celebrate the reappearance, after an absence of some hundreds of years, of the Basque flag flown by a Basque vessel.

L'Éscale was one of several bars ranged around the *place* offering comfort and conviviality to men from the fleets of France, Portugal, and Spain who fished the Grand Banks but came into St. Pierre for shelter from bad storms, for repairs, or for supplies. L'Éscale was most mariners' first choice, not because it had anything special to offer in the way of food or drink, but because of its proprietor, Madame Ella Geradin, a brassy blonde with a wicked sense of humour and a weakness for strays. Ella had decided at first meeting that Mike and I and our little vessel belonged in the latter category.

With Ella's blessing and connivance, the party celebrating *Itxaxozale Alai*'s christening became a prolonged and memorable occasion. I can't recall all of it. What I *do* remember is realizing early on that life without the ongoing companionship of Claire Wheeler would be an intolerable prospect. And I remember the way Mike Donovan resolved the problem of how to deal with my schooner's new name.

At some point in the evening Mike swayed to his feet to propose a toast that went something like this: "Cracking fine boat, that one. So what I say is" – he paused to refill his glass and hoist it high – "may the good Lord give her tight seams and a bloody good pump; and don't *ever* let the little bitch get far from shore. Here's to *Itchy-ass Sally*. . . ."

His version of the name was certainly easier to say and to remember, if altogether lacking in dignity. I became used to it in time, and even to its diminutive, which would follow the vessel almost to the end of her days.

Itchy.

The French Isles

I had assumed that *Itchy*'s new port of registry, emblazoned on her stern, would be St. Pierre, but I found Théo had painted *Miquelon* under her new name. When I asked why, he explained: "She is Basque, *n'est-ce pas?* So that is your new home port. You must sail her there at once to show the flag."

This sounded like a good idea, especially if I could persuade Mademoiselle Wheeler to come along.

Resplendent in her new paint, her new flag flying gaudily from her main truck, her compass adjusted, and her bullgine temporarily amenable, *Itchy* looked and even seemed to be a well-found little ship, worthy of admiration. I hoped her captain would be found deserving of some too, and when Claire accepted my invitation I was delighted, even ecstatic.

Itchy was seriously overcrowded but fine weather, good company, and much good food and drink made the outward voyage a convivial frolic. I put George Etcheverry at the vessel's helm so I could concentrate on posturing as the salty master of an ocean-going vessel for Claire's benefit.

Even with a brisk favouring breeze, it took us six hours to sail to Anse au Miquelon. As we rounded Chatte Rock, we could see people launching large, multicoloured dories from Miquelon's great sweep of cobble beach. By the time we were half a mile off the small and exposed wharf in the centre of the curving shoreline, we had an escort of several dories. Their crews appeared friendly, though not demonstratively so.

"That is the Basque way," Martin explained to me. "Cautious with strangers."

Only later did we learn that the dorymen had hurried to meet us in the expectation that we were customers from Newfoundland come to purchase firewater.

As we bore down toward the semicircle of weathered wooden houses behind the beach, our new Basque flag snapping overhead seemed to be exchanging greetings with a larger version flying from a staff at the end of the dock. We moored and went ashore to mingle with the few people and many dogs and horses straggling along a track that was the only "street." It led past a cavernous grey barn of a church to the wind-battered house of a fisherman of eighty-odd years who seemed to be the leader of this isolated community of some two hundred people. Martin explained who we were and why we were there, and we were gravely invited to make ourselves at home.

There being no hotel, my crew was offered quarters for the night in private houses, but I was uneasy about leaving *Itchy* unattended in her exposed position at the wharf so I returned there to keep her company. Near midnight Mike decided to rejoin me at the boat. By then the unlighted street had become a dormitory for the many small black ponies and large black dogs that roamed the village by day. It was Mike's misfortune to stumble over one of these.

Polite as always, Mike apologized.

"*Sorry*, doggie. *Nice* doggie. Won't happen again."

When the dog replied with a shrill whinny, Mike jumped backward and collided with a second slumbering beast. Again he apologized, but this time was careful not to mistake the creature's identity.

"*Sorry*, horsie! *Really* very sorry!"

Feeling his way with extreme caution now, he eventually reached the boat.

"Listen, Farl," he told me uneasily. "I think we oughta get the hell out of this place. It's bad enough being whinnied at by a goddamn dog but when the horses start growling at you, it's time to be on your way!"

Heavy fog rolling in on a light easterly made me so uneasy I was unable to sleep. Sometime in the pre-dawn hours I heard the distant beat of a make-and-break engine. Before long something bumped gently against *Itchy's* hull. I went on deck and helped two oilskin-clad figures clamber aboard.

They introduced themselves as John and Spence Manuel from Connaigre Bay on Newfoundland's Sou'west Coast. They were shy at first, but at length admitted they had made the thirty-mile crossing in their old trap skiff "to get a drop of the good stuff, you understand. They's three weddings on the go and nary a drop to be had around the Bay. Hard toimes, me son, 'less some of we don't do somethin' about it."

I warmed them with coffee and rum then accompanied them to the house of a fisherman who ran a small export business. We sat in his kitchen for a while sampling the goods and talking about the "trade."

I learned it had begun a century and a half earlier when the British authorities in Newfoundland decided to put an end to the age-old duty-free commerce between St. Pierre and Miquelon and Newfoundland. Revenue cutters had been built and manned, and a constabulary put on guard along the coast. With minimal effect. On foggy nights small boats had continued to put out from the little outports of southern Newfoundland to make their way in darkness to the French Isles, where the crews traded fish bait, salmon, firewood, caribou meat, and furs for sugar, flour, clothing, tea, and, by no means least, rum from the French islands in the Caribbean.

The pattern had changed somewhat in recent times. Although there was no longer a shortage of staples in southern Newfoundland, a shortage of alcohol persisted, so the trade continued to thrive. Customers arriving in Miquelon no longer bartered but paid spot cash for what they wanted. And what they wanted most was no longer rum but high-potency grain alcohol.

Alky, as it was called, came in wooden cases, each containing two ten-litre cans. It cost fifty cents a litre. One litre, well diluted, packed a wallop equal to that obtainable from three or four quart bottles of "store liquor" as retailed by the government in St. John's. There was no contest between alky and the government product.

Prior to Newfoundland's merger with Canada, efforts to prevent smuggling had depended on a few aging cutters crewed by men recruited from the thirsty outports. In consequence, few arrests were made. After Confederation, however, prevention became the responsibility of the federal government's Royal Canadian Mounted Police, who, as the Manuel brothers remarked, were "a different kittle of fish." The RCMP deployed a fleet of big, swift new vessels such as the *Commissioner Wood*, a gunboat built like a destroyer, manned by a dozen policemen, and armed with a quick-firing cannon. Fitted with high-powered radar and supported by aerial surveillance, she and the rest of the Mountie fleet should have been able to suppress the trade.

That they had signally failed to do so was a fitting tribute to the skills, hardihood, and thirst of the fishermen of southern Newfoundland.

I helped the Manuels load their skiff. The cargo consisted of six crates – twelve cans in all. As each crate went aboard, one of the brothers attached sacks filled with salt to it. This, they explained, was the "insurance."

"If one of they Mountie cutters happens onto we, us'll heave bags and all over the side. The salt sinks the boxes straight to the bottom, and there they stops 'til the salt melts into the water. How long it takes depends on how much salt you puts in to the bags. You can time it pretty close. When the boxes floats up they'll be a scattering of skiffs or dories handy, jiggin' cod as innocent as you please. And the Mounties never a whit the wiser."

Waking groggily soon after dawn, I decided to clear my head with a quick plunge from the end of the wharf. I was flailing about in the frigid water when I glimpsed several shark-like dorsal fins slicing toward me. For a terrible moment I thought I was under attack, then I realized that the fins belonged to dolphins.

They raced toward me like a spread of torpedoes. As I trod water, uncertain what to do, they went shooting past on either side so close I imagined I could feel the caress of their sleek bodies. I recognized them by their black and tan colours as white-sided dolphins. They seemed to want to play. As I waited in wonderment, the pod swiftly circled, sped seaward, then abruptly turned and came for me again, still at flank speed. This time the leader shot bodily out of the water and passed almost directly over my head, a hundred-pound projectile travelling so fast he, or she, was barely more than a flashing blur. One by one the followers repeated their leader's acrobatics.

Then they were gone.

I swam to the ladder, climbed up, and waited hopefully on the pier-head, but the dolphins did not return, nor could I see any further trace of them on a sea now glowing an opalescent rose under a rising sun. They had, as seamen say, "made their signal" and gone their way.

The bells of the gaunt old church intruded into my thoughts, which were not so much about the extraordinary behaviour of the dolphins as about whether Miss Wheeler would have been as moved as I had been. Somehow I thought she would have been.

Once all hands were aboard again we hoisted sail and set course back to St. Pierre. The wind proving fickle, I started the bull-gine. It decided to be recalcitrant, refusing to run unless I squeezed into the tiny engine room and, squatting beside it, opened and closed the igniter manually. This was an odious business for I was deafened by thunderous explosions and almost asphyxiated by exhaust fumes from a leaky gasket. Even worse was the apprehension that I would appear incompetent in Claire Wheeler's eyes. My fears on that score were put to rest when, unasked, she brought me a long drink of gin and gently squeezed my arm before going back up on deck. I knew then that whatever else she might prove to be, she would be a good shipmate.

It had been my plan to sail *Itchy* back to Newfoundland waters in mid-August so Mike could at least make the gesture of assessing library needs in the Burin Peninsula. Now I decided we could not leave St. Pierre until the engine had been completely overhauled. In truth I did not *want* to leave so long as Claire remained on the island, and she was supposed to continue her studies at the École Orale for another two weeks.

Through Paulo I arranged for a mechanic to deal with the bull-gine and was not unhappy to learn he would be unable to work on it for some days, so *Itchy* would remain moored to the wharf while the world unfolded as it ought.

One afternoon Mike, who was at least as observant as the next man, informed me he intended to spend a night ashore. He told me

Ella Giradin, Mistress of l'Éscale.

he and Paulo had arranged to give a dinner at l'Éscale in honour of some of the lady students of l'École Orale. Blandly he inquired if I would care to come.

It was a perfectly splendid party attended by a lot of Detcheverrys, Dutins, and other local people. And by Claire. This time Paulo acted as *chef de protocol* and when he judged the time was right (sometime before dawn) spirited Claire and me out of l'Éscale and escorted us across the dark and silent Place to *Itchy*, drowsing at the dockside with her head under her wing. Paulo, Mike, and one or two other worthies then mounted guard at a discreet distance from the vessel to ensure there would be no untoward disturbances for the remainder of that magic night.

There followed halcyon times.

In the mornings I would waken to the sound of the harbour waters slapping gently against the hull where we lay snug against the jetty. I would climb lazily out of the bunk to stick my head out through the fore hatch and sniff the mingled aroma of cod, coal smoke, and cooking from the town, then go back below and make a cup of tea for my sleeping love.

When she was up and ready we would amble across the *place* to l'Éscale, where Madame Ella, having seen us coming, would have freshly baked croissants with honey waiting for us. Quiet fellows wearing dark blue berets and sitting at little iron tables having coffee or a drop of something stronger would give us a smile and a casual *bonjour*, and we would listen respectfully while they discussed all manner of things dealing with the world of ocean, which was the only world they really cared about.

Later my love would go shopping for hot and crunchy bread from the tiny *boulangerie*, and fresh milk from a wooden cart pulled by a big black dog and loaded with old wine bottles filled with still-warm milk. Or she might amble to the fishermen's stalls for fresh halibut steaks, a chunk of salmon, or some sole fillets, before visiting the *épicerie* for cheese from some far-off vale in the French Alps.

After lunch, if the fog held off, we might climb the treeless hills behind the town and walk through fields of blue lupines and scented grasses to the high dome of Cap Diable. From there we could look southeast over the neat rectangles of the weathered little town below, across the double harbour past Galantry Head to a distant curl of foam marking the haunted reef called les Enfants Perdus, beyond which lay the grey shores of Newfoundland.

If the fog came rolling in we might make our way through ghostly streets to Le Select, from behind whose long bar Jean Corbier would pour us a noggin and tell us yarns of the great days of *le whiskey* when St. Pierre and Miquelon were targets of interest and sometimes of the guns of prohibition-smitten Americans. Jean brought to life for us the row of windowless concrete warehouses, built like wartime bunkers, that lined the waterfront but were now hollowly empty. In the 1920s and early 1930s they had been stacked to the rafters with thousands of cases of whiskey, brandy, rum, and wines. He recalled for us the elusive, hard-faced men who had manned swift and sometimes nameless vessels that came and went from St. Pierre by night to rendezvous with black-painted motorboats off the coasts of the New England states. And he showed us the table in Le Select where legendary U.S. gangster Al Capone had held court when visiting this outpost of his empire.

There was much to do and see and hear in the days when Claire and I were weaving the first strands of the tapestry that would become our lives together.

One day Théo came by to invite us along on an expedition in *Oregon* to Miquelon's Great Barachoix. He had agreed to deliver Martin Dutin and his friend Bernard and their wives to their campsite there. Mike could not join us. He had to return to work and since *Itchy* was unable to carry him back to Newfoundland, the local ferry would. We said a fond *à bientôt* to him, with never a suspicion that this was the last voyage he would ever make with us. All too soon cancer would take him.

It was warm and sunny on the morning that Claire and I made our way to *Oregon*, where the rest of the party had already assembled, laden with camping gear and hampers of good things to eat and drink. Smoking a large cigar and wearing a khaki-coloured boiler suit and a tropical pith helmet, Théo greeted us grandly. He was a man with many heroes and on this day was honouring a rather unusual couple: Britain's Winston Churchill and Nazi Germany's Field Marshal Erwin Rommel.

Under Théo's direction we slacked off the capstan and *Oregon* bumped noisily down her rollers into the sea. We boarded and the ladies made themselves comfortable under rugs up in the bow while the men slouched in the stern sheets, close to the make-and-break. A smaller version of *Itchy*'s bullgine, this one was not so temperamental. Théo had kept it running for more than thirty years, during which it had become a weird melange of brazing, welding, soldering, and grafted-on parts. It drove *Oregon* hissing and plunging through the ocean swell at the speed of a trotting horse.

Passing out of the North Channel, we soon came under the loom of Grand Colombier, which, though a mere dot of an island, rises almost sheer out of the sea to a height of six hundred feet. Flocks of puffins wheeled away from its cliffs as we approached. It seemed such a forbidding fastness that Bernard decided he and I should climb it. Théo laid *Oregon* alongside with consummate skill and quickly backed the dory off to safety as soon as the two of us had leapt from the bow to the rocks.

We had a hard scramble up the cliff, made even more difficult because it was riddled with holes originally dug by puffins but now mostly in the possession of brown rats. Survivors of some long-forgotten shipwreck, the rats fed on puffin eggs and young. According to Théo the puffins retaliated by digging out and gobbling up baby rats.

Gaining the crest, Bernard and I found ourselves on a plateau perhaps three acres in extent surrounded by what looked like a ruined wall five or six feet high. A lush growth of grasses and flowering plants coated the enclosed space. I thought the wall must have been man-made. Théo agreed.

"Has nobody ever dug up there to see what they could find?" I asked.

"*Oui.* In my *grandpère's* time five men climb up with shovels and go to work, but soon the ground begin to shake. Those men, they try to come down the cliff but the island shake them off into the sea and three of them are drown. Nobody try since then."

Now *Oregon* pounded on through a violent tide rip across the channel called *la baie* into the lee of the massive cliffs of the island of Langlade. With the rising sun warming our faces, we coasted along to Percé Rock, an out-thrust bastion of high cliffs pierced by a tunnel through which *Oregon* barked an echoing passage that sent flights of storm petrels flitting around us like monster butterflies. At Anse aux Soldats we went ashore on a pebble beach under the sea cliffs where during the summers two families made their livings fishing lobster and capelin.

Each July millions of sardine-like capelin came to this hidden place. Gleaming masses of green-flanked males and less flamboyant females allowed themselves to be washed ashore by each incoming wave to form a living carpet on the gravel. As the wave withdrew, it left the capelin shimmering in ecstasy as females discharged their eggs and males drenched them in milt. The next wave would wash most of them back into the sea, leaving behind so many fertilized eggs that the beach became as resilient under foot as if made of rubber. During the two or three weeks of the run, enormous numbers of the little fishes were shovelled up by men, women, and children and spread to dry in sun and wind on wire racks high up on the beach. Autumn found tons of silvery dried capelin ready to be shipped to France, where, lightly toasted and served with fresh-baked bread and new wine, they were a gourmet delight.

The fishers, jovial men and stout women, did not see many visitors. They welcomed us with laughter and good-natured badinage. One small boy put to sea in a miniature dory no longer than a bathtub to welcome us. Daily he dared the surging breakers in this pumpkin seed to fish for lobsters among the very claws of the sea cliffs.

To my delight Claire was as enthralled by this tiny community isolated at the end of the world as I was, and appeared happy to remain indefinitely. But our safari leader insisted we push on. Laden with gifts of capelin and two fine lobsters, we continued on our way, motoring past the ominous bulk of Cap aux Morts (a place of many wrecks) until a vast bight came into view at whose far horizon lay La Dune, the seven-mile-long isthmus of saffron-coloured sand connecting Langlade with Miquelon. Our destination, the Great Barachoix, was a vast salt-water lagoon at the northern end of the isthmus. We beached *Oregon* on the gleaming sands to the south of its entrance to await the rising tide so we would could enter.

Meanwhile I took Claire off exploring. Skeins of shorebirds, including rare piping plovers, scampered along the beach, where stranded purple-and-gold jellyfish melted in the hot sunlight. In from the water's edge lay a waste of rolling sand dunes seemingly devoid of life except for sparse clumps of sand grass, forage for a few herds of wild horses who threw up their shaggy heads and snorted at us before streaming off into the distance.

We came across the remains of a dozen wrecks, including the jutting ribs of wooden ships, some of which must have been of great age. A hundred yards back from the beach, storm seas had built windrows of wreckage around the skulls and baleen plates of blue and fin whales. One skull half-buried in the sand was so huge Claire and I could lie side by side on the sun-warmed bone of its broad brow. When we slid down, Claire turned and lightly caressed it in a gesture of respect for one of the great ones.

We had brought along wine, a yard of fresh bread, cheese, and tinned anchovies, on which we picnicked while two harbour seals watched from the water's edge. Afterwards we stripped and swam, then lay naked in the hot sands making angels with our arms and legs. We made love while flights of terns swooped close above as if delivering a benediction.

Walking for miles through sand and flotsam, we found such strange objects as a little wooden pig with a sand-polished brass ring in its nose; the jawbone of a human being; and part of a cork life preserver bearing an inscription in the Cyrillic alphabet.

Returning almost reluctantly to *Oregon*, we found an impatient Théo, for the tide had risen and begun to fall again. Herding us aboard, he started the engine and we plunged through the shallows guarding the entrance to the lagoon. On this fine summer's day the

On the beach at Langlade.

barachoix was a mystical place. A faint indigo haze made objects waver and fade and mirages shimmer in the distance. As *Oregon* made her way up the channel, the water surrounding her boiled and eddied – not just with the current's turmoil but with the comings and goings of hundreds of seals whose sleek black heads bobbed high as they watched us.

The Great Barachoix belonged to the seals, especially grey seals whose crowded rookeries once gave life to a thousand reefs and islets from Labrador south to Cape Hatteras, but who had been almost exterminated by sealers before the middle of the twentieth century. By 1940 the few North American survivors were mainly concentrated around St. Pierre and Miquelon, principally in this lagoon. In the 1950s they began recolonizing some of their old haunts in the Atlantic region. By the 1960s fishermen were complaining that the greys, along with harp and hood seals, were eating too much fish, so the Canadian government placed a bounty on them and once again their numbers began to decline. A public outcry in Canada and abroad, in which I was involved, resulted in a temporary halt to the slaughter, but in 2003 Canada again bowed to the demands of the fishing industry and authorized a "cull" – the weasel word for butchery – of twenty to thirty thousand grey seals together with close to a million harp and hood seals. By then human fishers had effectively exterminated most commercially valuable fish stocks so this was a double victory by humankind over life in the sea.

When we visited the barachoix in 1960, a good many grey seals were summering there. This salt-water lake, which even at high tide was nowhere more than six feet deep, was also home to numberless clams, crabs, and other shoal-water fauna that provided an inexhaustible source of food for the grey seals and for smaller harbour seals. Both species shared the riches of the lagoon with island fishermen who for several centuries had dug clams here with which to bait their trawls. Piles of clam shells left by them formed squat white cones as much as twenty feet tall.

A myriad of seals surrounded us on all sides. We stared at them – and they stared back with equal intensity. They were of all sizes and ages, from pups thrusting their wrinkled faces high to peer at us myopically to ancient bulls weighing several hundred pounds and equipped with teeth that could have given a tiger pause. Some of these dove under the dory, surfacing so close we could have touched them. I was enormously pleased when Claire did not flinch even when one broke the surface only inches from where she sat.

It took Théo an hour to work his way across the lagoon to where a hunting cabin stood on the north shore. Here the others disembarked, but Claire, Théo, and I had no time to go ashore for the tide was now falling fast and if we did not quickly get clear of the lagoon we stood a good chance of being marooned in it until the next high tide. Heading for the exit, we were frequently forced out of shrinking channels and had to retract shaft and propeller so we could pole the dory over intervening sandbars. We were still far from the exit when Théo failed to haul up the shaft in time. There was a shuddering impact and the engine stalled. I stripped and went overboard, to find that the propeller had been jammed against the hull and the shaft badly bent.

There was nothing we could do here to repair it so Théo and I got out the two pairs of massive sweeps and began rowing. I assumed we would row back to the north shore of the lagoon, where we had left our passengers, then walk the ten miles cross-country to Anse aux Miquelon for assistance, but I reckoned without Théophile's adamantine nature. We rowed to the mouth of the lagoon, frequently going aground, and eventually reached the exit, where the current swept us out through a wild tide rip into the open ocean.

If Claire was worried by our predicament she gave no sign of it, except to wonder aloud how we were going to get back to St. Pierre.

"*Bien*," said Théo with Gallic confidence. "We will sail." He dug out a triangle of dirty canvas worn so thin it resembled a piece of lace. This we rigged using one of the sweeps for a mast and set our slow course for home. The breeze was no more than a zephyr. This was fortunate because the rotten halyard supporting the sail tended to break when a strain came on it. Idling along in a generally southerly direction, we stretched at full length on hatch boards warmed by the late afternoon sun, drank wine, ate canned pâté de foie gras, sometimes snoozed, sometimes chatted, all with an insouciance I can only account for as a consequence of Théo's absolute confidence in his own infallibility.

We were content – until the breeze began to strengthen out of the sou'east and the sky began to darken ominously. Théo and I exchanged glances. A storm was brewing. We did not speak of it to Claire.

At first I wasn't much worried because the massive hump of Langlade was only about five miles off. I assumed we could reach a landing place below its cliffs but *Oregon* had no keel and would not go to weather under sail. In fact, while we were trying to beat in toward the lee of Langlade, the dory was actually being pulled in the opposite direction. Worst of all – a black fog was now bearing down upon us. Without a word Théo and I downed the sail, picked up the sweeps, and began to row toward the disappearing island as if our lives depended on it.

When we caught sight of a powered dory hugging the Langlade shore, we pulled toward her with the concentration of brute beasts while Claire did her bit by clambering up on the tiny bow deck to wave Théo's yellow oilskins tied to the end of a boathook. The men in the distant dory either failed to see us or were themselves in too much of a hurry to come to our assistance.

Fog was now pouring over Langlade's cliffs and before long the island vanished. We were alone in the gathering dark. Then a hard puff out of the southwest hit us and the sail, which we had again hoisted, blew away in rags and tatters.

This left just Théo and me and the sweeps to keep us from being driven to the shores of Newfoundland. Claire had remained crouched in the bow as lookout. Suddenly she swayed precariously to her feet and began waving her makeshift flag for she had spotted a vessel at the edge of the fog bank. We dropped our oars. Théo roared like a wounded bull. I blew my lungs out into the big conch shell that served as *Oregon's* foghorn, and Claire flailed the yellow oilskin above her head. Long minutes passed. The distant vessel vanished into a swirl of fog. Then she miraculously re-appeared, heading toward us.

She was the *St. Eugène*, a passenger launch belonging to the commune of St. Pierre. As she surged up alongside and took our tow rope, her skipper told us how lucky we were. He had just received a radio message that the first hurricane of the season was on its way and an all-ships warning had been issued. He himself had turned back from his trip to Miquelon in obedience to the warning.

Although she did not show it, Claire must have been mightily relieved to be headed for St. Pierre at the end of a stout rope. I certainly was. Not so Théophile Detcheverry. As the tow got underway he stood dourly at *Oregon's* tiller, head hunched between his massive shoulders and his great nose arrogantly cocked as if in defiance of the fates that had inflicted this ignominy upon him. I have a sneaking suspicion that, had it not been for Claire's presence, he might have slipped out his sheath knife and cut us adrift to sink or swim by our own efforts.

That evening as the wind roared among the chimney pots of St. Pierre, hundreds of fishermen-sailors swarmed ashore from Spanish trawlers taking shelter in the harbour. There were lively times in every café and bistro and Claire and I joined in for a while. Théo did not. He spent most of the night down on the hard, in driving rain and screeching wind, repairing the damage done to his beloved *Oregon* and ensuring that no further harm came to her.

Mike Donovan (right) and Itchy at St. Pierre.

Hard Times

The end of August and of our too brief time together was upon us. Claire had to return to Toronto and her job. I was a married man so she did not anticipate a long-term future with me, nor I with her: yet both of us nurtured the hope that next summer we would somehow be able to bring our own happy adventure back to life. Meantime, I did not have the heart to continue the voyage without her so I decided to leave *Itchy* in St. Pierre for the winter.

When I broached the idea to Paulo and Théo they both assured me they would take good care of her. Probably they would have done so had I not made a stupid blunder. Instead of appointing one or the other to take charge of my vessel I asked *both* of them to do it, thereby putting two captains in command. My stupidity would prove disastrous.

Claire flew sadly off to Ontario while I crossed to Newfoundland on the *Spencer*, a retired fishing schooner now serving as the ferry between St. Pierre and Fortune. Making my way to Ferryland, I reclaimed my Jeep and headed west in a morose state of mind, torn between my reluctance to leave Newfoundland and my little ship, and a burning desire to see Claire again as soon as possible.

While crossing the barrens of Newfoundland, I picked up a hitchhiker, an unremarkable-looking fellow who told me his name was Simeon. He said he was from St. John's and on his way to the "mainland" to look for work. He also claimed to be an expert driver, ready and willing to spell me off at the wheel.

At dawn of our second day Sim was driving. Dozing in the seat beside him, I was awakened by a horrendous crash as the Jeep broadsided a sedan that had pulled out of a side road. Nobody was seriously injured and the Jeep was essentially undamaged but the sedan looked like a melon that had been kicked by an angry giant.

The car's owner did not wish the accident reported, which was a piece of good luck because, as we drove away from the scene, Sim confessed he did not have, and never had had, a driver's licence. Furthermore, he confided that he was a resident, albeit absent without leave, of "the Mental," the hospital for the insane in St. John's. This was his first venture into the world beyond the Rock and he hoped I wouldn't send him back.

He did no more driving but his companionship for the rest of the journey kept me from brooding over my own problems. When I bade him goodbye in downtown Toronto, he told me earnestly: "If ever ye finds yerself in the Mental, say as you're Sim's buddy an' they'll be bound to treat you right."

I paused long enough in Toronto to unburden myself to Jack McClelland, confessing that I did not know how I was going to resolve the conflict of loyalties and passions.

"You're such a stupid bastard," Jack snorted. "Bloody romantic nincompoop!"

Nevertheless, he dealt with my problem in typical style. Giving me the key to his parents' modest mansion in Forest Hill (they were away on vacation), he instructed me to take Claire there, wine her, and tell her how much I loved her.

Somewhat hesitantly I phoned Claire at the office where she worked as a commercial artist. She was astonished and bewildered by my call. Later she would tell me: "I never expected to hear your voice once we were back in Ontario. I did very much hope we'd see each other again sometime, but was sure it could never be more than a summer romance. How could it be, when you were a married man with two small children?"

Despite her uncertainty, we did meet that evening and, in consequence, I spent the next three days and nights in Toronto. Then I went home to Palgrave, where I failed to screw up my courage sufficiently to tell my wife I wanted to leave her. My two small boys, Sandy and David, proved to be the mooring lines that held me and I could not muster the strength to break away.

Claire made no attempt to persuade me to leave my family for her, but resigned herself to the situation as it was. So the two of us spent the winter in a kind of limbo, lightened by an occasional loving rendezvous.

I immersed myself in work and by March had completed two books: *Owls in the Family* and *The Serpent's Coil*. My state of mind was not improved by a cryptic note from Martin Dutin that same month. Martin wrote to say *Itchy* had sunk, but had been raised and, assuming she was insured, he thought there should be no problem restoring her. I promptly cabled that she was insured (though not for much) and asked for details. When none were forthcoming, I feared the worst but hoped for the best.

Early in June I brought Jack the manuscripts for both books, ready for the press.

"You've been a good chum," I told him. "In a couple of days I'll be heading east to St. Pierre. With luck Claire will join me later on. I don't know when I'll be back. *If* I'll be back. But I'll keep you posted."

Jack grinned his crooked grin and wished me well.

On July 1 an old DC-3 biplane flew me to the pasture airstrip in St. Pierre. It was not a happy landing. Neither Théo nor Paulo was at the strip to greet me, and when I tracked them down they were constrained and evasive. It was a while before I learned the whole story of the disaster that had befallen my vessel.

After my departure from St. Pierre the previous autumn, Théo and Paulo had been unable to agree whether *Itchy* should be hauled out at the shipyard where Paulo worked or on the beach where Théo wintered his dory. Since neither would defer to the other, she was not hauled out at all but was left moored to an abandoned wharf.

In February arctic pack ice laid siege to St. Pierre and a hard westerly gale pushed some of it into the harbour, where it stove *Itchy's* stern and sank her in twelve feet of water.

Worse was to follow. Blaming each other for what had happened, Théo and Paulo both declined to do anything about it. In consequence, my poor little ship remained in the muck at the bottom of a filthy harbour for two months, sinking ever deeper into the ooze of fish-plant debris and town sewage. Not until nearly the end of May did my two friends, spurred by the knowledge that I would soon appear, declare a truce. Only then was *Itchy* finally refloated and hauled up on the slipway for repairs.

The shipwrights refused to touch her until she had been cleansed of the noxious slime that filled her bilges and cabin. Since nobody could be found to tackle this noisome task, she had been left as she was, pending my decision as to what should be done with her.

Ella Geradin at l'Éscale had no doubt what that decision should be.

"You should sink her again. A lot deeper and farther out to sea. I can smell her here at the bar when the wind blows the wrong way. Ugh!"

There being nothing else for it, I cleaned her out myself – an experience I would not wish to repeat. Then I had difficulties getting the damage repaired. The shipyard's owner agreed to do the work – but had his own agenda. So long as there was other work for the yard (and in spring there was plenty of it), none of the shipwrights went near my vessel. She could wait until they had nothing else to occupy their time.

July was one of the bleakest months I have ever lived through. Théo's family had abandoned him after accusing him of trying to make love to his daughter-in-law. He was shunned by almost everyone in St. Pierre, as were those who admitted to being his friends. Since I was staying in his now otherwise empty house with him, this included me.

He and I and my vessel were virtual pariahs.

Nevertheless, *Itchy* slowly recovered. Repairs were made and several improvements implemented. Among these was the installation of a new engine – a twin-cylinder diesel of the type used in British lifeboats. And, with Claire very much in mind, I rebuilt the cabin, installing a homemade toilet consisting of a pail with a seat and a cover, and improving the galley. *And* the bunks.

One day a telegram was delivered, telling me Claire would arrive in Sydney by train on July 29, hoping to travel on to St. Pierre aboard the small French freighter *Miquelon*. The telegram also told me she had taken two weeks' leave from work, which, along with her annual holidays, meant we would have almost a month together.

St. Pierre had been solidly fogged in for a week, but on the twenty-eighth the sun broke through, literally and figuratively. I had heard that Henri Moraze, a Basque who had made a fortune out of *le whiskey*, was setting up an air service to ferry tourists to the isles, and that his one and only aircraft, chartered from St. John's, was expected to arrive next morning for the inaugural flight to Sydney. This was too good a chance to miss. Next morning I was waiting on the wet grass of the strip as the mist parted and a four-seater Comanche zipped in beneath the cloud cover. Almost beside myself with impatience to see Claire again, I asked the pilot, a rangy young man called Charley, if he would take me on the flight to Sydney. Happy to have company, he agreed to do so.

We landed in Sydney an hour and a half later and when the train pulled into the station at midnight I was there to meet it. Off stepped the golden girl of my dreams. I hustled her off to the Isle Royale Hotel, where I had booked the best room, overlooking the harbour. It was a still and lovely night and the moon shone full into our windows, spilling its light over the double bed with such intensity we never did bother to switch on the electric lights.

Late next morning – a sunny Sunday – we went walking hand in hand along the esplanade past a row of superannuated steamships to where the *Miquelon* was moored. She seemed abandoned too, but we found her second mate aboard. He told us the vessel had broken something vital in her engine and would not be going anywhere for at least ten days. As an apology he gave us a packet of dried capelin and a bottle of wine.

I phoned Charley at the airport to see if he could take us back to St. Pierre, only to be told the fog was too thick for him to fly.

Claire and I hardly cared. We were together, and the day was fair. We ambled happily about Sydney, a coal-mining town not much celebrated for its beauty. We found it charming. That night we dined excellently at its premier restaurant – Joe's Steak House – after which we idled along the esplanade, where we joined an extraordinary assembly of dogs, young and old, large and small, of all colours and both sexes, who seemed to be staging their own promenade. We were the only human participants.

After a time the moon began to rise so we went back to our room, where, when we grew a little peckish, we toasted capelins on candles provided by the hotel in case of emergency and drank the bottle of wine from the *Miquelon*. Bathed in moonlight and love, we did not care if we had to spend the rest of our lives in Sydney. Claire whispered in my ear: "This might be the closest we ever get to a honeymoon, darling. If it is, I won't mind a bit."

In the middle of Monday morning, Charley called to say the fog had lifted and St. Pierre might be found if we moved fast. After hurrying to the airport, we discovered we were the only passengers, sharing the plane with Charley and several bags of mail.

It was a perfect day for flying. At my request Charley took us close enough to the south shore of Newfoundland so that Claire could see something of its mighty fiords, its tiny settlements, the Blue Hills of Couteau floating on the vast inland plateau, and the Annieopsquotch Mountains rearing on the northern horizon.

We made landfall at Miquelon, and Charley gave us a guided aerial tour of the French Isles, flying so low over the Great Barachoix and over La Dune that we sent seals and wild horses splashing and skittering away in all directions.

The farmer whose cows grazed St. Pierre's airstrip (and sometimes had to be herded off so a plane could land) drove us into town and to the wharf where *Itchy* lay waiting, all freshly painted and smelling of attar of roses (thanks to a gift of perfumed soap from Ella) to welcome Claire back aboard.

That night when we climbed into our new bunks (into one of them) and blew out the small flame of the oil lamp, the manifold trials and tribulations of the past several months vanished out of mind. At midnight the ship's clock struck its round of bells and I sleepily murmured the watchkeeper's ancient chant:

"Eight bells . . . and all is well."

Toward dawn I came suddenly awake to the sound of stentorian breathing from somewhere close at hand. Groggily I poked my head out the companionway and shone a flashlight into the murk. Its pallid rays revealed a school of pilot whales circling the inner harbour.

The sleek black creatures, some of them fifteen feet in length, cruised slowly past the stern of the boat, blowing great gusts of fishy breath as they passed. Puzzled by their presence but relieved to know the source of the strange sounds, I saluted them and went back to Claire.

We woke, somewhat belatedly, to the clatter of pounding feet and went on deck to find what seemed to be most of the town's population scrambling to find vantage points from which to watch an extraordinary spectacle.

Twenty-two whales, including several great bulls and a number of cows accompanied by their calves, were being harassed back and forth and around the inner harbour by men in motorboats led by Louis Paturel, son of one of the town's richest merchants. The men were armed with stabbing weapons, mostly contrived from butcher's knives with wooden staffs as handles; one of the men, a visiting sportsman from France, was wielding a stiletto-like blade two feet long.

Running their boats alongside the panic-stricken whales as these rose to breathe, the pursuers thrust at them indiscriminately. Their crude weapons were unable to deliver mortal blows, but several whales were soon spouting geysers of blood from their blowholes while others gushed crimson fountains from backs and flanks.

At this juncture Théo appeared and pushed through the crowd to ask if I wanted him to bring *Oregon* into the harbour so we could enjoy a better view of the sport. He seemed surprised and somewhat offended when I brusquely refused his offer.

Although Claire was revolted by what was taking place and I was infuriated, there appeared to be little we could do about it except chase away the spectators who were trying to use our vessel as a vantage point.

We were foreigners here. When I saw Martin in the crowd, I asked him to do something to stop the butchery. He replied, with some embarrassment: "Farlee, the St. Pierrais, they are fishermen, *non*? This is their harbour. So it is for them to do what they please."

What they were pleased to do was spend the remainder of the day tormenting the whales, driving them round and round the harbour in which they were being contained by a fusillade of bullets fired by riflemen posted at the harbour entrance.

By noon some whales were so injured or so exhausted they could no longer flee. These became targets for ramming. Unable to sustain herself, one cow with calf ran herself up on a shoal and, as she lay there, was attacked by men wielding axes.

It was too much for us. Cravenly, we abandoned ship, hurried through the town, and climbed into the hills until we could no longer hear the growl and snarl of boat engines. We did not return to *Itchy* until dusk had sent the sportsmen to their homes – or to the cafés and bars to relive the day's entertainment and to plan what they would do on the morrow.

When darkness had fallen, I undertook a quixotic attempt to avert what promised to become a massacre. As Claire quietly cheered me on, I took our little dinghy and rowed into the night, hoping to herd the whales to freedom through the now-unguarded harbour entrance.

They were not difficult to locate for they were clustered close together, blowing so loudly I had only to row toward the whistling rush of their laboured breathing. I approached them nervously, very much aware of their size, of the mystery of them, and hoping they would not turn on a member of the species that was tormenting them.

As I shipped my oars and slowly drifted in among them, my apprehension dissipated, to be replaced by something akin to the sense of oneness I had felt during my brief meeting with the white-sided dolphins at Miquelon.

I found myself talking to them.

I told them they must leave – *begged* them to leave, telling them that in the morning they would be slaughtered. I told them to follow me, then, picking up the oars, I began rowing slowly toward the lighthouse at the harbour entrance.

For a time I thought they *were* following, but the darkness was almost absolute and I could see nothing clearly. Nearing the entrance I stopped and listened. I could still hear their sonorous breathing but there were no rippling water sounds.

The whales were not with me.

I tried again, and yet again, but they would not follow, choosing to remain in the illusory safety of the middle of the harbour. Eventually I returned to Claire and when I told her I had failed, she took me in her arms and we wept together.

Early next morning the holocaust began. The sullen roar of speedboat engines rose to a crescendo. Someone organized a dozen boats into a semicircle to drive the exhausted whales into shoal water at the end of the harbour and to hold them there until the falling tide had stranded them in viscous, stinking mud.

Once the whales had been immobilized, thirty to forty men and boys (some as young as ten or twelve years) waded into the muck and began butchering them with knives and hatchets. The waters of St. Pierre harbour ran red with blood as, one by one, the whales perished.

It was as berserk and gory a spectacle as any I have ever witnessed, more terrible than anything I saw even during my years as an infantryman at war. It was the ultimate Killer Animal at his demonic worst.

The aftermath was as demented as the massacre had been. Louis Paturel later claimed to have had expectations of selling the giant corpses, but nothing came of this, there being no market for whale flesh.

The dead whales began to rot. In the end, the carcasses had to be laboriously winched ashore, loaded onto trucks by means of a mobile derrick, and carted across the island to the cliffs at Savoyard, where they were dumped into the ocean for wind and current to carry away.

Perhaps the bodies of some of the victims drifted onto the beaches of La Dune, where their bones may still remain.

﹐ 7 ﹐

Pushthrough

The troubles that had beset *Itchy* (and me), combined with revulsion at the massacre of the whales, soured me on St. Pierre. I was ready and anxious to depart. Though still romantically enamoured of the place, the whale butchery had deeply upset Claire, and when I proposed that we sail immediately to Newfoundland on a shakedown cruise to test the new engine and to ensure our little ship was again in good order, she agreed.

Early one morning we set off for Fortune some thirty miles distant on the northwest shore of Newfoundland's Burin Peninsula. The day was bright and clear, the wind light and fair. I experienced a powerful feeling of relief as St. Pierre fell astern. A small voice in the back of my head was muttering that there was really no need for us to return to St. Pierre at all. All Newfoundland lay ahead inviting our exploration.

At noon we met the *Spencer* outbound for St. Pierre. As we passed one another, the French Isles dropped astern and we sailed into a different world. The water soughed under *Itchy's* forefoot as she shouldered her way through sparkling seas. She was fully alive again, doing what she had been built to do, and doing it superbly. Claire sat at the tiller, the wind in her face and her eyes as bright as the dazzle from the sunlit waves. Once in a while we looked at each other, laughing with the sheer joy of being alive on such a day. The hours slipped by until at seven o'clock we were abeam of Fortune Head, close enough to shore to wave to a woman who came to the door of the light-keeper's cottage. The sea ahead was full of dories whose crews were jigging squid. They beckoned us on as if we were one of their own little schooners returning out of the past.

Entering Fortune was not quite the same thing as entering Paradise. An enormous fish plant had so poisoned both air and water that even the gulls appeared sickly. We found a mooring at the *Spencer's* home wharf and before long were found by officialdom in the shape of George Squires, Canada Customs officer.

George was apologetic. Because we had arrived from a "foreign port" we could not simply step ashore – we first had to be cleared back into Canadian jurisdiction.

"Damn foolishness!" George muttered as he passed me yet another paper to sign. "Never ye mind, skipper; when we gits done with all this balderdash, you and your Missis'll come along of me to the house for a scoff."

I glanced at Claire to see how she took the assumption we were a married couple. When she met my anxious look with the flicker of a smile, I felt I had just been given carte blanche to enter a new world.

Having done what he absolutely had to do, George forewent an examination of the ship for contraband. Which was as well, for I had stowed a good many bottles in lazarettes and lockers and even under the floorboards.

Regretfully George informed me that *Itchy* could not, however, enter Canadian waters as a Basque vessel, or under any but her properly registered name. We would therefore have to lower the Basque flag and replace the name boards. However, though our little ship again became *Happy Adventure*, she never did entirely succeed in shucking off her sobriquet. Those who knew her intimately would continue to call her *Itchy*.

Our official re-entry into Canada strengthened the secret hand I was playing. That night as we sat in the little cabin I remarked to Claire, "Since we're here anyway and it's going to be a hell of a nuisance clearing out of Canada again, why don't we spend a few days cruising the coast? It's a world of wonders."

I had powerful memories of the great tangle of fiords called Bay Despair not far to the west of Fortune Bay that I had glimpsed from the deck of the *Baccalieu* four years earlier. Claire was receptive. She knew next to nothing about Newfoundland and wished to know more. Although not exactly enthralled by the ominous sound of the name, she agreed that we should make a sally into Bay Despair.

I had no large-scale chart of the Sou'west Coast so early next morning I went aboard the *Spencer* for a chat with her skipper, a white-bristled old seadog who took me into his wheelhouse, where he unrolled a yellowed chart so defaced as to be almost illegible. Ignoring the chart, he then proceeded to recite from memory the courses and hazards lying between Fortune and the head of Bay Despair.

It was the way of such as he. As children, they had memorized the compass bearings between their small outports and those they needed to visit and had continued to do so as they grew older, until the memories of those who became skippers embraced the courses to almost every port in Newfoundland as well as many in the Caribbean and even in Europe.

Such men could afford to treat the charts in cavalier fashion, but I was not similarly blessed. Humbly I accepted a gift of the *Spencer's*

The P and W Davis *and* Happy Adventure *at Pushthrough.*

old chart. With it in hand, Claire and I set off next morning across the wide mouth of Fortune Bay. A spanking sou'wester filled our red sails until they were drawing taut as the proverbial drum. We rollicked along at six or seven knots, lee rail almost under and salt spray whipping into our faces.

The breeze fell light as we approached Brunette Island midway across. That was as well since Brunette was guarded by a veritable minefield of reefs and sunkers through which I navigated very nervously indeed while Claire exclaimed over Brunette's massive sea cliffs worn into weird shapes, crowned with patches of green turf, and cleft by black hollows and sea caves where seabirds wheeled. This, her first real glimpse of the Sou'west Coast of Newfoundland, gripped her as it had me.

"I think," said she presciently, "I'm going to like it here."

Six-mile-long Brunette had been home to more than a dozen fishing families until recently. No one lived upon it now. Abandoned houses at Mercer Cove were greying bones, and even the great light at Mercer Head, once so vital to coastal navigation that it had been tended by two families, was now an automatic robot, heedless of human hands.

Claire was incredulous when I told her the people had been removed from Brunette by Joey Smallwood as part of his centralization policy and had been replaced with buffalo!

"Harold Horwood told me about it," I explained. "One of Joey's wild schemes was to turn the spruce barrens in the middle of the Burin Peninsula into a buffalo ranch to provide Newfoundland with a homegrown supply of beef. So the government brought an entire herd of buffalo from out west somewhere and just turned them loose on the barrens. Trouble was, there was no grass, and buffalo don't eat spruce trees. They were soon starving so the local lads went out and shot most of them, 'to put the poor things out of their misery,' is what they said. Then Joey had the last dozen or so rounded up and ferried out to Brunet, where the trees had all been burned or cut off centuries ago and there was some grass."

If Claire had reservations about this improbable tale, so, I must admit, had I. But a few weeks later, while passing Brunette's western cape in a dory, I saw a huge black creature standing on a distant headland. And in the spring of 1963 a fisherman found a shattered and rotting buffalo carcass at the foot of Brunette's sea cliffs where it had fallen or, perhaps, jumped. It must have been the last of the herd.

At day's end we were approaching the entrance to Hermitage Bay and Bay Despair. By then the wind had gone sou'easterly and was making me anxious to find a port before darkness and the inevitable fog could overtake us. According to the chart, the nearest harbour was a tiny indentation with the improbable name of Pushthrough. I set a course for it. Sure enough, the fog caught up with us and we had to feel our way blindly the last few miles, steering toward an eerily wailing diaphone on Pushthrough's invisible lighthouse.

Our first intimation that we had arrived was a near collision with a spidery wharf from which three startled boys peered down at us. Perhaps they thought *Happy Adventure* was the reincarnation of one of the pirate ships that haunt the Newfoundland coasts and the imagination of every boy who lives there. Instead of taking our lines, these three fled into the night, presumably to spread word of what the sea had washed up on Pushthrough's doorstep.

This was Claire's first outport and nothing would do but that we immediately go ashore for a walk-around. Darkness, and a fog which by then was "thick as molasses," combined to prevent us from seeing very much. We did, however, get a good whiff of Pushthrough's pungent aroma of salt fish, wood smoke, barrels of fermenting cod liver oil, and rotting sea-wrack, and we heard a few sounds of life, notably the scuttle of spectral sheep from close underfoot, and the foghorn's ceaseless dirge.

Feeling our way past wooden houses that glistened with moisture, we tried to peer through heavily curtained windows but failed to discern more than indistinct shadows. Nor did we encounter a single human being.

Claire had had enough.

"This place is spooky. Let's go back to the boat."

We stumbled back to the wharf and to our own little cabin warmed by our Peanut stove and brightly lighted by two oil lamps in gleaming brass gimbals. While Claire cooked supper, I told her what little I knew about Bay Despair.

"It's a bit like the fiord country of Norway, only without high mountains – an enormous water hand with spread fingers thrusting deep into the rocky vitals of Newfoundland. It isn't *really* a bay at all – more a maze of fiords, inlets, runs, and passages. A fantastic water world all of its own.

"Nobody knows when Europeans first saw it or who they were, but Basques, Portuguese, French, Spaniards, Englishmen, and Yankees have all poked around in it. At least four centuries ago they were fishing and whaling near its mouth, and a few sailed deeper in, looking for hideouts probably. They included brigands, pirates, deserters from naval ships, and runaways – indentured men and women who were virtually slaves – from fishing stations along the outer coast.

"Of course they weren't the first people here. The first comers seem to have been a people ancestral to the Beothuks – the Red Indians of the history books – who were exterminated by white Newfoundlanders before the end of the nineteenth century. I'm told the bay still has a few Indians but they are Mi'kmaqs who came here from Nova Scotia in the eighteenth century.

"Until about 1850 the Mi'kmaqs were the only people living far back in the bay, though by then there were two dozen little fishing settlements near the outer coast, each with from one to a dozen families, cut off from everywhere except by water, making their livelihood mostly from catching and salting cod.

"Most of those little places are gone now and the rest are, as Newfies say, 'fast going out.' Pushthrough's one of the survivors.

"Lumber companies began using the bay after the last war to reach the inland forest country. Some settlements – mostly of loggers' families – grew up at what's now called Head of the Bay. But even they are shrinking away now because Newfoundland's forests have been pretty well stripped.

"The settlements have been like limpets, clinging here and there without ever really getting their toes or their claws in. About all that's left of most of them now are names on charts, and a few bones and relics buried under the moss where people used to live."

Claire shivered slightly.

"You make it sound very bleak. Perhaps Bay Despair is a good name for it!"

"No. It's full of life, really. Not a lot of people, but lots of life. And Despair isn't its real name anyway. On eighteenth-century charts it's called Baie d'Espoir – Bay of Hope, itself a corruption of the first name on record: Baie d'Esprits – Bay of Spirits – which seems to have been what the aboriginals called it. Baie d'Esprits – Baie d'Espoir – Bay Despair – it's a name-changer. We'll just have to find out for ourselves what it's really like."

At the mouth of the bay on that first night I wrote in my journal:

> *After dinner of ham and eggs we read for a bit then went on deck to pee over the side and make the water sparkle with a billion tiny stars of phosphorescence. The fog pushed down making us shiver so we hustled below, where we made love before gently falling asleep to the sound of the foghorn endlessly repeating its message to vessels wandering on the sea:*
>
> *C-o-m-m-m-m-to-me . . . C-o-m-m-m-m-to-me . . . C-o-m-m-m-m-to-me . . .*

When we woke next morning the horn was still going strong, warning us not to even think about trying to sail. I stuck my head out the companionway and the fog seemed almost impenetrable. Then out of the murk loomed the shadowy shape of a big schooner bearing down on us and only a few yards distant. My heart was in my throat as she slipped by about an arm's length away, to thump against the wharf where we were moored.

The *P and W Davis* was a rough-built, big-buttocked coaster from Head of the Bay bound for Fortune with an immense deckload of fresh-cut timber, and her holds stuffed with firewood. Her crew consisted of two fourteen-year-olds who, I decided, must have been among the luckiest boys alive, spending their summer moseying in and out of little harbours from Port aux Basques to St. Pierre under the amiable eye of their uncle, Skipper Hubert Bullen.

The boys went off visiting friends ashore while Hubert, a long-faced fellow with a lugubrious air but an amiable smile, came aboard of us for a gam.

Born at Man O' War Cove near Head of the Bay, Hubert had grown up at his father's small shipyard there. However, he preferred sailing to building vessels and by the age of twenty had earned his Master's coasting ticket. Now, at forty-five, he built dories and skiffs during the winters, and in the summer skippered the *Davis*, carrying lumber and firewood to little places along the Sou'west Coast that had long been denuded of their own stands of timber.

"'Tis nought but the barest kind of a living. Hard toimes now, me son. They's but four lumber hookers left in the Bay. Was a dozen or more when I were young. All of they be old and going out now, though I hopes the old *Davis*'ll last me toime."

Hubert talked sadly too of the decay of the salt-cod economy that had sustained the thousand or so small communities on the coasts of Newfoundland through at least three centuries, and of its replacement by the frozen fish industry operating factories in a few widely separated communities and fed by company-owned deep-sea draggers and seiners instead of by inshore fishermen in their own small boats.

Claire had been sketching him while he talked. Now Hubert peered with astonishment at the result.

"Well, me dear! You've took me off right proper! And skipper here says as you can handle a vessel, too." He turned to me. "You'm some lucky man, is what I says."

The *Davis*'s arrival seemed to awaken Pushthrough. Men and boys drifted down to the dock to look us over. They were a polite if somewhat distant lot who did not speak until spoken to. I couldn't tell what they thought of *Happy Adventure* but there was no doubt as to their admiration for my crew. When Claire went on deck to hang a dish towel in the rigging, I overheard one young fellow tell another: "*Yiss*, me *son*! I'd be some pleasured going to sea along of *she*!"

By noon the murk had thinned a little so Claire and I went for an exploratory walk. We followed a stony path almost to the lighthouse, which was so veiled in fog we could hardly make out its shape. We did not approach too closely because of the diaphone's stomach-shaking whoops.

Cautiously making our way back along the cliff edge, we came upon the whitening skeleton of what had once been a sailing vessel on the rocks below, then a scattering of grey, unpainted houses crouching askew among enormous, dripping rocks. Here we encountered a covey of cats, who eyed us suspiciously, and a few people, most of whom also seemed to eye us askance. However, one elderly man greeted us and then asked us to his home for a mug of tea.

Sandy Kemp was another retired skipper of the once-innumerable sailing ships, which now were almost gone. He had spent most of his adult life at sea, largely as master of trading vessels going to and from "the Boston States." We were surprised to learn that he and his wife, Millie, who had often sailed with him, had made more than a dozen visits to New York and were far more familiar with its urban sophistication than either of us were.

Why, I asked, had he continued to live in Pushthrough?

Skipper Sandy considered the question while his "crackie dog," a pint-sized mongrel named Pinch, considered whether or not to chew me up.

"To tell the truth of it, skipper, I hardly knows. P'raps 'twas because this is where us belongs. . . ."

Sandy and Millie refused to let us leave until we had shared a boiled dinner with them. Then, accompanied by the indefatigable

Pinch, Sandy took us on a walkabout of Pushthrough, ending at a large abandoned house on the outskirts of the settlement.

It had been built by a Massachusetts man named Chambers, who, down on his luck (or in flight), had found his way to Pushthrough aboard one of the local schooners and settled here. An avaricious entrepreneur ("he had silver dollars for eyes") he had gained control of the only local commercial enterprise, Pushthrough Trade, with its retail store, fish flakes, and plant for making salt cod; its three big schooners; and the largest wharf in the harbour. To crown his enterprise, Chambers had built a twelve-room mansion – in an outport where the next largest of the three dozen houses could boast only five small rooms.

"A right quare fellow," Sandy remembered. "Married two maids and both died on him with nary a child. At the end he lived all by hisself in that big old house. The salt fish business went under. Pushthrough Trade was took up by a St. John's merchant. The schooners was lost or laid up. Just after the war, he give it up and died. When his will was read it said for him to be shipped back to the Boston States. Because, you understand . . . he never did belong to Pushthrough."

Peering through uncurtained, salt-encrusted windows, we could glimpse dark, heavy furniture, including a parlour organ. Nothing except the body had been removed and no heir had ever put in an appearance or made a claim on the house or its contents.

"She'll stand like that 'til she rots, like the old schooners that was run ashore in Rotten Row at the bottom of the harbour," Sandy told us. "One thing is certain sure. They's nobody here likely to go aboard of this one."

On our third day of being fogged in Hubert came aboard to warn us that the coast steamer was due sometime after dark and he and I would have to shift our schooners or risk being squashed. We shifted across the narrow tickle to a ruined wharf on the other side.

I was just making fast there when another timber hooker, the *Winnie Pearl*, emerged out of the murk heading toward us at full speed. Transfixed, I watched her skipper give such a demonstration of seamanship as I have seldom witnessed.

Foaming full tilt down a tickle less than a hundred yards wide, the *Winnie Pearl* never slowed until she was her own length away from a horrendous collision. Then she smartly dropped *both* her anchors and, in the manner of a runaway horse, surged to such a sudden stop that she sagged back on her haunches. As she did so someone aboard flung a line ashore, where someone else quickly snubbed it around a rock. Then, *still under full power*, the eighty-foot vessel pivoted right around and came gently to rest alongside the Pushthrough trade wharf, her bows pointing toward the harbour entrance.

"How the bloody hell did he *do* that? And *why*?" I demanded of Hubert, who was standing calmly by.

"Well, skipper, he got no reverse gear on that old engine, and he don't dare slow her down for fear she'll quit. So that's the only way he could a-done it. And ain't he going to be some wild when he hears he got to move again to let the steamer in!"

Claire drifted off to sketch Pushthrough in the mist, but I had a task below. This was a special day for us – the day one year earlier when we first knew we were in love. In celebration I was preparing a feast of fresh codfish caviar, cold mackerel salad, and codfish bouillabaisse, all to be washed down with bottles of white wine cooled in the bilges.

After the dinner we were galvanized from post-prandial stupor by the rude bellow of the steamer's horn. We hurried on deck to watch the thousand-ton *Baccalieu* ease into the berth being vacated by an indignant *Winnie Pearl*. Then we joined most of Pushthrough's population on the dock, for this was "steamer time," the chief event of the week in any outport on the Sou'west Coast.

Baccalieu's decks were crowded with people and cluttered with deck cargo ranging from a big new trap skiff to a one-ton truck. Passengers and residents mingled on the wharf, where Claire and I were spotted by Captain Riggs, waved aboard, and taken to his cabin for a drop of brandy. He was gloomy about the weather.

"Radio's callin' for a sou'easter and heavy fog, me Little Man. Seems like 'tis all they got for us this season. Don't say as how I could get along at all in this one but for the radar."

I took this with a grain of salt. I was convinced Skipper Riggs could have *smelled* his way into every nook and cranny on the coast of Newfoundland.

Unfortunately, I could not. *Baccalieu* steamed off into the murk but we remained weather-bound in Pushthrough for the next three days.

The damp became so pervasive that green mould was sprouting on much of our food, on the wet and slippery planks of the cabin floor, even on our clothing. When Claire undertook to examine my beard for signs of greenish growth, I understood she had had enough of Foggy Hollow and I had better take her somewhere else.

Great Jervais seemed a possibility. This was a now-abandoned settlement a mile or so to the north of Pushthrough where, according to Sandy Kemp, the weather was quite different.

"Near always warmer there," he told us, then added darkly: "Some says 'tis because 'tis closer to the Other Place, being as it was purely papish, you understand . . . afore the Devil chased they out of it."

Settled in the nineteenth century by a few fugitive Roman Catholic families from St. Pierre who had fallen foul of their own people, Great Jervais had been remarkably successful, growing to some forty families and rousing envy and suspicion in the neighbouring communities, all of which were staunchly Protestant.

According to Sandy, something fell and mysterious happened to Great Jervais in 1937, something that caused a number of deaths, followed by the total abandonment of the place.

"None of we ever knowed what it was. Some thinks it was sickness carried them off. Others says 'twas the Devil come to claim his own. I only ever knowed one fellow from there. Name of Joe Rose [originally LaRue]. Was a deckhand on my schooner for a voyage or two. A proper jinker he was. Nothing he ever done come right.

"One toime him and the mate had a fight and that night – we was in Gloucester and a big starm was called for – he loosed our lines from the shore bollards and made them fast to some oil barrels waiting shipment on the dock. Well, sir, along about midnight she began to blow a gale, and the first we knowed the schooner had pulled the barrels into the harbour and we was adrift and like to end up on the rocks. We'd have lost her that night, only she took the ground on a mud bank. That was the last time I saw Joe, but not the last I heard about he.

"One winter evening a year or two later he undertook to row a young woman teacher over to Pushthrough for to catch the steamer. Halfway across Great Jervais Bay he stops pulling and tells her what he wants. When she says no, Joe pulls out the plug in the bottom of the dory and it begins to fill. When 'twas half full the maid must have changed her mind 'cause he put back the plug, bailed out the dory, and after a time landed her on a rock near Pushthrough harbour mouth, where it took her half the night to call somebody to help her git ashore.

"I never heard tell of Joe Rose again. But if you goes over to Great Jervais, take a care."

Before we could attempt the trip the fog began to thin. Pushthrough was slackening the chains and we wasted no time making our escape. Claire cast off the lines while I started the engine. We had no more than cleared Dawson's Point when the blatting diaphone at the still-invisible lighthouse fell silent. The shroud began to part and pale streaks of sunlight gave us our first glimpse into the yawning throat of Bay Despair.

The opening before us had a stunning majesty: a great gulf slicing into a thousand-foot-high rocky plateau whose cliffs plunged into dark waters of almost unimaginable depth; although we were enclosed by land, we were now sailing over the deepest abyss to be found anywhere adjacent to the shores of Atlantic Canada. The sea floor here lay an extraordinary *half a mile* below *Happy Adventure's* keel – a plunge cauldron scoured out by the melting of mile-high glaciers fifteen thousand years earlier, but now a void of darkness, silence, and unknown things.

The names on the chart indicated that earlier arrivals may have felt much as we two did: that they were entering a world beyond the provenance of ordinary mortals.

Three miles to starboard of us Wreck Cove gaped hungrily. Three miles off the port bow was Old Harry Head, Old Harry being the pseudonym seafarers gave to the Devil. Behind the Head was a black-walled cove called Davy Jones's Locker, the traditional mariners' name for the place where drowned sailors gather. Four miles directly ahead of us towered Goblin Head, with three brooding clefts in the wall behind it called Great, Middle, and Little Goblin Bays.

Such was the vestibule of the Bay of Spirits.

We set course across it under power and as we putt-putted along were accompanied by three playful minke whales, each about *Happy Adventure's* length, who demonstrated their agility by surfacing and blowing almost under our bowsprit, then swooshing off at flank speed before the cutwater could touch them. Claire was engrossed in their performance, but I was looking over my shoulder at a fog bank that was following us into the Bay. When I drew

Claire's attention to it she remarked, "I should call you Foggy Farley! It seems to follow you around like a pet dog."

"Take the helm!" I ordered brusquely and went below to see if I could squeeze another knot out of the engine.

Here I should explain that the new diesel behaved with the utmost fidelity, but since it had no controls on deck one of us had to go below to the "engine room" to change pace or to start or stop it.

The great eastern arm of the Bay is split by a ten-mile-long island. The main passage, to the southward, is called Long Reach and the much narrower one to the north, Lampidose Passage. The strangeness of that name attracted us, as did the promise of an escape from the pursuing fog, so we headed for it. This meant hugging the southern shore of the Goblin Peninsula, whose cliffs, towering high above us, were stained with impressionistic swashes of colour – gold, silver, sulphur, bronze – the leachings of unseen mineral deposits.

The Lampidose was an awesome place, a spectacular gorge winding sinuously between other-worldly hills. When a faint breath of wind touched us from astern we stopped the engine, hoisted all sail, and ghosted along in solitude and silence. There was no indication that anything human had ever passed this way. Nor were any natural inhabitants visible – not even an errant gull.

When I wondered aloud if we might not have passed through the gates to the underworld and be caught in the implacable current of the River Styx, Claire accused me of morbidity. In truth, I felt exalted, as if we were in the presence of the elder gods.

However, the fog demons still pursued us and by the time we passed Margery Head were so close that I started the engine and shamelessly ran before them. When a narrow opening in the cliffs to the northward offered a haven, I turned into it, and so we found ourselves in Roti Bay.

Hubert Bullen had described Roti Bay to me as "a worm-gut off the Lampidose. Full of wind as a horse's belly. You go in there, you wants to be good and certain you got good anchors and plenty chain . . . or that little hole-in-the-wall'll fart you right back out again."

Although the fog did not pursue us into Roti Bay, the wind was rising and the sky darkening ominously. The chart showed only one tiny cove, Clay Hole, where we might hope to find safe anchorage. We eased *Happy Adventure* into it between two rocky arms and over kelp-covered shoals until we had only three fathoms under us, then I let go our biggest anchor, praying that the flukes would dig deep into a bed of clay.

Ebony clouds were soon swooping down to mast level as a sou'easter gathered strength, storming over the high surrounding hills, whining and moaning in our rigging. I furled the sails, made all shipshape on deck, then ducked below, slamming the companion hatch tight shut behind me.

Claire already had the galley stove roaring and dinner cooking. The lamps flickered cheerily, steam filmed the portholes, shutting out the gathering storm, and I poured us both a drink.

So began one of the most memorable nights we ever spent together. We seemed divorced from the rest of humankind. It was almost as if the last trump had sounded and we alone were left. The sou'easter boomed and bellowed like the voice of God. Mighty gusts struck us, heeling the vessel over while her rigging keened like pagan pipes. She tugged at her chain like a restive horse, surging forward in momentary calms, then sagging back as new gusts struck her.

She was alive! The night was alive! And so were we!

Implausible as it may seem, we felt no fear of the imponderable forces raging around us. As the gale rose to a crescendo of sound and fury, we made love then slept sweetly in one another's arms while *Happy Adventure* surged under us.

Once during the night the wind veered suddenly, spinning our little cockleshell around and making the chain growl in the hawse pipe. Claire did not awaken, and soon the wind veered back and all was well again.

The gale dropped before dawn and I went on deck at first light, to be greeted by a chorus of ravens' and gulls' voices echoing and re-echoing around the enormous amphitheatre of the surrounding hills. A moose came splashing along the shore, glanced at *Happy Adventure* lying a boat's length away, nodded as if to itself, and wandered on. Claire joined me with a pot of tea and we sat contemplating our spectacular haven. It was a transcendental moment.

After breakfast we rowed ashore looking for fresh water to fill our tank. We had been unable to fill it at Pushthrough because a drought had emptied the wells there. The drought had also afflicted Roti Bay so that all the little streamlets draining into it seemed to have dried up. We followed one of them – a staircase of clattering white stones ascending a steep slope through a tunnel of wind-stunted spruce trees. To our delight it led us to a rock pool filled with crystalline water.

We were hot so we stripped off and took a bath surrounded by giant fern. Descending the staircase hand in hand we found a little beach and became children again, chasing around in search of scallop shells to use as shovels, then squatting naked while digging in the sand and mud for clams. We filled a bucket with clams before rowing back to the vessel to cook a chowder for our lunch – a chowder that turned out to be full of mini-pearls.

The sun shone brilliantly and the bay underwent a sea change. The formerly grey and brooding hills glowed with a delicate green sheen, and the indigo waters below them were stilled, except for a friendly little riffle on the surface. A harbour seal swam to within a few feet, then bobbed half out of the water in order to satisfy its curiosity about us. A pair of ravens swooped down from a high peak to the north where they perhaps had their nest, and they bombarded us with raucous questions until they were distracted by an intruding eagle and flapped off to chase him away.

It seemed to me that the ravens were not just guarding their own bit of territory – but the heart and, as it may be, the very soul and essence of the vast watery world of Baie d'Esprits.

Michael and Emilia John at Conne River.

· 8 ·

Head of the Bay

On a warm and sunny morning hazed by pungent wood smoke drifting south from the island's interior, which was then ablaze with wildfires, the friendly harbour seal escorted us out of Roti Bay.

We had no particular destination in mind, only the desire to sail deeper into the mystery. The breeze was light and favourable as we ghosted through a broad reach hemmed in by eight-hundred-foot hills that grew increasingly wooded the farther north we sailed.

We saw plenty of life: gulls, eagles, waterfowl, and a pod of porpoises, but no sign of mankind. We had sailed a good twenty miles into the land and begun to wonder if we had sailed out of human ken when we opened a cove to the westward fringed by little houses and dominated by an enormous church. The chart told me this was St. Alban's. We had returned to our own kind again.

Sailing on through a narrow tickle we headed somewhat reluctantly for another cluster of houses with a sprawling lumber mill in its midst. This was Milltown, the premier community in Head of the Bay. We tied up at the government wharf.

One of the people who drifted down to look us over was Dolph Roberts, a slightly built, fair-haired man I had met and travelled with for three days in 1957 aboard the *Baccalieu*. Now he took Claire and me under his wing Newfoundland style. Loading us into his old car, he drove us to Deepwater Point, where Head of the Bay's road system (it amounted to about three miles of dirt-and-gravel "moose trail") terminated at what had been a thriving shipyard built by Dolph's uncle, Morgan Roberts.

Basques, French, and Portuguese had all made good use of the tall and vigorous stands of white pine, spruce, and hardwoods originally found inland from the head of the bay. Those who followed did even better. Between 1900 and the end of the Second World War, local shipwrights launched more than two hundred sailing vessels here, some of them being as much as three hundred tons. Most of these had been employed in the "three-cornered trade": fishing on the Grand Banks or down the Labrador in summer; voyaging to Europe in autumn with salt fish; returning home early in the winter via the Caribbean, where they took on cargoes of sugar, salt, and rum.

The man who built some of the best of the bay schooners (and the last of them – a ninety-tonner launched in 1953) was Morgan Roberts. Eighty years old when we met him, he was a massively built man still "full of piss and vinegar," as his nephew admiringly put it, who welcomed us to a sprawling wooden house built in the grand manner and furnished with a semblance of mid-Victorian pomp and splendour. It even boasted a bathroom, complete with a huge, claw-footed iron tub in which Claire and I were invited to luxuriate.

Sadly in need of paint and repairs, the house overlooked a placid cove and the ruins of the sawmill and shipyard upon which the now-exhausted Roberts family fortune had been built. At Morgan's benevolent command, we dined with him and Dolph at an elaborate mahogany table set with strangely assorted but genuine silver and oddments of imported chinaware. The meal consisted of canned Spam accompanied by a pallid salad made from sliced onions and bits of wild watercress. It was served with panache by one of Morgan's cousins, a heavy-set woman with a moustache and a great, gurgling laugh, who, after the death of Morgan's wife, had become the doyenne of the establishment.

While we were eating, the *Glimshire* (another of the surviving quartet of lumber hookers) eased in on the rising tide and anchored just offshore to load a cargo of "sticks" (pulp logs) Dolph had cut during the winter and rafted ready for her. The rusty music of her old winch and of men's voices echoing over calm waters became the background for Morgan's story.

In the mid-eighteenth century three Roberts brothers with their wives and children had fled from the French occupation of Placentia Bay in thirty-foot open bully boats propelled by oars and lug sails. Sailing west along the coast they became the first English to settle at Hermitage Cove, a harbour that had formerly served as a summer fishing and whaling station for Basques and Portuguese.

Hermitage Cove was not far enough west for two of the Roberts brothers so they set sail again. One was never heard of afterwards; the other settled in what would become Pushthrough, and it was there in the year 1800 that Morgan's great-grandfather had been born.

Morgan's branch of the family lived in and fished out of Pushthrough for three generations, carrying their salt cod to Placentia or St. Pierre to trade with the French for what they needed.

"Everybody lived out on the coasts, them times," Morgan explained. By which he meant everyone of European blood. Except for an occasional renegade from the coast fishery, nobody except Indians lived in the labyrinthine interior of Bay Despair.

However, in 1856 a transatlantic cable company began constructing an overland telegraph link from St. John's to Port aux Basques, running just inland from the foot of the great fiords and bays of the southern coast. Soon a relay operator and his family were established at Head of the Bay, and another at the inner end of the arm called Bay the North. Thereafter, Englishmen who had been working as indentured labour (and hating it) for Jersey fishing companies along the coast began slipping away inland to try making a livelihood felling trees, pit-sawing the resultant logs, and floating the timber out to the coast to sell. Some even tried to establish little farms.

By 1870 two such families were living at Head of the Bay. One of these traded a barrel of gunpowder to the local Mi'kmaqs for the "use of" some three hundred acres of foreshore. In a similar exchange the other settler attempted to pass off a barrel of spoiled flour mixed with coal dust. When the Mi'kmaqs spotted the swindle and complained, the settler ran them off "his" land with a pitchfork, and when they returned to argue their case, he shot one of them stone dead – a not unusual way of settling disputes with natives in Newfoundland, as elsewhere in the Americas.

In 1890 Morgan's father decided to abandon the fishery at Pushthrough for the life of a logger and sawyer. He sailed his family to Head of the Bay, where they lived in a log shanty for the two years it took to cut and saw enough logs to build a proper house. There were several strong-backed sons, so the family made rapid gains. They acquired an old sawmill from one of the Jersey merchants at the coast and before long the Robertses were sending shiploads of lumber as far afield as St. Pierre. From this it was no great leap to establishing a small shipyard.

Between 1904 and 1948 the Robertses built at least one vessel a year – mostly fore-and-aft schooners, but some square riggers, including a 190-ton three-master. Most of the lumber hookers Claire and I became familiar with in the bay and along the coast had been built in the Robertses' yard from models carved and whittled by master ship-wrights who never worked from paper plans. Morgan showed us several of the models he himself had designed and made. They were in fact half-models, each lovingly fashioned to a shape determined by the eye of the carver and by the infinitely long tradition of the sea. Morgan explained that he would work at a half-model, a touch here and a shaving there, until "she *looked* just right." He would then slice the model into sections and, with dividers, take measurements, which he would multiply by whatever scale was required and apply directly to the planks and timbers waiting in the yard.

Because the water behind Deepwater Point was very shoal, large vessels had to be launched on their sides and at high tide. It some-times proved necessary to dig a channel as much as a hundred yards long through the muddy tide-wash to get them afloat. No matter. When they finally floated free they did their builders proud. One of the Robertses' schooners won international renown by making a passage laden with salt fish under sail alone to Portugal in just nine days, returning in eleven: a round trip of some five thousand miles.

The last vessel off the Robertses' ways was the 140-ton *Shirley Rose*, built in 1944; and then the Age of Sail was dead.

The Robertses had also engaged in the thriving trade, legal and illegal, between the bay and St. Pierre. Produce from the bay shipped to the French islands consisted mostly of lumber, firewood billets, and barrel hoops and staves but also included turnips and potatoes, salmon, and game, especially caribou and moose. Return cargoes included sugar, French cloth, household goods, and barrels of Martinique *rhum*, little if any of which was ever seen by the govern-ment excise cutters patrolling the waters between the French Isles and Newfoundland.

"Give us a good puff of wind and we could show our heels to any of them, even the fastest steam cutter they ever had," Morgan happily remembered.

His memories were sadly at odds with the present. The shipway below his house was now a graveyard of abandoned hulks – "come home to die." A rank growth of underbrush almost completely hid the marine railway. The smithy and the sail-maker's loft had collapsed. The mill, where lumber for the shipyard had been sawed, was still recognizable as such for Dolph had managed to keep it going until a few years previously.

"Time was," Dolph told me as we stood outside watching the night overwhelm the ruins below us, "when they was Morgans aplenty hereabouts. We worked as a crowd, you know. One for all, and all for one. Nobody got too big for their britches, and nobody went without. We was our own co-op. After Confederation, with schooner building going out, Smallwood's government give us the concession for cutting timber in the country roundabout Head of the Bay.

"We kept two mills busy – here, and at Little River – and we done very good with it. Then the Strickland brothers, them as is the merchants at Milltown, along of the Church of England minister and the Roman Catholic priest at St. Alban's, wanted a share in the concession. We was agreeable – but what they had in mind was to take full charge.

"The Member [of the provincial parliament] for the Bay was on their side. They put in their own manager, a very religious man he was too. He set up a new kind of bookkeeping and within the year our co-op was belly up. Bankrupt, they says nowadays."

The provincial government withdrew the Robertses' concession and gave it to the Milltown consortium, which also acquired the co-op's other assets. Loggers, haulers, and millers who had made their livelihood inside the co-op now found themselves beholden to Strickland Brothers, who paid fourteen dollars a cord for finding, cutting, and bringing wood out of the interior and rafting it to Milltown, where the Stricklands sold it "in the water" to foreign freighters at twenty-four dollars the cord.

"Cutting pulp these times is starvation wages," Dolph continued, "but people got no choice. The government welfare officer has his orders. Either you cuts for Stricklands at Stricklands' price or you loses your welfare benefits. So it's take what's offered or be cut off sharp. No unemployment insurance. Nothing but the bare-naked dole to keep you and yours from starving."

Dolph's description of the state of affairs was confirmed by the welfare officer, an earnest young man named Selby Moss. He told us that of the thousand-odd adults living in and around Head of the Bay, 80 per cent of the able-bodied were unemployed and living on the dole, as last-ditch relief has long been called in Newfoundland. Moreover, most families had been on it for several years.

"Bowater [the British-owned pulp-and-paper company that dominated the industry in Newfoundland] closed down its operations around the bay four years ago, without so much as a thank-you-and-goodbye. A good many people here had come in from the coast to work for Bowater when the salt-fish racket went under. Now they got nowhere to go. Nothing for them anywheres on the Island. Only the dole. I don't rightly know where 'twill end. My wife and me belongs to Bonavista Bay. Been here two years and I don't say as we'll stick it much longer. If the department don't shift us out we'll pack up and go. This place's got the creeping sickness."

The hospitality extended to us at Head of the Bay had been generous to a fault but this bleak re-entry into the real world was leaving a sour taste.

Milltown had few attractions. One morning at two I was rousted from my bunk to shift *Happy Adventure* out of the way of the coast steamer *Bonavista*. Then I had to shift again when a big RCMP cutter nosed alongside demanding mooring space. The policemen who formed her crew came sniffing about, patently curious about what my business on the Sou'west Coast might be. As if this was not enough, we had barely finished breakfast when a float plane full of prospectors thundered in and wanted our berth. The pilot was brusque in his demands and I lost my temper. By the time I rejoined Claire down below, I was seething.

"Goddamn world is too much with us here. Let's get the hell out of it."

"Could we go back to St. Pierre?"

"Not yet, damn it. We haven't begun to explore the bay. Let's go visit the Mi'kmaqs."

An hour's easy sail brought us into the broad mouth of the Conne, the second-largest river flowing into Bay Despair. The only native settlement extant in Newfoundland stood on its banks, inhabited by descendants of Mi'kmaqs brought by the French to the Sou'west Coast from Nova Scotia during the eighteenth century to trap the furs so much valued by Europeans.

The existing native settlement consisted of about thirty families whose houses, widely dispersed along the shore of the river estuary, ranged from typical Newfoundland style – nearly flat-roofed, two-storey, wooden structures – to one-room log cabins.

There was no wharf, for these were not people of the sea. As we rowed ashore, several girls came down to the beach. Dark-eyed, dark-skinned, and black-haired, they greeted us shyly but with warmth. Geraldine and Adeline, pretty ten- or twelve-year-olds, undertook to guide us to the home of their uncle Sylvester Jedore, who, we had been told in Milltown, was chief of the band. The sandy trail leading through the settlement was crowded with people of all ages, none of them apparently in any great hurry. Men, women, and children sauntered past and, though they did not speak, all gave us friendly looks.

Our young guides led us to their uncle's house only to learn that he and his whole family were off on the inland barrens picking berries. So the girls took us to the log cabin of Michael

John, another uncle. His wife, sixty-seven-year-old Emilia John, welcomed us into her little kitchen. She was, as she put it, "blind as Old Tom" (their rangy, half-wild cat), and had been so for a decade. She told us she was a "white woman" from St. Alban's on the other side of Short Reach.

"When Michael marry me I come to live here with his folks, and never had no cause to wish I didn't. He never give I a cross word in all our life. I'd never let nobody touch a hair o' that man's head."

The girls had gone to fetch Michael, who came hurrying in with an armful of wood to stoke up the stove and "bile the kettle" so the visitors could have tea. In his seventies, with deeply creased mahogany skin and the sparse, tight body and walk of a woodsman, he was voluble and active. Although going deaf and suffering from fainting spells because, as Emilia told us, "the poor man finds his heart," he did most of the indoor as well as the outdoor work.

Now he scurried about seeing to our comfort. Had we eaten? There was bottled moose meat in the pantry and freshly baked bread . . . or would we prefer bannock? He would have the tea on the table in a minute; meanwhile, here was a plate of raisin cookies.

The tea was strong but lavishly laced with condensed milk. Bread, which he had baked himself, was slathered with his own raspberry jam. He apologized for the quality of the bread, explaining that he and Emilia preferred bannock and made bread mainly for the chickens, because bread made the birds lay better.

Grateful as we were for what was put before us, what we really wanted was to hear their story.

They talked freely and without a trace of self-pity even as they told us of the loss of four of their children. One son had been killed when a saw "exploded" at Strickland's lumber mill, another had died in action with the Canadian army in Italy, and two daughters had died in their teens during a diphtheria epidemic.

Trapping and hunting had provided their livelihood.

"Even in the Hard Times the country fed us. Them times the government was giving the white folks as was fishing on the coast or working in the woods six cents a day dole, and they was hungry. We got plenty caribou, patridge, and rabbits in the woods and out on the barrens. Duck, fish, and seals from the bay. Salmon and trout from the brooks.

"We travelled wherever the animals was. Come dirty weather we stayed snug in our tents and tilts. Nowadays most everyone lives in houses. The woman and me don't care for that, but we can't go onto the country no more, so here we stays."

A brisk easterly breeze had risen while we were talking. Combined with the fast-rising tide, it made our anchorage unsafe so I decided to run back to Milltown for shelter. Michael and Emilia were as loath to see us go as we were to leave, but there was no help for it.

After we were again moored in Milltown, Dolph came aboard to suggest we visit John Barnes, a tidy little man who had been a local teacher for forty years and was renowned for his unbending rectitude. "Sooner be et by a bear than tell a lie," was how Dolph characterized him.

A natural-born historian, John Barnes had a great deal to tell about early days at Head of the Bay, where his father had settled in 1869.

He told us that the first settlers had made a large part of their income from cutting spruce and birch "rind" (bark), used to line the holds of schooners carrying salt-bulk fish to foreign markets.

"There was no money on the go them times. You traded for what you needed. The people took the rind to Gaultois in rowing boats. Later they built bigger boats and sailed they to Harbour Breton and St. Pierre.

"Michael Collier come to the bay same time as my old dad and settled close to the Indian camp at Conne. He pretty near became one of them and had six sons by an Indian wife. He planned out, and him and his sons built, a forty-ton schooner specially for the shoal waters of Conne and Little River. Flat-bottomed she was. Very shoal draft. Very broad, and no keel at all so she would stand on her own feet when she dried out. When the tide rose again she'd float off good as new.

"Mainly she was rowed with six great sweeps, one for each of the sons, but she was rigged with a leg-o'-mutton and square sails too. Having no keel she could only run before the wind, but Michael and his boys would take that ugly old thing all the way to St. Pierre loaded to the gunwales with billets of firewood, barrel staves, lumber, and country meat.

"If the wind was foul, they'd row her all the way. Six men rowed four hours at a stretch, then they'd take a break and have a scoff in their little galley in the forepeak.

"They'd take six gallons of rum aboard at St. Pierre, but never land a drop of it at Conne because the Indians never knowed how to drink, and Michael respected that. 'Twas said him and the boys would drain the kegs before they come ashore, then the lot of them would sleep for a week."

We had some reservations about this account but Dolph again assured us John Barnes was incapable of lying. In proof thereof he told us another story:

"Geese used to pitch at Head of the Bay and John's brother Obie was a great gunner. One day a fellow in a motorboat was heading up the bay when he came across John rowing his dory.

"'Did your brother get any geese this year?' the fellow asked.

"'I believe he did get a couple,' John replied.

"The fellow went on his way but, glancing astern, he saw John rowing after him hard as he could row so he stopped the engine and waited till John come up, huffing and puffing something awful.

"'I may have told you a lie,' John says when he finds his breath. 'I believe one of they was a gander.'"

Time was now running out for Claire, who had to return to her job in a week's time. First she was anxious to revisit St. Pierre and our friends there but I was so enamoured of the Bay of Spirits I did not want to leave. This was an impasse that could have festered. Claire would not let that happen. She deferred to my wishes, but with such grace that I became ashamed of myself and changed my mind. So one fine morning we let go our lines, crowded on all sail, and went scudding down Short Reach bound for the French Isles.

We had a magnificent run until we entered the head of Long Reach, where we were struck by a ferocious squall roaring out of the canyoned mouth of Little River – a gust that laid *Happy Adventure* over until her lee rail went under and water was pouring into her steering well.

Thrusting the tiller into Claire's hands, I leapt to free the main sheet from its cleat so the vessel could right herself, but I had foolishly made the line fast with a half hitch and this had jammed as the sheet came bar-tight. I had to cut it free, while Claire clung to the tiller for dear life, wide-eyed and certain we were going to go all the way over.

Once the wind had spilled out of the mainsail, the schooner regained her feet and we skittered on past the long, rocky finger of Cape Mark to the safety of open water.

"You all right?" I asked as I took the tiller back from Claire.

"I *think* so," she replied somewhat shakily, "but please let's not do that again."

This was our first experience with a blow-me-down – an unexpected squall of hurricane strength that seems to come out of nowhere and can dismast a big ship or overturn a small one. Blow-me-downs are among the least attractive features of fiord country, where narrow waterways surrounded by high hills form natural wind tunnels.

Once things had settled down, I got us both a belt of brandy. In doing so I realized I had forgotten to pour a libation to the Old Man of the Sea, a ritual learned from my father, who claimed to have learned it from a white-bearded ancient in Liverpool who had sailed the world in clipper ships. Tradition has it that the Old Man – Neptune, some call him – likes his drop and so, before setting out on a voyage, it is wise to pour a healthy dollop over the side for him.

"Insurance," was what Angus called it. And I had forgotten to pay the premium. I made up for that neglect and a hard but steady quartering breeze whipped us south through Long Reach to Little Passage. This was a narrow-gutted twister several miles long and no place for the faint-hearted, especially when wind and tide were fighting as they were this day. The coast steamers used Little Passage, and two weeks earlier the *Bar Haven* had failed to make an especially tight bend and had shoved her bow into a mountain. Fortunately the shore was so sheer she had been able to back off with no more serious damage than a crumpled prow – and the temporary loss of her skipper's dignity.

Rounding Margery Head at the end of the passage, we opened Hermitage Bay to find it frothing white, for the wind had now built to a sou'west gale. We made no attempt to buck our way across the bay but unabashedly ran for shelter in nearby Gaultois.

Once a major whaling port, Gaultois now boasted (or was afflicted by) a big modern fish plant that had turned the harbour into such a stinking stew as might have offended even old-time whalers. We moored at a wharf where a covey of small boys took our lines before running off to the plant to fetch us a pail of freshly cut cod tongues and cheeks. These I fried in salt pork fat while Claire contrived a salad made from blanched asparagus tips (out of a can, of course) and homemade mayonnaise. The whole was washed down by a bottle of Sauterne from *Happy Adventure*'s cellar.

I noted in my journal:

> *Surely there is no more pleasant thing than to moor in a safe harbour, well fed and well lubricated, after an exciting voyage with a really good companion.*

We sipped coffee and Drambuie, recalled the blow-me-down, wondered over the flight of a dozen eagles who had soared close over us in Little Passage, and enjoyed the glow of unabashed admiration for one another.

> *I feel I am ready to go anywhere with Claire, though she may have some legitimate reservations about doing likewise with me.*

The gale blew itself out and a lovely evening ensued so we went for a cross-country walk to investigate the neighbouring outport of Pink Bottom. Claire had accused me of having invented the name but there it was – a handful of houses near the bottom of a deep gulch originally settled by a man named Pink. This superb natural harbour boasted a newly built government wharf and a fleet of ten or twelve dories, none of which was being fished. Everyone here, so we discovered, had given up fishing to work on the assembly (or disassembly) lines at The Plant in Gaultois.

Even the name of the community was being changed. Like so many Newfoundland place names of character and colour, Pink Bottom had been officially rejected by bureaucratic Mother Grundies, in favour of Picarre, which had no significance for anyone.

Returning to the Gaultois wharf, we found it overrun by about twenty children playing on teeter-totters they had made for themselves from heavy construction planks balanced over a stone retaining wall. On these they soared up and down, fearless of the rocks below on one side and the rising tide on the other. As they soared they sang (more or less in harmony) children's songs that had crossed the Western Ocean centuries earlier from seaports in Devon and Dorset. We pondered how enormously lucky they were to have been born in a corner of the world where they were free to be themselves and where adult sanctions had not deprived them of the right to live at risk.

We woke next morning gasping and choking. I struggled on deck, to discover it was dead low water. Very, *very* dead. The fallen tide had exposed such a collection of rotting fish carcasses from the plant that the very air seemed to resonate with the stench. And there appeared to be no escape, for we were aground.

Claire dealt with this emergency. From somewhere in her meagre baggage she produced two sticks of incense. Not then, or ever, has she volunteered an explanation of how or why she had them. No matter; they did the trick, enabling us to breathe until the rising tide refloated us and we could flee from Gaultois.

We had a lovely sail across Hermitage Bay, whose deep bight fell away to the eastward of us in majestic grandeur. We slipped between a pair of massive headlands on the far side, experiencing the never-failing excitement of entering a new harbour.

Hermitage Cove's outer anchorage was filled with fishing boats. We sailed past them and through a tickle into a small barasway forming one of the snuggest harbours in Newfoundland. Here we anchored and rowed ashore to look for the brothers Sandy and Kent Hill, who, according to Dolph Roberts, were particularly knowledgeable about Bay Despair. They were away at their nets but before long their thirty-five-foot motorboat came chugging into the harbour and dropped anchor near *Happy Adventure*.

I rowed across to them, bearing the heel of a bottle of brandy, introduced myself, and was welcomed aboard by a burly pair of wind-and-weather-worn men with red faces, gleaming teeth, and the calm certainty of twin Buddhas. They had been fishing cod with nylon gill nets – a major innovation on a coast whose waters had for centuries been fished with jiggers, handlines, cod traps, and baited longlines, until the massive post-war surge of industrial-scale fishing dependent on ocean-going draggers and factory ships had so depleted fish stocks that inshore fishermen could no longer make a living with traditional gear.

The Hill brothers had done something about that. First they built a small sawmill. Then they spent a winter in the woods at the foot of Bay Despair cutting the timber needed to build a big, partly enclosed motorboat along the lines of the Nova Scotian Cape Islander, a vessel capable of fishing almost any species in almost any weather and in all seasons. Next they bought five hundred dollars' worth of nylon twine and made a fleet of deep-water gill nets.

Then they went back to fishing.

Starting early in the spring, they netted salmon followed by herring, then cod, turbot, sole, and halibut. *And* they fished lobster with four hundred wooden traps they had also made themselves.

Spring, summer, and autumn, they spent every day (except Sunday) working as many as twenty nylon nets wherever the fish were to be found in Hermitage Bay and Bay Despair. Evenings they gutted and otherwise prepared what they had caught, either aboard their vessel or at one of their several camps throughout the region. Twice a week they sailed to the plant at Gaultois to sell their catch. Live lobster and fresh salmon fetched ten cents a pound; cod in salt brought six cents a pound; fresh cod ready for filleting, one and a half cents per pound.

Hardly munificent earnings, but for the Hills it was enough.

"We don't want for nothing," Sandy told us. "Got good houses over our heads. Don't owe nobody nothing. All our youngkers – Kent's got seven and I've six – gets proper schooling. Two of them's already teaching and I've a girl away at university in St. John's. We eats well. We dresses warm. And we never goes short of a drop, or of friends and neighbours to help us down it. You could say we was pretty well contented."

They gave me a fat cod they had caught that day and, when their work was finished that evening, came aboard *Happy Adventure*. While Claire quietly "sketched them off" they talked warmly of their younger years lived in a community of five families at Barasway de Cerf, a cove in Bay Despair. There they had enjoyed such a satisfying life that they and their families had remained at Barasway de Cerf until their children's need for greater education in the modern world became paramount. Only then had they (reluctantly) moved to Hermitage Cove. They continued to spend their summers at the barasway and returned to it during the rest of the year whenever the opportunity arose.

"'Tis home, you understand. And I'll tell you, skipper, and you too, Missis, they's no better place upon this earth."

The next day being Sunday, the Hills insisted Claire and I accompany them and their families to morning service in the sparse old Anglican church, then join them at Sandy's house for an enormous meal prepared by his wife, Irene, and three stunning daughters.

Ruddy-complexioned like her husband and brilliantly blue-eyed, Irene had been a beauty – was one still. Before her marriage she had "belonged" to Brunette Island, where her father had been one of two lightkeepers caring for one of the most important lights on the Northwest Atlantic seaboard. The light tower, an immense inner cylinder of stone surrounded by a second cylinder, contained living quarters for two families that, in Irene's time, had numbered twelve children between them.

"One for each of the twelve brass oil lamps that give out the light," she told us. "When we was growed enough, we was each allowed to care for one of the lamps – fill and clean it and polish the mirrors and the lenses to the satisfaction of our dads, as was the keepers. So you see, we helped make the light shine out across Fortune Bay so sailor-men and fishermen could find their ways safe home.

"If I never does nothing else, I'll always be some glad I could do that much for they."

The Hills adopted us into their community, apparently without a second thought and without reservation. Our problems became their problems. One evening I explained that we must soon sail to St. Pierre so Claire could fly back to Toronto, but that I was most reluctant to leave *Happy Adventure* on the French Islands for a second winter and, moreover, reluctant to leave the Sou'west Coast at all.

"No need to, bye," said Kent. "Take the missus on the coast boat to Fortune and the *Spencer* out to St. Peter's. Then you come back the same way. Winter your vessel here in Hermitage. You can be certain sure we'll keep a sharp eye onto her. Or you could sail her back into Bay Despair. Visit Sandy and me at the barasway on the way. Look around so much as you like and when you *has* to go back up-along, you could haul her out for the winter at Head of the Bay. Dolph'd look after her like she was his own."

To my delight, Claire agreed. "We could start off again in Bay Despair next summer, Farley, and you've said Harold Horwood wanted to sail with you on the Sou'west Coast. Perhaps if you wired him, he could come down and keep you company until it was time to haul *Happy Adventure* out."

Harold Horwood.

, 9 ,

Bay of Spirits

We boarded the *Bonavista* on a Tuesday evening. One of a newer breed of coastal boats, she was eastbound under the command of Captain Roland Penney, a ship-handler of legendary skill whom we had already met. As we stood hand in hand by the rail bidding a sad adieu to our little ship forlornly tugging at her anchor in the barasway, Skipper Ro came out of the wheelhouse to welcome us aboard. Following our gaze, he murmured just loudly enough for me to hear: "Maid or a vessel . . . don't pay to leave ary one too long on their own. Could be gone out of it when you comes back again."

The warning brought me no solace, since not only was I about to part from Claire but within a few weeks would also have to part from *Happy Adventure*. I would as soon Skipper Ro had kept his maxim to himself.

Our voyage aboard the *Bonavista* was pleasant enough. She was crowded with sociable people. Some were destined for medical treatment in St. John's; others (mostly men, but some women) were bound "away" looking for the work they could no longer find in the outports. One middle-aged fellow from Jerseyman Harbour was going home after spending eleven months on a scallop boat fishing out of Lunenburg. A score of younger men were off to lumber camps in the interior of the island in hopes of finding a few weeks' winter work cutting pulp. Several teenagers were heading for boarding schools in the capital. Few of these travellers would see their homes again for many weeks or months, yet all were in good spirits. Two harmonicas and a guitar were seldom silent, and the passenger saloon was a babble of song and gossip.

When we docked at Harbour Breton so many people crowded aboard to visit that it became almost impossible to make one's way along the decks and alleyways. One visitor had no difficulty doing so. He was a big black water dog who boarded every steamer to collect scraps from the cooks. He made his way rapidly to the galley, clearing a path for himself by using his nose to goose everyone who stood in his way.

Because Claire and I were preoccupied with thoughts of what our futures might portend, we did not take much pleasure in the voyage. Although Claire's prospects must have been dauntingly uncertain, she was more worried about those confronting me and how I was going to deal with them. My stated plan was to spend September in Bay Despair aboard *Happy Adventure*, nominally gathering material for a prospective book. But Claire rightly guessed I was deliberately delaying my return to Ontario while I tried to resolve the problem of whether or not to abandon my marriage.

We disembarked from the *Bonavista* at Fortune and next day the venerable *Spencer* ferried us across the narrow waters to St. Pierre, where we spent two foggy and miserable days waiting for a plane.

On the third day I stood beside the sodden runway and watched a lumbering DC-3 disappear into the murk, carrying Claire away to what seemed like an unimaginably distant place.

The deprivation I felt was so overwhelming that my first inclination was to get mindlessly drunk. Then it occurred to me that something of Claire's presence might still linger aboard *Happy Adventure* and I was filled with a consuming compulsion to return to Hermitage.

This turned out to be easier said than done. That night St. Pierre was pummelled by a sou'easter that grounded planes, locked fishing vessels in harbour, and disabled a passenger liner a hundred miles east of Miquelon.

For hours I paced, prowled, and growled through the storm-lashed streets of St. Pierre, unsuccessfully seeking a way to rejoin my little ship. The *Spencer* remained securely moored to her wharf at Fortune. The skippers of the *St. Eugène* and the *Attaboy* (the latter a retired rum-runner), which were the two most seaworthy launches on the islands, would not even consider putting out in such weather. Even the usually indomitable Théophile Detcheverry failed me for he would not commit his beloved *Oregon* to the turmoil raging in the waters between St. Pierre and Newfoundland.

Two days after Claire's departure I happened on Pierre Tenier, a gaunt sometime-fisherman (more usually a handyman around the harbour), who owned a decrepit power dory of *Oregon*'s lineage and who was always short of money. Pierre had been drinking at the Joinville bar when I encountered him. Without much hope I asked if *he* would ferry me to Hermitage.

"*Peut-être . . . peut-être.*" Maybe – he said muzzily. "*Combien?*" – how much?

Thirty dollars was all the cash I could command. It proved enough.

Pierre agreed to start at dawn next day by which time the storm was expected to have moderated. Indeed it had, though it was still blowing half a gale and, as he pointed out, the seas were *très formidables*. He suggested we might postpone our departure until the following day but when I snarled at him – threatening to drown my frustrations in booze paid for with the charter money – he reconsidered.

Before we were even clear of the Passe du Nord-est, his dory, *Petite Céleste*, was pitching and rolling like a demented pony desperately anxious to rid herself of a rider. Her motion was so extreme that I was ready to turn back but, astonishingly, Pierre was not.

We were not alone. He had shipped a crew consisting of his own nine-year-old son together with a fourteen-year-old lad who today would be described as "learning disabled" but who, in those times, was just called simple. The dory had no pumps so it was the boys' task to keep her afloat by bailing her out with wooden scoops.

To help maintain her trim, I huddled in the bow (where the motion was worst) while the others crowded into the stern sheets, attempting to shelter from spray and driving rain under a piece of tarpaulin that soon enough was torn from their hands. Clustered close around the tiller, the three of them seemed diminished to the size of hand puppets by the mighty seas rolling up behind us.

I was having serious second thoughts about this voyage but, unimpressive as she may have looked, *Petite Céleste* was a staunch little vessel and her three-horsepower, single-cylinder engine was as resolute as the heart of God. It never missed a beat, which was as well for if we had lost steerageway the dory could readily have broached, rolling over in the troughs and pitching the four of us into the dark depths.

But as frightened as I was, I was exhilarated too. Although my stomach sank as the dory plunged through the breaking crests, my spirit soared. If there can be direct communion between man and the world womb, this was as close to it as I was ever likely to come. I still retain a vivid image of the rocks of les Enfants Perdues as we drove past. I can smell the rank tang of sea-wrack on them, feel the driven spray from towering pillars of foaming waters thundering skyward like aqueous volcanoes, and hear and feel the dolorous clamour as they fell back into the ocean.

I also remember the only meal we attempted: chunks of salt-water–soaked bread with uncooked sausages and stinking cheese that had to be hacked up with a large, sharp knife while the bucking and kicking dory tried to send us flying. Pierre and the boys appeared to relish the fare. I limited myself mostly to brandy.

Heaving and plunging through a chaos of cross-swells that kept us all bailing, it took the best part of the day to make good the fifteen miles between St. Pierre and Danzig Head on the Burin Peninsula. From there we had a relatively sheltered run into Fortune harbour, which we found packed with fishing vessels waiting out the storm.

The wind fell out that night so next morning we set off across the mouth of Fortune Bay in calm but misty weather. The mist soon thickened to a proper fog and Pierre's ancient compass, whose needle showed a decided preference for southwest no matter which direction we were actually heading, was little help. We were guided instead by the extraordinary hearing of our young *simple*. Perched in the bow, he could detect the vibrations of distant diaphones at a distance beyond any normal human hearing, first on Brunette Island, then on Pass Island, enabling us to steer a course toward each in turn.

When we had approached close enough to Pass Island to be able to make out the dim outline of the coast near Basse Terre Point, I took over the navigation using an old White Rose Gasoline road map of Newfoundland in lieu of a chart. It was of some slight assistance in finding our way along the south side of the Hermitage peninsula to Dawson's Cove, an outport only five miles distant across the peninsula from Hermitage. I chose to go ashore here. Pierre and his crew lingered only long enough to refill their fuel tank before heading for home, some fifty miles to the south.

Harold Horwood had reached Hermitage by coast boat two days earlier and was waiting for me aboard *Happy Adventure*. We wasted no time getting underway and by next evening were back in Milltown, whose post office would provide my link to Claire during the succeeding weeks.

Harold and I made a number of short local voyages out of Milltown, then he wanted to take a look at the outer coast so one fine morning we sailed to Long Reach and headed out toward the mouth of Bay Despair.

A spanking nor'west breeze made *Happy Adventure* fly along like a water witch, her red sails taut as drumheads and the water swooshing under her forefoot. As often happened in Long Reach, we were accompanied by dolphins. Land, sea, and sky seemed possessed of a vivid vitality that moved Harold (who normally eschewed displays of sentiment) to say he had never felt closer to the primal essence of his native land.

Next morning we ran past Pushthrough out into the open sea, where we encountered a terrific swell and a stiff nor'wester. *Happy Adventure* bucked into it, keeping closer than may have been wise to the lowering coastal cliffs as we looked for the hole in the wall called Richards Harbour.

I was afraid we might have overshot it when Harold spotted a crack in the massive coastal barrier. Since daylight was almost gone, we could not tell whether the opening led to a safe haven or to a dead end. I started the engine while Harold got the canvas off and we nosed into the narrow gut on a rising tidal stream that shot us into a mountain-ringed basin a quarter mile across. A few houses

Richards Harbour.

and a dwarfish church clung to the steep southern shore and several trap skiffs rode uneasily at anchor.

Richards Harbour was an outport with a murky reputation, according to Skipper Riggs:

"Quare folks there. 'Tis the only place on the coast where folks don't come running to the wharf when the steamer calls. Seems like they shuts their doors and draws their curtains. They's a saying you might hear: Dogfish [a small species of shark] makes better company than Richards Harbour folks."

Certainly our arrival triggered no apparent interest. When we moored at the head of a rickety stage, nobody came down to help us with our lines; when I went ashore to see if I could buy some fish for supper, the few people I met seemed distant to the point of rudeness. A worried-looking woman running the settlement's one and only store in the front room of her house sold me some salt cod but, as I left, hastened to shut the door behind me, as if relieved by my departure.

"Unfriendly bunch," I told Harold as we ate our meal. "I wonder why."

I would not get an answer until January 1965, when a small helicopter arrived in Burgeo, where Claire and I were then living, to fly the doctor from Burgeo's cottage hospital to Richards Harbour. The doctor invited me to go along for the ride.

"St. John's wants me to evacuate a patient from there but I know in advance he won't be going out, so you might as well have the seat."

We had a rough flight along a wind-lashed coast to land on the only level spot in Richards Harbour, the site of a house that had burned to the ground a few months earlier. We were met (*not* greeted) by three glum men who ushered us into the kitchen of an unpainted house half-buried in drifted snow. Here we found ourselves facing several more grim-faced men, and a very angry woman of about fifty.

"Simeon's not going wit' ye!" she shrieked as we came through the door.

The doctor sought to calm her.

"All right, my dear. You're his mother. If you won't let him, then he won't go. But since I'm here I must have a look at him so I can tell St. John's he's all right."

Beckoning me to follow, he headed up the narrow stairs before either the woman or her formidable escort could intervene. We found thirty-six-year-old Simeon Pink locked in a small room whose one tiny window had been boarded over, leaving only a narrow slit to let in some daylight. There was no furniture other than what had presumably been a mattress but was now so ripped as to be unrecognizable. Simeon was squatting on it, naked except for the torn remnant of a shirt. He blinked and smiled at us as we stood in the open doorway, smiled and drooled.

"Mad as a March hare," the doctor murmured. "Born that way. He should have been shipped to the mental hospital years ago but the people here would never let him go." The doctor's examination was superficial and our stay short. As we hurried back to the helicopter, I felt as if many eyes were watching us depart, none of them friendly.

I would later hear more about Richards Harbour from an Anglican minister who spent three decades on the coast. According to him, the community was afflicted by a genetic defect resulting in one and sometimes two or even three children in each generation being born "idiots."

"It was and is a tragedy, not just for the poor children but because most people on the coast have always believed insanity was a curse – the Devil's work. So Richards Harbour people tried their best to conceal what was happening there. They hid the idiot children away. They cared for them as best they might, but kept them out of sight. They thought if other people found out, Richards Harbour folk would become pariahs. They kept their secret so long as they could, and even now won't face up to it.

"Well, that's about over now. The government is bent on closing out Richards Harbour. Everyone will be moved out and resettled somewhere else. If poor Simeon Pink is still alive, he'll finally finish up in the asylum in St. John's."

We had intended to sail west as far as Francois, but our plans changed when we heard that Hurricane Betsy was heading for the Sou'west Coast. I decided we had best run back to Bay Despair for shelter. Harold was somewhat contemptuous of my timidity.

"You really are a mainlander, Farley. A proper Newfoundlander doesn't run from bad weather – he revels in it."

"Good enough, Harold, but I'd rather be improper than fill a watery grave. Let go the lines."

We made a fast run eastward, putting in to Pushthrough as night fell. There we waited for Betsy to strike. She never did, but the threat she posed gave Harold a chance to get to know Pushthrough. And vice versa. Coming back from the lighthouse one morning we encountered a bevy of small boys. As they sidled past us, looking askance at our bearded faces, Harold lunged at them barking fiercely – "BOW-WOW-WOW." Without hesitation they leapt over the edge of the path and went rolling down into the land-wash below. They would not soon forget Harold.

One of the adults we met was Skipper John Foote. A massively built man in his eighties, now reduced to skeletal proportions by cancer, John lived in a four-square little cottage overlooking the entrance to the bay. The bedroom where he spent most of his time was painted sky-blue and was fitted out like the cabin of a ship – except for flowered curtains on the window. Though too weak even to wash himself, he remained in full command of his faculties and was delighted to have visitors.

A granddaughter, whose husband had been lost at sea only a year after their marriage, was sharing the cottage with Skipper John. She brought us tea and hot biscuits while John relived fragments of his life for us.

Born in Little Goblin, he had spent his early years at Rams Passage – called Raymonds Passage on the charts – at the junction of Bay Despair's two largest fiords, Bay the North and Bay the East. At that time Rams had been home to eight close-knit families; four more lived at nearby Victoria Harbour and three at Little Goblin. All considered themselves part of the same clan.

John's father had owned a small schooner of the kind known as a western boat.

"Summer times us fished the offshore banks in her. Was nothing out there to bother we but a gale or two and foggy weather. Always fish aplenty. Jigging and trawling we filled the holds two or three times a week, then we'd carry the fish back to Rams for to split and gut afore the women salted it and laid it out on the flakes to dry.

"Winters was the bestest times. Come October us'd shift to the head of Bay the North to winter in our tilts. Once the ice made thick enough all hands fished through it for herring and turbot as we put down in brine in barrels."

He told us that when the weather was "clement" men and older boys would range far into the interior "furring" and hunting caribou. As late as 1915 there were still wolves in Newfoundland, and John remembered being followed by a little family of three that may have been one of the last surviving packs on the island.

"I knowed they was hungry but I was never feared. When I come to a cache of deer meat I had near to Indian Pond, I cut out a frozen brisket and left it for they. 'Twas turnabout, you understand, because one time my old dad was away back in the country and broke his foot and couldn't hunt. When he come upon a fresh wolf kill with seven big wolves on it, he were so hungry he dragged himself right to the wolves and they parted for him and left him to it, and saved his life."

During the first decades of the twentieth century, winter used to come early to the Sou'west Coast. John told us that by mid-December the inner reaches of the bay would be frozen hard. Youngsters and many older folk would don homemade double-bladed skates. With racquets (snowshoes) slung on their backs in case they wanted to go inland, they were as mobile as the caribou. Accompanied by their water dogs hauling "slides," Rams Passage people skated almost everywhere they chose to go in Bay Despair.

"Ah, yiss, us was the real winter men. And what a time it were for visiting. I minds one Christmas a crowd of maids and lads from Rams and Goblin skated all the ways up to Mr. Morgan Roberts's house at Head of the Bay. Took two days and nights because, you understand, we had to stop every place along the way to have a scoff and sing a song and have a dance. 'Twas the same going home. Except we would pick up a good many youngkers from the Head, and St. Alban's, and Conne River who'd come back for to have a time with we at home.

"Summers we could get about near as fast in sailing skiffs. They was only eighteen foot on the keel, open decked, but with four sails: a driver, mainsail, foresail, and jib. Me dear man, they could surely fly!

"Free as the birds we was them times, and Bay Despair were a wunnerful fine place to live, sheltered from heavy weather, handy to the deep-water fishery. Enough ground for turnips and potatoes. Grass enough for sheep and a cow or two for every family. Most days from October to March there was caribou within sight. They al'ays followed the same passes, and they come in hundreds. Winter time we'd shoot what was wanted and haul some on our slides to Gaultois to trade at Newman's, the Jersey merchant, for whatever 'twas we needed.

"The hills all about was thick with chickens [ptarmigan] and rabbits to fill the pot, and ducks and turrs [guillemots] on the ponds and out on the bay. Yiss, and trouts and salmon! Bay the East river had the biggest kind of salmon run. 'Twere nothing for we to fill a skiff from one net strung at the river mouth with salmon ten, fifteen, twenty pounds weight. Sea trout and mud trout was thick enough in every little brook and pond so's you could pretty near scoop up what was wanted with an old rubber boot.

"If any man went hungry those times, 'twas because he wanted to.

"Codfish? Me dear man, they was so plenty in Long Reach two fellows jiggin' could fill a dory in an hour. Out along the coast they was plenty enough to fill the holds of every vessel in Newfoundland. I knows they's gone down a good deal since, and I don't say as they won't go down a good deal farther yet, but when I were young you'd have thought they was no end.

"'Course, we never had much money. The way the merchants rigged things, you never saw the cash. What odds. We had near everything we wanted. And they was al'ays some fellow slipping over to St. Peter's for baccy and rum to keep the men jolly, and cassie wine and fancy cloth for the women. Ah, yiss, byes, we never suffered from the lack of what we needed, unless it were from lack of trying."

As with most settlers who spent a good part of their time in the country, Rams Passage people maintained good relations with the Mi'kmaqs. John mentioned this in passing and I asked him if he knew of any contact in times past with the Beothuks.

He did not personally know of any, but had heard Peter Benoit, one of the Mi'kmaq elders, tell of finding remnants of a Beothuk birchbark wigwam around the turn of the century near Long Pond, thirty miles northwest of Head of the Bay. The crumbled tent had contained the skeletons of three adults and a child.

"The bones of the young one was covered all over with the red ochre they used for to colour most everything they valued. It looked to Peter Benoit like the young one died first, and they'd done what they could for he afore they died theirselves."

Harold thought these might have been some of the last surviving Red Indians, fleeing the genocidal fishermen of northern Newfoundland.

Listening to John's stories led me to suppose his life had been lived mostly in virtual isolation from the world I knew. I was quite wrong about that.

"Plenty of young fellows from Rams and most other places round the Bay made voyages across the water in schooners carrying salt fish. Afore I were thirty I'd been to England twice, Spain three times, the Azores once, and half a dozen times to the Caribee Sea. Then I bought a forty-ton schooner of me own and in the next thirty year fished and sailed her pretty well right around Newfoundland and to Canada and the Boston States.

"About the time Father were born, in 1856 that were, the telegraph come overland to the bottom of all the big bays along the coast on its way from St. John's to Port aux Basques. They was a repeater station at Head of the Bay and another at Bay the North. The one at Bay the North was run by a chap named Thomey. His son was still the operator when I fished turbot there fifty year ago.

"Once a week, winter or summer, a repairman walked the line between the stations, which was thirty or forty miles apart. They kept the wire in order and they carried the Sou'west Coast mail on their backs, passing it along from one station to the next. It could take a good few days for a letter to make the trip in or out. The operator at the station would tell us the news of the country and of the world too, when we come to visit he or to get mail. I supposes we knowed as much as we cared to about what was going on.

"The first teacher on this coast were Jacob Sims, who come out from England to Mosquito on Newman's steamer *Greyhound* in 1861. Jacob give over teaching pretty quick, got himself a maid, and now they's near as many Sims on the coast as fish in the sea. They never was a school at Rams. Most of we learned reading and writing from the women. They took turns at it, between making fish, looking to the animals when the men was off fishing, picking berries, growing gardens, raising children, spinning wool, making clothes, and cooking for all hands.

"They was no clergyman in the bay until after 1919; only, four times a year old Canon Bishop – that were his real name – sailed over from Hermitage to marry and baptize them as needed it. We al'ays had a deacon of our own could bury the dead, so we was well enough looked after."

Harold was curious about what medical aid had been available in the bay in those times. John laughed when asked about it.

"For the most of it we cared for ourselves. They was only one doctor on the coast. He were stationed at Hermitage. If you was sick you could go to him. If you was dying, he might come to you. Mostly we doctored ourselves. The operator at Bay the North was a right good hand at doctoring, and the Indians knew a thing or two, but our women folk could cure a good part of our ailments.

"That were a good thing 'cause getting the doctor from Hermitage was nigh as hard as finding pirate gold. One time when I were a boy, a woman at Rams got sick to death so two men set off in a skiff for Hermitage to fetch the doctor. When they got there they found he were carried off to Head of the Bay to look at a sick man there, so off they went behind him. They waited at Head of the Bay till he done what he could, then took him aboard their skiff and sailed for Rams. On the way they met a crowd from McCallum – that's out on the coast past Pushthrough – come for the doctor too. They had to follow our boat to Rams and wait till the doctor was through afore they could carry him off to McCallum. He were nigh two weeks afore he saw Hermitage again. Come spring of that year he took passage to St. John's and never *was* seen after in Bay Despair."

John's stories made us want to visit his old home ourselves. September had brought clear, cool weather, so one still morning with the sea gleaming like oiled silk and the air soft and buttery, we started the engine and set off for Rams.

Our course was north-by-east to Goblin Head, whose cliffs loomed like the ramparts of a titan's fort, reducing *Happy Adventure* to the stature of a water bug. She was, however, still big enough to startle a pair of six-foot sharks of a kind known locally as squid hounds who were blissfully following one another at the surface, perhaps with amorous intent, until our cutwater sliced between them.

This bold coast abounded with eagles – we counted more than forty in a few hours. The white heads and tails of the adults stood out like signal flags against the cliffs upon which they perched in little groups. As we came abeam of them, they would plunge from their roosts, sweep down over us for a look, then ride the updrafts back to their high perches.

Barely rippling the still waters at quarter-speed, we eased into Goblin Bay. Cradled by eight-hundred-foot crags, it was a forbidding place. Except for two slits in its lowering northern shore, called Middle and Little Goblin, there was only one place – Pot Hole – where even a dory could have safely sheltered.

We decided to see if Middle Goblin was any more hospitable and found it well protected by surrounding hills. It looked like a perfect harbour. Yet, according to Skipper John, it had never been settled. When I had asked why, he had been vague, except to say with a small smile, "Some thinks 'tis where they goblins lives."

Giving its two guardian islets a wide berth we entered Middle Goblin through a narrow passage between five-hundred-foot peaks. We did so cautiously for John had warned us of a one-fathom shoal in the channel. It turned out to be a submerged stone "bridge." The water over it was so crystal clear we could see legions of very big scallops massed upon it looking, Harold thought, "like a defensive army of alien beings."

Once over this sunken rampart we found ourselves in a per- fectly landlocked and spectacularly beautiful basin with a bald hill looming over it to the northward and wooded glens running out of its eastern and western ends. There was not a breath of wind inside this walled sanctuary and the silence as we anchored off the mouth of the eastern glen seemed oppressive. It was growing dark by then so we did not go ashore. Instead we feasted on a cod given us at Pushthrough then crawled into our bunks and slept.

Not for long. Shortly before midnight a terrible gust exploded out of the eastern glen, spinning the vessel around her anchor and bringing me tumbling up on deck, where I was almost blinded by a rain squall. With the help of a flashlight I could see foam boiling on the shore rocks less than twenty feet under our stern. Harold scrambled out beside me. What to do? If we stayed where we were and the anchor dragged, we would drive ashore and almost certainly lose the ship. If we raised anchor and tried to run for it, where would we go in the nearly pitch-black night? We decided to stay put and, if the anchor dragged, start the engine and hope to claw off shore.

Blow-me-down gusts battered us throughout the remainder of the night but by dawn an uncanny calm had returned to Middle Goblin. We could see some odd-looking stone structures on shore that looked as if they might have been man-made, but we did not linger to investigate. Though nothing was said about how we felt, I believe we were equally anxious to get out of Middle Goblin. Resisting any temptation to examine nearby Little Goblin, we headed for open water.

Coasting farther north, we came at last to Rams Passage, a mile-long tickle separating Rams Island from the mainland. We anchored and went ashore in the dinghy for a look-about. As recently as 1952, eight houses had faced each other from both sides of the narrow tickle; now nothing remained of them except a few "shores" – supporting posts. Skipper John had described for us how one calm summer's day the houses had been "launched off" and hauled south to take up residence in Pushthrough. Heeling to port or starboard like drunken sailors, and towed at a snail's pace by motorboats, the two-storeyed houses must have constituted as strange an armada as ever sailed the Bay of Spirits.

The next day brought a headwind booming out of Bay the East, which we had intended to explore. We decided instead to try Bay the North, which appeared relatively calm. Bay the North turned out to be a gargantuan rock-cut roughly half a mile wide, walled by towering cliffs. By noon *Happy Adventure* was gingerly poking her bowsprit into Second Brook Cove, a niche in the rock wall beside which we were able to anchor so close in we could almost step ashore and climb the cliff to search for a stone construct in the shape of a huge cross said to be laid out on the high plateau overlooking the cove. According to Michael John, the boulders of which the cross was composed were far too large and heavy to have been arranged by human hands. He also told me the Mi'kmaqs made annual pilgrimages to it in the belief it had miraculous healing powers.

Harold was skeptical about its being a cross at all, believing it would turn out to be a random arrangement of erratics – boulders deposited by melting glaciers. We never found out because a north wind got up, threatening to blow *Happy Adventure* right out of Bay the North, and we had to skip back aboard and leave the cross in possession of its mystery.

With the engine running full out, we made a very wet run to the head of Bay the North. The fiord changed its nature at its northernmost extremity. Beetle-browed cliffs were replaced by rounded hills covered with conifers. Low shores nurtured patches of level ground once cleared for pasture, now resplendent with rippling waves of hay – hay nobody would ever harvest and no cattle would ever graze. Of the telegraph station and the winter tilts that had once given a human aspect to this portal into Newfoundland's interior, nothing visible now remained.

Next morning we scudded out of Bay the North heading for Milltown, where I hoped to find letters from Claire. As we changed course for the run up Long Reach, we sailed through a covey of dories from Pushthrough whose two-man crews were jigging cod. They waved and shouted greetings. It must have been a long time since they had seen a schooner, even such a small one as ours, go driving up the bay under full sail.

As we left them astern, I thought of Skipper John Foote's last words to us.

"'Twere in 1952 the government chased we out of Rams and closed her down. At the last of it I sailed me schooner over to Pushthrough. She lays in the tickle down by the wharf. No doubt you'll see her there when you goes out."

We had seen her. The merest skeleton of a vessel, her planking mostly gone and her naked ribs curving out of the landwash like those of some long-dead whale.

· 10 ·

Stormy Passage

Three letters from Claire awaited me on our return to Milltown, each more unhappy than the last. These tipped the scales so that I finally mustered the will to go home. Together Harold and I decommissioned *Happy Adventure*, and I made arrangements locally for her to be hauled ashore and looked after for the winter. Then we took the next eastbound coast boat as far as Terrenceville at the head of Fortune Bay.

Once there, forty or fifty passengers raced off the boat in a mad rush to grab a seat in one of several "taxis" waiting to make the long drive to St. John's. Shoving and pushing in proper mainland style, Harold and I got berths in a battered sedan belonging to young Jimmy Hickey, together with (very *much* together with) seven others. Somehow we all got stowed aboard, though our luggage overflowed the trunk and festooned the roof.

151

Four people occupied the front seat and five the rear one. There was a pregnant woman; one baby; one twelve-year-old with what sounded like whooping cough; a garrulous and weighty woman heading for hospital because she had "wind in me bowel"; two young male teachers; and a young woman prone to car sickness. Harold and I shared the back seat with one of the teachers, the pregnant woman, and the one with the delicate stomach.

As Jimmy Hickey cheerfully put it, the car was "dragging her arse" before the four-mile stretch of pavement leading out of Terrenceville ended and we began the hundred and seventy miles of gravel-surfaced track leading to Newfoundland's capital city.

The re-entry into modern life was not easy to take. During the six hours required to reach St. John's the radio blared rock and roll at full volume. We had to stop countless times for the pregnant lady to relieve herself; for the lady with the delicate stomach to throw up; and for we males to repair or replace burst tires. I longed to be back aboard *Happy Adventure*!

I was now determined to face and force the decisions that had to be made if Claire and I were to have a life together, but the way was not easy.

Frances would not agree to an uncontested divorce, and in those times obtaining a contested one was a horrific ordeal entailing such unsavoury expedients as having oneself photographed committing adultery in a sleazy motel room. Neither Claire nor I was prepared for that; having canvassed all the possibilities, we concluded that the only solution for us was to live together common-law.

To ease the embarrassment this would create for Claire and for her family, and to make it harder for me to backslide, we decided to travel to England. There I could begin researching my next book – a history of Newfoundland. Claire would join me as soon as she could disentangle herself from familial and other obligations in Toronto.

This old tub is certainly no Blue-Ribbon Liner. Her cargo holds carry Yankee onions, Nova Scotian apples, and Newfoundland salt fish. She also carries the Royal Mail, which is likely the only thing enabling her to pay her way. If she was solely dependent on what freight and passengers she's got, her owners would soon be bankrupt.

Apparently they're going to be in any case. My cabin steward, whose name is Harry Mathers, tells me the scuttlebutt [rumour] is that this is the SS Newfoundland's *last voyage. The crew of fifty-five are to be laid off after we dock at Liverpool and the old lady herself will then go to the breakers' yard to be cut up for scrap.*

Harry is phlegmatic about it:

"In this world if a thing don't pay hard coin, somebody's going to suffer. And it won't be the owners if they can help it."

Does all this seem pretty grim? Well, it likely would be if I was travelling away from you, but that isn't how I see it. We're coming together . . . the long way round maybe . . . but together, for good and always. And together we'll vanquish fear and solitude and all such bleak uncertainties, and dark shadows will be put to flight. . . .

It's noon now, and there's been a calamity. While I was in the first class lounge, attempting to lighten the bartender's gloom (I seem to be his only customer), a heavy sea struck us broadside and nearly rolled the ship on her beam ends. When I scrambled back to my cabin I found my trusty portable typewriter had been flung against a bulkhead so hard the keys were bent and the ribbon was festooning the space like a funeral decoration. Fortunately, it's a tough little thing. After a lot of cursing and fiddling I seem to have it working again.

The gale continues. It is now keening at Force 8 and we are practically stopped in the water, probably not making any headway at all. Everyone, even the crew, seems to have disappeared leaving me in possession of what feels like a derelict. I haven't seen the captain since we left St. John's. I'm alone in the dining saloon at mealtimes except for a couple of waiters who, in view of what awaits them in Liverpool, act more like undertakers as they slither about trying to keep crockery and cutlery from being turned into lethal flying objects. I'll bet they wish I'd do the sensible thing and lose my appetite too, but I seem to have a cast-iron stomach.

There's a dog aboard, quartered in a kennel under a shelter on the boat deck. I went out a little while ago to see if she is surviving. Found the poor thing – some kind of a spaniel – sprawled in a corner of her cage and doubtless sure her time had come. Holding onto a stanchion with one hand, I held out the other to her. She gave it a thorough licking, after which she seemed a little happier. When I left her she howled despairingly but the sound was lost in the roaring of the gale. I'd sneak her into my cabin, except she'd be flung about like a rag doll there.

This is one hell of a storm. I climbed to the lower bridge and watched, appalled, as the old girl drove her bows right under, sending a deluge over the upper bridge. I wonder if she's seen the copy of my book about the salvage tugs I brought with me, and wants to show me that anything a salvage tug can handle, she can too.

2300 hours. It is now blowing Force 10 on the Beaufort Scale, which means around seventy-five miles an hour. I tried to visit the bar but got slung about like a ping-pong ball so I clawed my way back to my cabin, physically encountering the first mate in the corridor en route. We clung to each other as he told me the forecast is for more of the same for the next two days! We are now hove-to and being blown backward toward Labrador, which, I hope and trust, is a safe distance to leeward. I'm wedged into my bunk, trying to type with one hand while holding onto the typewriter with the other. Wooooops! The chair just broke loose and committed hara-kiri against the washstand.

For the first time, and I never thought I'd say this, I'm glad you aren't with me. When you do come across, make sure it's on the Queen

Mary, *and pray her skipper has the sense to take the* southern steamer track, *not the* northern *one as our suicidal captain has done.*

Wednesday. Last night was the worst I've ever spent at sea. Around midnight I was flung out of my bunk and if it hadn't been for a pile of life jackets that had spilled out of their locker onto the floor, I might well have done myself some damage. But I'm fine, though cured once and for all of any mad dreams I ever had about sailing around the world. Bay Despair will be big enough from now on.

Thursday morning. This old bitch is now in the troughs and rolling like the proverbial drunken sailor. I inched my way down to B-Deck and peered into the Tourist section. Not a soul to be seen though there were ominous crashes and bangs from the narrow little cabins. And the sounds of straining stomachs. And odd little moans, and yips of pain, or ultimate resignation. Also one shrill scrap of conversation.

"Oh, Fred! We're sinking! I know *we're sinking!*"

To which Fred replied:

"Lay still, you bitch!" *I don't know if he was talking to the lady or to the ship.*

The cold grey dawn found us hove-to in such a sea as I hope never to witness again. The first mate said some of the waves were cresting at a height of forty-five feet or more. Their tops were being blown clean away as if sliced off with a knife. The noise was fearsome as the wind, at Force 12, which is a full hurricane, ripped through the vessel's top-hamper. The mate told me we rolled past 40 degrees several times last night, but the worst roll – the one that threw me out of my bunk – was closer to 45 degrees.

That happened because the radar was useless – just a clutter of wave reflections – and suddenly the dim lights of a very big, west-bound tanker glimmered through the murk almost dead ahead. She was bearing down upon us with the full weight of the hurricane driving

her. Our lookouts on the bridge saw her just in time. The skipper rang for full ahead on both engines and ordered the helm hard over. This brought the ship from being head-to-the-seas, to broadside in the troughs. She came as close as billy-be-damned to rolling over and everything aboard that wasn't nailed down came adrift.

Evening. The wind is dropping off some and we are actually underway and making about three knots. The vessel's motion is so extreme the only safe place to be is in the bunk or wedged into a chair that's bolted to the floor. Harry and I managed a sally to see how the dog was making out. We took her food and water since her owner, whoever he may be, seems to have vanished. Surprisingly, she was in pretty good shape. There are advantages to having four feet and being low to the ground. But she was so glad to see someone she had hysterics. With difficulty we moved her, cage and all, and now she is snugly settled in a spare First Class cabin. As Harry says, "Who's to know?"

I spent much of today reading a book by Alex Waugh about middle-aged men screwing young women. It's full of superficialities and viciousness, and almost devoid of tenderness or compassion. I thought Waugh seemed to have no concept of what love is all about. Then I reflected that not so long ago I would have been inclined to share his cynical delineation of love as being little more than a transient and foredoomed evocation of the flesh.

But that was B.C. – Before Claire. You've changed all that. You are a sorceress or, at least, an enchantress who has utterly enchanted me and given me some understanding of what love is all about. You are so vividly with me at this moment, turning your dark eyes on me and making me yearn for you as for life itself. Slim little one with a maiden's breasts and a woman's warmth; that happy nymph who is Claire Angel Wheeler to most people. But who is my beloved!

Friday. The storm has moved on and life is again stirring in this old vessel. The Manchester ladies actually appeared for breakfast. They

are of indeterminate age and neither is pretty though one has a pert appearance and a sense of humour. Harry told me they had been in the U.S. of A. for two years working as domestics (his word) and had intended this homeward journey to be the crowning event of their sojourn in the New World – a triumphant return, travelling First Class and sitting at the Captain's table! Alas, they have yet to see him. He has been on the bridge or in his quarters since we sailed.

They've had a bad time of it. Their bathroom door burst off its hinges, shattering a full-length mirror whose shards showered all over them as they rolled about in their bunks. Then their washbasin tore loose and flooded the cabin and all the pretty clothes and mementoes from lotus land they were bringing back to Manchester.

This afternoon the sun shone briefly and we had lifeboat drill! When I jokingly suggested to one of the officers this was like locking the barn door after the horse had fled, he did not smile.

"Not really, sir. There's another storm coming up astern. Might not be as bad as the last one, but one never knows. . . ."

By suppertime the new storm had caught up with us and now all hell is breaking loose again. The passengers have all fled to their cells. The ship is pounding along through mammoth swells, chased by a heavy following sea. At noon today the chart posted in the saloon showed we had made good just five hundred miles of easting, and still have fifteen hundred to go. If I was the superstitious type I'd suspect that old Father Neptune doesn't want to let this one go to the ship breakers and is determined to take her for himself.

[This second storm proved less fearsome than had been predicted. By Saturday we were clear of the worst of it and conditions were returning to relative placidity, both on the sea and on board.]

We have a mystery passenger or rather two mystery passengers, husband and wife, who came aboard at Boston. Harry has confided their secret to me. The husband is not present in the flesh; only his ashes are, contained in an ornate bronze urn that, at the beginning of the voyage, occupied the upper berth in the couple's two-berth cabin. But the first big storm pitched the unfortunate fellow onto the floor, where he rolled noisily about, smashing furniture and wreaking havoc in the cabin until Harry roped him back into his bunk.

When he broke free again, and yet again, his wife took drastic action. Here is as much of the story as Harry has confided to me.

The husband, whose name was George, originally came from a village near Leeds but had lived most of his adult life in the States, where he had made a good deal of money. Late in life he married a younger woman, but died not long thereafter leaving her as his sole inheritor. However, he had specified that she should take his ashes back to his natal village and bury him in ancestral ground.

The widow told all this to the cabin stewardess who looked after her while she was sick as a dog during the storms. The stewardess told Harry, who believes the widow must have become a bit unhinged because she offered the stewardess fifty dollars to rid her of what remained of her spouse. The stewardess accepted and, in the dark of night, she and Harry pitched George overboard. I wish I'd been there. It must have been a scene such as even Joseph Conrad could hardly have imagined.

Sunday morning. We've now been nine days at sea and have made a huge diversion to the south to avoid a couple more major depressions. Now we are plowing northeast at fifteen knots and expect to raise Cape Clear on southern Ireland this afternoon. Eureka! This voyage is almost over, and I can't say I'm sorry.

2000 hours. Famous last words! Almost over? Holy Mother! Before noon today we were up to our ass in another bloody storm. We are again hove-to and again being blown westward!

The ship is rolling her guts out and the passengers are emptying theirs. I'm wedged into my bunk after a fantastic exercise in the dining saloon – a Farewell Dinner for all the passengers to celebrate our pending arrival in England but the only people present were the ship's doctor and me. We two sat there, grimly hanging on while the poor bloody waiters engaged in a nightmare ballet. I don't know why arms and legs didn't get broken; but when I met the purser in the corridor as I crept back to my cabin he told me a hundred pounds' worth of crockery had been smashed.

That was the climax of a dreadful day. At 0800 this morning some barrels of diesel fuel stowed 'tween decks broke loose. One drum smashed itself open against a bulkhead and forty-five gallons of diesel oil ran down into the air circulation fans. Within minutes they had shoved the fumes all through the ship. The stink was especially bad in Tourist, where the situation was absolutely hellish.

I went below to try to help the doctor and could only stand it for a few minutes at a time. I thought one young woman, reportedly seven months pregnant, was surely going to die, but some of the crew hauled and slid her on a mattress up to an empty cabin on A-Deck where a port could be opened to let in some fresh air.

The stench down below and the awful motion of the ship convinced some passengers this was the end. They crawled and scrambled up to A-Deck, where a ship's officer endeavoured to turn them back, until the doctor intervened, insisting they be allowed into First Class, where the stench was less terrible and the ship's motion less extreme.

That's how things stand. I'm going to pack up the typewriter and put it under the mattress before I lose it. The gale is still blowing like billy-oh; but the forecast calls for it to abate after midnight. With luck we'll be under the shelter of the land by morning. Then it'll be Liverpool, and the end of the voyage.

The end of one voyage . . . but, soon, the beginning of another: yours and mine together. We'll make it the most splendid one in all recorded history. By God we will!

· 11 ·

Searching for an Anchorage

Claire joined me in mid-January of 1962, and we began our lives together in a frigid stone shepherd's cottage on the Dorset coast. As the weather warmed toward spring, we drove north to John o' Groats at the uttermost extremity of the Scottish mainland to spend a month in Caithness, land of my paternal forebears.

When spring came, we felt ready to return to Canada and face the music so I booked passage to Montreal on the SS *Laurentia*. We drove to Glasgow to board the ship but when we presented ourselves at the offices of the Donaldson Line to collect our tickets, the manager stared long and hard at our passports then sternly informed us we could not share a cabin because we had no proof we were married.

He refused to accept my assurance that we were wedded Inuit-style, by mutual consent, so I demanded our money back. This was a prospect he found more repugnant than abetting an illegal relationship, so he reluctantly handed over the tickets.

The *Laurentia* was a war-built, steam-turbine-driven freighter converted to carry general cargo and passengers. Considering my crossing in the *Newfoundland*, I really should have known better than to take Claire aboard a packet, even one a lot bigger, newer, and more powerful than the *Newfoundland*, but I counted on the tempestuous winter season on the North Atlantic being over.

It wasn't.

In mid-Atlantic we encountered a Force 9 gale whose mighty seas made *Laurentia* roll like a log in a millrace. This storm lasted three long nights and days. After it ended and Claire had recovered her sang-froid and her appetite, she slyly suggested I must be what Newfoundlanders call a jinker – a jinx aboard ship.

Maybe so. *Laurentia* landed us at Montreal after a spectacular arrival involving a collision with a visiting French destroyer – a mishap that slammed our vessel against a concrete dock with such force as to snap off one of her massive propeller blades. Claire made no overt comment, but I knew what she was thinking.

Except for the contretemps with the Donaldson Line, living in sin had not posed much of a problem in Britain, where people seemed remarkably permissive about unsanctified relationships. We anticipated less tolerance in Canada, where it was still virtually impossible to even get a divorce without an act of Parliament and where two people living together without benefit of marriage were pretty generally regarded as being outside the social pale.

We went first to Port Hope to apprise my mother, Helen, of the state of our affairs, for although Angus knew about it he had not told her. Helen gave us her heartfelt blessing, after which we drove on to Toronto to see Claire's family. None of them disapproved (openly, at any rate) of what we were doing. To the contrary, Claire's mother, forthright Winnie Wheeler, was so delighted she mixed a bucket of orange blossoms – gin and orange juice – with which all hands could celebrate our union.

The question of where we would live was temporarily solved by my parents, who offered us the family cottage not far from Brighton on the shore of Lake Ontario. Indian Summer, as it was called, was a thin-walled cabin consisting principally of one room that served as kitchen, dining room, and bedroom. Furnished with shabby castoffs, it lacked plumbing though it did have a good well a few hundred feet away in one direction and a somewhat rickety outhouse the same distance in another direction. It was hardly much of an improvement over the mouldy shepherd's cottage that had been our first home together, yet Claire was delighted with it. We reclaimed her little Morris Minor from her parents' garage, drove it to Indian Summer, and settled in for a few wonderful weeks.

Since we were well in advance of the annual invasion of summer residents we had the lakeshore and the greening southern Ontario countryside mostly to ourselves. We did not work too hard. Uninhibitedly amorous displays by spring birds, frogs, snakes, skunks, and rabbits outside our windows provided a constant challenge. Nor did we spend a lot of time worrying about our future, or even planning what we would do next. We were agreed that as soon as I finished the young people's book I was working on, we would reclaim *Happy Adventure*, then, if we were lucky, find a more permanent place for ourselves in Newfoundland or somewhere in the Atlantic provinces.

In early June Claire and I set off eastward in the Morris. In order to make room for all our gear we folded back the convertible top and piled the rear seat so high with boxes and bags that the little car was like a cartoon donkey, overburdened to the point where little of it was to be seen except legs, a head, and a tail.

Our progress was pleasantly slow. We took three days to reach Nova Scotia, where we spent two days exploring the Celtic eccentricities of Cape Breton Island. One of the oddities we encountered was a tourist cabin consisting of two bedrooms separated by (and sharing) one bathroom. In order to give the occupant some privacy, a contraption made of rope, bicycle tubes, and pulleys had been rigged in such a way that when one bathroom door was opened, the other would be pulled shut and would remain so until the first door was closed again – whereupon the second door would swing open to welcome a new occupant. This arrangement allowed the owner to rent each bedroom separately while claiming that each had its own bathroom. It was a vivid demonstration of the ingenuity that so distinguishes Cape Bretoners.

Next day we made the five-hour ferry crossing of Cabot Strait to Port aux Basques, where the newly built Trans-Canada Highway across Newfoundland theoretically began. Knowing that the TCH was still more of a dream (a nightmare, actually) than a reality, we bought tickets on the antique, narrow-gauge, trans-island railway known sardonically as the Bullet. Claire and I had an upper and lower berth in the sleeping car while the Morris made the journey lashed to a flatcar.

Our transit of Newfoundland took thirty-six hours, which was considered a swift passage for the Bullet. In winter it sometimes took three days and nights and sometimes had required as long as a week. While crossing the high interior, progress was sometimes so plodding that passengers were able to jump off the lead car and pick a can of berries before climbing aboard the last car as it came abreast of them. Or so we were told. We were also told the salutary story of the young woman from Port aux Basques en route to St. John's who, as the Bullet neared Gambo two-thirds of the way across, accosted the conductor demanding to know when they would reach their destination because she was perilously near her time.

The conductor, a regal and intimidating figure in a gold-braided blue uniform, reproached her.

"Maid, you was some foolish to git aboard the Bullet and you in the family way."

To which she replied, "Ah, sorr, but I weren't in the family way when I got aboard."

The Bullet's leisurely pace gave us time and opportunity to absorb something of the feel of the vast wilderness interior of the island and to be regaled and entertained by our fellow travellers, a marvellously uninhibited and amiable lot. Every male seemed to have a good supply of rum with which he was insistently generous. Bottles were freely passed up, down, and across the aisles and if the conductor happened to be passing, he would be invited to wet his whistle too. Some passengers had fiddles or accordions and all hands tended to join lustily in singing the narrative songs and old sea shanties indigenous to Newfoundland. It was not hard to imagine how a female passenger might indeed find herself in the family way before the conclusion of such a journey.

The Bullet finally crawled across the narrow isthmus connecting the Avalon Peninsula with the rest of the island, passing close by two outports whose names especially caught Claire's fancy – Pinch Gut and Famish Gut – before coming to a final halt in St. John's. Reclaiming the Morris, we drove to Beachy Cove on the shore of Conception Bay, where Harold Horwood had a little house that he invited us to share for as long as we wished.

Harold's generosity was not without drawbacks. He had quit his job with the *St. John's Evening Telegram* to become a freelance writer but was also in the process of becoming chief guru for the island's restless youth, whose counterparts on the mainland would become known as flower children. Flower children was hardly an adequate description for Harold's variety. His small bungalow was overrun day and night by hordes of youngsters, some of whom were the offspring of dysfunctional neighbouring shanty dwellers with Irish names. Others were older and tougher versions of the same from the seedier districts of St. John's. They were an interesting lot but their comings and goings were not conducive to sustained literary endeavour on our part.

We delayed at Beachy Cove partly because we were looking for a possible replacement for *Happy Adventure* – something a little more comfortable and considerably more seaworthy. Harold suggested a vessel that had once been his – the *Fort Amadjuak*, a power schooner built many years earlier for use in the Canadian eastern Arctic. He had owned and sailed her for a time on the Labrador. After he sold her, she fell on hard times, and by the time Claire and I saw her, at Bay Bulls just to the south of St. John's, she was hauling capelin to a fertilizer plant.

Although Harold did not actually pressure me into buying her, the upshot was that I forked out five hundred dollars, and what remained of the *Fort Amadjuak* became mine. I arranged for her to be berthed at St. John's until Claire and I had found a home port for ourselves, to which we could bring her for refitting.

In mid-July we set out to rejoin *Happy Adventure*. This entailed making a two-hundred-mile bounce ("drive" is not a suitable description) to Fortune, during which Claire became intimately and painfully familiar with thank-you-ma'ams (as Newfoundlanders pithily describe potholes in their roads).

A few hours after arriving in Fortune, we boarded the *Bar Haven* for the trip to Milltown. She was crowded to the gills with passengers ranging from a gaggle of teenaged girls returning from a Salvation Army camp, to a horse named Herbert who was being sent to haul logs at Head of the Bay.

Claire and I enjoyed a splendid little holiday aboard while Captain Charlie Brown, a remarkably well-read man with a perverse sense of humour, nursed *Bar Haven* in and out of the score of outports along the way. One stormy night off Point Rosie we stood on the bridge and apprehensively watched the skipper do his work. It was too rough for him to dock the ship, so cargo was discharged into two wildly pitching dories bouncing around like beach balls in the heavy sea. The freight being dropped into the boats consisted almost exclusively of cases of soft drinks, cartons of cornflakes, toilet paper, and chocolate bars.

Charlie Brown shook his head sadly.

"Only Newfoundlanders'd be daft enough to risk their lives – and my ship – to put junk like that ashore. If 'twas cakes and ale, like the poet fellow said, it might be worth the doing. But *this*!" he snorted. "Ah well, what odds. We does it anyhow."

In due course, the *Bar Haven* eased alongside the Milltown wharf and we could see our little schooner high and dry on shore, looking pathetically forlorn and neglected. Having been abandoned for months, she was in sorry shape. Her black hull paint was cracked and mottled and her copper bottom paint conspicuous by its absence. Her interior dripped moisture and stank of mildew, long-departed fish, and the slime of St. Pierre harbour.

Aided by three local boys who nurtured their own dreams of going to sea, we set to work scrubbing and repainting her and attaching two three-hundred-pound bars of iron to the keel to help stiffen her in heavy weather. Then, as a spring tide flooded the land-wash, we launched her off and moved aboard.

Having no fixed plans, we thought to spend a few weeks cruising the fiords of Bay Despair, then visit Hermitage, and possibly make a run back to St. Pierre. After that we would begin a serious search for a more or less permanent anchorage for the vessel and for ourselves.

Shortly after we moved aboard, a motorboat arrived from the tiny outport of Cape la Hune, fifty miles to the westward of Bay

Despair. In place its normal cargo of nets and fishes, it bore a wedding party consisting of bride- and groom-to-be, three bridesmaids, and four groomsmen. They were seeking a minister to perform the wedding ceremony. Cold and wet, for they had spent many hours bucking a rising sea, they tied up alongside us. As we warmed them with tea and rum, they described how they had gone first to Pushthrough, only to find that the local vicar was away on holiday. Undaunted, they had continued on to Hermitage hoping to find the only other clergyman on this section of the coast. When told he was visiting Head of the Bay, they had followed him to Milltown.

Claire helped the wet and wind-whipped bride rearrange her finery, then we loaded the lot of them onto the back of a lumber truck whose owner volunteered to carry them to the church, where the hurriedly summoned minister joined them. The ceremony over, they piled back into their boat and set off for distant Cape la Hune.

The truck driver came aboard *Happy Adventure* for a chat. He told us this was the first time any of these young people had been in a motor vehicle, for La Hune had no roads. He explained that the couple was determined to tie the knot that day because the groom had to leave Cape la Hune next morning to spend six or seven months aboard a Nova Scotian dragger, and his sixteen-year-old bride-to-be was already four months pregnant. "Didn't want the babe born with a broken arm trying to hang on 'til after the wedding," the truck driver said without so much as a smile.

Before leaving Head of the Bay, we made a short shakedown cruise to Conne River to visit Michael and Emilia John again. When they saw *Happy Adventure* entering the river mouth, Michael hurried to the shore to take us home for tea and talk.

Having read that around 1764 the French had brought a party of Mi'kmaq Indians from Nova Scotia to Newfoundland to help consolidate French control of the southern coast, I wanted to hear more about the history of his people.

Michael told us his forebears had been put ashore at Long Harbour near the head of Fortune Bay. They had not settled there, however. Settlement was not their style. Instead, they had established a traditional nomadic pattern, penetrating deep into the forests in winter to hunt caribou (later to trap furs for their French patrons), and in summer returning to the coasts for fish and other sea foods. Early in the nineteenth century, they had picked the Beothuks' Bay of Spirits to be the heartland of their new country and Conne River as their main pathway to and from the interior.

In 1900, the year Michael turned fourteen, the Bay of Spirits Mi'kmaq clan, comprising forty or fifty families, had become less nomadic. In winter they inhabited more or less permanent log cabins in and around Hackleberry Lake deep in the interior. In spring they travelled south to live in birchbark wigwams at Head of the Bay and the mouth of Conne River, where they were visited every midsummer by a priest from St. Pierre who came to reaffirm their allegiance to Roman Catholicism.

Michael told us that, in his youth, people travelling in the country before freeze-up or after break-up used small canoes framed with willow withes and covered with caribou hides sewn together with sinews. However, while at their summer homes they would build large birchbark canoes in which they went fearlessly to sea, travelling east to St. Pierre and west to the vicinity of Port aux Basques, from where they sometimes crossed Cabot Strait to visit their ancestral clans in Cape Breton Island.

I asked Michael how these seafarers managed to navigate so far from land and in the fogs endemic to these waters. He said his people imitated the Beothuks, who used to carry bundles of spruce boughs in their canoes. In thick weather, or when far from land, they would throw branches overboard and steer a course by looking *backward* so as to always keep two or three in line astern, thereby ensuring that they steered a course straight ahead.

Michael himself had never seen a Beothuk but gave us a vivid description of a meeting between these now-vanished people and his father and grandfather. His father had been about ten when the two Mi'kmaqs encountered a party of Beothuks on the west branch of the Long Harbour River. The Beothuk group included one old man, two or three younger ones (one of them very fat), two or three women, and several children. The two groups were only about a hundred yards apart when they first saw each other, and Michael's grandfather immediately cocked his old muzzle-loader and ordered his son to take cover. The Beothuks seemed equally apprehensive. They had been roasting deer meat on sticks over an open fire but now they hurriedly began breaking camp.

Michael remembered minute details of what his father had told him.

"They had two bark canoes, made high in the middle, not like ours. Bows and arrows, but no guns. Had piles of deer hides and many bark baskets. They left all them things and even their wigwam and canoes and hurried off into the woods, only taking what they could grab quick and looking back a lot. I believe they was as scared of Granddad and my dad as they two was of them. After they was gone Granddad looked at all their things, but never took nothing. Said them people would come back for them. After that it was quite a time before any of our people went near Long Harbour."

This seems to have been the last occasion when Conne River Mi'kmaqs encountered living Beothuks. The last to be seen alive by European settlers in Newfoundland seems to have been a woman known as Shawnandithit who was captured in the Northern Bays and taken to St. John's, where in 1829 she died of tuberculosis. The little group seen by Michael's father and grandfather must have been among the last Beothuks alive upon this earth.

We returned to Milltown to pick up mail. While we were there, a handsome power skiff crewed by a middle-aged couple from Stone Valley, a little settlement on the outer coast not far east of Pushthrough, arrived for a load of lumber. Cecil and Clara Dominie, who "had heard tell of us," came aboard to invite us to visit them at home and at another place, within the bay, called Raymonds Point, which they frequented in summer. We decided to make Raymonds Point our next destination.

By the time we let go our lines on the following day, it was already duckish (dusk) and Short Reach was hazed in purple mist. We ghosted through it like disembodied spirits until, just off the entrance to Roti Bay, we met a familiar motorboat towing a raft of logs.

Well met by chance! It was the Hill brothers in their Cape Islander. As we came alongside them, Sandy passed us a bucket of cod tongues and sounds (swim bladders, from under the cod's backbone) for our supper. We arranged to rendezvous for the night in Roti Bay after Sandy and Kent had delivered their logs to the sawmill at Milltown. Next morning we sailed with them down Long Reach to their fishing station at Barasway de Cerf, a cove of singular loveliness so well protected by sunkers that only the initiated could hope to pilot a vessel into it.

Happy Adventure went nowhere next day because I was afraid to take her out of the Barasway on my own and the Hills had gone off to haul their nets in Long Reach. When they returned in late afternoon and began gutting their catch, Claire and I rowed over and hung about waiting, like gulls, for a handout.

Their catch included a number of brilliantly hued redfish, a deepwater species that instead of laying eggs gives birth to living young.

Sandy slit one of these open to reveal thirty or forty tiny reproductions of the parent. The bulk of the catch consisted of immense cod, some weighing twenty or thirty pounds. These were mostly female and stuffed with roe – hundreds of thousands of eggs in each fish. Kent told us the cod and redfish had come into the bay to spawn in the deeps of Long Reach, as their kind had doubtless been doing since time immemorial. Now, however, they were encountering gill nets for the first time and the resultant slaughter was so great that the Hills, who were under no illusions about what they were doing, predicted that the fishery could not last.

"Nylon nets be terrible fish killers," Sandy said, shaking his head. "I don't say as they won't clean out the inshore fishery same way the draggers is cleaning out the Banks."

Next morning the Hills headed for Gaultois with a ton of gutted cod aboard. The plant would pay them two and a half cents a pound, less ten cents from every dollar, which was the interest levied on the cost of two nets supplied on credit. Taking into account the time spent going to and from the plant, I estimated that between them the brothers were earning about $8.50 a day, out of which they had to pay for their gear and fuel and the maintenance of their boat.

We rowed away from Hills' Floating Fish Market, as Claire called it, with one pail half-full of cod roe and another overflowing with fillets of redfish and grey sole. Claire parboiled the roe-filled ovaries then lightly fried them in bacon fat. She poached the fillets in canned tomatoes, adding a soupçon of condensed milk and some scruncheons – bits of pork skin sautéed a golden brown – to the sauce.

When all was ready, the Hill brothers joined us for supper and stayed to sit for Claire while she sketched their portraits.

"If ever you goes away from the bay again, skipper," Kent said as the brothers got back into their dory, "see you leaves the maid behind. Us'll take the finest kind of care of she."

We spent some time exploring the neighbourhood on foot and in our little dinghy. One morning we rowed to the head of a hidden arm of the barasway that culminated in a freshwater stream beside which stood two log shanties with an old dory pulled up on shore in front of them. This was the summer residence of Leo Wilcox, a lean, tough little man of indeterminate age who greeted us by waving an axe (which he just happened to have in his hand) in our direction. No menace intended. Leo was part Mi'kmaq and part white countryman – a widower who welcomed visitors, though he rarely saw any. But he was not lonely for he had with him three small and gloriously dirty grandsons who clearly were enjoying the time of their lives.

On this day all hands were busy unsnarling a tangle of ancient trawl lines and baiting the rusty hooks with fresh squid – an unexpected gift of the morning when a school of the creatures had jetted into the stream on a rising tide and stranded themselves in its shallows when the tide fell. The boys had collected about a hundred of them, which Leo intended to transmute into codfish.

That evening after setting the trawls in Long Reach, he came aboard *Happy Adventure* for a noggin and to tell us tales of how he had tramped and trapped the interior as far as Gander Lake, eighty or ninety miles to the northeast of Conne River.

In the early spring of 1946, Leo lingered a little too long on his trapline near Meelpaeg Lake deep in the interior. Normally he would have come out on snowshoes before the spring thaw began, hauling his winter catch behind him on a slide. This time he had delayed in order to make a last attempt to trap a silver fox that had eluded him all winter. By the time he gave up on that an early thaw had begun making cross-country travel very difficult. Almost out of ammunition and "store-bought" grub, he dared not linger until the thaw was over and he could make himself a country canoe to travel out in, so he cached his fur and set off to walk back to Conne River.

Day after day the thaw grew more intense until melting snow slowed his progress to a virtual crawl. The rivers started to break up, and lake ice began giving way beneath him so that he had to cross some lakes by crawling on his belly through pools of slush, sometimes swimming through melt ponds. Other lakes had to be bypassed, and detours around them sometimes took him a day's march out of his way.

By the tenth day Leo had nothing left to eat, yet did not dare halt long enough to make a hunt. Although wet through much of the time, he refrained from building fires big enough to dry himself, fearing he would not be able to summon the willpower to leave their comfort.

On the twelfth day he reached the Salmon River and found it in full spate. There was no possibility of surviving an attempt to swim it, yet somehow he had to cross. Recalling that, downstream near the river mouth, there had once been a cableway to enable telegraph patrolmen to overleap the torrent, Leo set off to see if it still existed.

He found it a day later. It consisted of a single rusty cable strung between two tall poles planted on opposite sides of the river. Normally the poles would have been standing on dry land. Now, however, the Salmon was in full flood and a hundred-foot-wide turmoil of white water and ice floes swirled *inshore* of each pole.

The cable had originally been equipped with a breeches buoy – a kind of suspended chair by means of which a man could haul himself across – but this had long since disappeared. There being nothing else for it, Leo waded into the frigid water, struggling desperately to keep his footing, and managed to reach the nearest pole. He climbed it by means of some slippery footholds axed out long ago . . . lashed himself to the cable with the leather tumpline from his pack . . . then slid down the curve in the wire to mid-river, where the cable sloped up toward the farther pole.

Hanging just above the surface of the cataract, he hauled himself hand over hand *up* the wire, which, rusted and frayed, tore off his gloves and ripped the flesh from palms and fingers. Reaching the second pole, he slid down it and thrashed his way through the torrent to shore.

Two days later he walked into the Conne River settlement. Three weeks after that, when the spring thaw had ended, he went back into the country by canoe and retrieved his fur.

"Pretty good catch, too," Leo remembered with a grin. "When I come out that second time I could buy the woman a washing machine drove by a gasoline engine. She were some pleasured!"

· 12 ·

Stone Valley

Easing *Happy Adventure* out of Barasway de Cerf, we ghosted south
and west with just a breath of a breeze to Cape Mark, where the
Hills were hauling their nets. Naturally we went alongside and naturally they gave us a fine big cod already skinned and ready for the
pot. They also issued an imperative invitation – almost an order –
to visit them in Hermitage.

"The women'll cook a scoff of patridge and moose meat," Sandy
offered. To which Kent added, "And they'll be a drop of white stuff
to make the fiddles jump."

We could not have refused, but first we wanted to see Raymonds
Point. Long Reach's resident school of harbour porpoises escorted us
for several miles to a high ridge terminating in a low point upon
which stood a white-painted building too large to be a house. Jutting
out from the point was the ruin of a once-substantial wharf, now

reduced to dangerous-looking wreckage. Gingerly we came alongside and threw our lines to a nimble, middle-aged man who shyly introduced himself.

"Phil Dominie. Welcome to Raymonds Point."

When I asked after Cecil Dominie, Phil explained that his cousin Cecil was still at Stone Valley and not expected for a week or two. "Told we you might be along and said for you to make yerselves at home."

This turned out to be one of the most seductive places we encountered in all of Newfoundland. About fifty acres of the point had long ago been cleared and was now a luxuriant meadow. In the centre stood a little conical hill about a hundred feet high commanding an unparalleled view of almost the whole of Long Reach's sinuous coasts and rugged surrounding hills. This meadow was aglow with both native flowers and domestics that had gone wild. There was even a blue spruce copse that looked as if it might have been transplanted from some English country estate.

The white building, once a herring factory, was still in good condition as was a one-room frame school. But of the houses that had once sheltered the people of Raymonds Point, not one remained. The only evidence that they had ever existed was scattered and abandoned belongings: a sofa bleeding horsehair stuffing; several cast-iron stoves; a rusty tin trunk containing mouldy clothing; bits and pieces of spinning wheels; handmade wooden chairs; and a wheelbarrow with a broken wheel. Upon its abandonment in 1952, the residents of Raymonds Point had either cut their houses into sections small enough to be loaded aboard boats or had floated them off whole and towed them away.

Nevertheless the Point had stayed vigorously alive, populated by birds, rabbits, voles, and a family of foxes. There were also two small tilts, or cabins, belonging to people who once had lived here all year round and still returned in summertime.

First settled in 1850 by an English fisherman named Charles

Strickland, the place was almost surrounded by the fecund waters of Long Reach and superbly situated for the making of salt cod and pickled herring. Strickland, his associates, and their descendants had specialized in herring, some of which they salted and dried, but most of which they packed in brine-filled barrels and carried to the Caribbean in schooners they built themselves, exchanging their fish for rum, salt, and a little cash.

Phil Dominie had been born at Raymonds Point. Like all the rest, his family had kept milch cows and sheep; had made their own butter and cheese; and had sheared, carded, and spun wool enough to provide most of the family's clothing with enough over to pay for a few such extravagances as an Edison gramophone.

The Point was one of the few places in Newfoundland where community whaling had been carried on. This had begun as an accidental enterprise when Phil's grandfather and a great-uncle, jigging for cod off Fox Island, "went afoul" of a twenty-foot minke whale that swam under their dory and became entangled in their anchor line. The whale towed the dory for miles down Long Reach while the two men repeatedly stabbed it with a boat hook. When the animal eventually bled to death, they towed the corpse back to the Point and "cut it in." Then they tried the oil out of the blubber, poured the oil into herring barrels, and sold it to some Norwegian whalers who were then appearing along the coasts of Newfoundland.

After that the Point men regularly hunted smaller whales (mainly minkes and Brydes), using harpoons they hammered out on their own forge. For a time it was a sustaining "fishery." However, by the time Phil's father died whales were all but gone from the bay and even from the coastal waters, having been nearly exterminated by the Norwegian whalers.

During Phil Dominie's lifetime, the herring had followed the same path. Only a few years before our visit they had still been so abundant that, as he recalled, "when the rale big schools come into

Long Reach to spawn, they was so many that the ile come off they made the Reach shine like a rainbow." During the 1950s these teeming multitudes were assailed by a fleet of modern seiners: hundred-ton vessels, many of which had come all the way (via the Panama Canal) from British Columbia after having almost completely destroyed their own herring stocks there. They did the same along the coasts of Atlantic Canada, delivering tens of thousands of tons of herring to industrial rendering plants, which turned them into fishmeal for livestock feed.

Deprived of the sea creatures that had provided a major portion of their sustenance, the Point people found it increasingly difficult to sustain themselves. They also faced mounting pressure from the Smallwood government to abandon their "uneconomical and backward outport" and move to "growth centres" far from the sea, where they could, in Smallwood's words, "help transform Newfoundland into a modern, industrialized country."

The pressure on the people of Raymonds Point grew ever more intense. The government-subsidized coast steamer service was withdrawn. The regional doctor (employed by the province) became a rare and reluctant visitor. The school was closed because the Department of Education claimed it could not find a teacher for it.

These were nails in a coffin. There was also a carrot. As with many other recalcitrant outports, the people of Raymonds Point were offered a cash subsidy if they agreed to move – but only if *all* of them agreed to go. This pitted the families who were prepared to leave against those determined to remain. The resultant rancour mortally wounded the essential unity that sustained all outport settlements. In the end, Raymonds Point "went under."

The government's victory turned out to be pyrrhic. Although the Point itself was abandoned, most of its residents resolutely refused to go inland to one of the so-called growth centres. Instead, they went the other way – moving *closer to the sea*. They shifted lock, stock, and (literally) barrel to a deep cove on the outer coast of the bay, where they joined fates and fortunes with the dozen families of Little Bay Harbour, people who were so implacably opposed to the resettlement program that, Phil Dominie told us, they renamed their outport Stone Valley to proclaim their immovability.

Phil, his wife, Meg, and two sons in their early teens had been among those who moved to Stone Valley. Yet they still belonged to Raymonds Point and returned to it every summer. Their tilt was a rough, tarpaper-covered shack only large enough for all of them because they were seldom all in it at one time. Cooking was mostly done on an ancient cast-iron stove set up outside the door. Phil and his oldest son, Ralph, spent most of their time on the reach fishing cod, which they carried to the plant at Gaultois in their powered dory. They retained some of the catch, however, and the entire family took part in the familiar ritual of making salt fish.

"The plant don't pay hardly nothing for fresh fish," Phil told us, "so we salts a good bit like the old folks used to, some for winter eating and some for to sell."

In their spare time the Dominies picked berries (the Point was lush with strawberries and raspberries) which Meg preserved, went trouting in the brooks and ponds, gathered mussels and winkles, and dug clams. The boys went hunting armed with a rusty old .22 and brought back ducks and rabbits.

The Dominies' summer life seemed so idyllic we had no difficulty sympathizing with their yearning to return permanently to the Point. Meg told us it had been the closing of the school that had finally "drove we out of it." One day, accompanied by the boys and their black water dog, we went to look at the abandoned school. The blackboard was still in place and it bore a number of farewell messages, mostly sad, but some angry.

"THEY KILT THE SCHOOL BUT CANT KILL WE," said one. These carefully printed words were heavily underlined with red chalk.

The boys also took us to visit the graveyard on the hill in the centre of the Point. Standing among the wooden markers we could look up and down the entire reach, blue-hazed in the evening light. Jack, the younger son, pointed out other, now abandoned, settlements: Fox Island, Snooks Cove, May Cove, Patrick Harbour, Jack Daws Cove, Harbour la Gallais, Hatchers Cove. Nothing visible to us now remained of any of them.

As we made our way back to our vessel Claire picked a small bouquet, which she placed on our little galley table. There were tears in her eyes as she poached cod fillets for our supper – tears that did not come from cooking.

One rainy day we sheltered in the Dominies' dimly lit tilt listening to Phil talk about his life while Meg made pots of tea and baked biscuit bread for all of us.

Phil's story was essentially that of most outport fishermen: a struggle to endure, not against the sea and the land but against the rapacity of merchants, large and small, upon whom the settlers depended for what they could not find or make for themselves; such things as flour, sugar, molasses, tea, fishing gear, guns and ammunition, oilskin coats and rubber boots.

Phil had been a fisher since the age of nine, handlining from a dory with his father. By the time he was fifteen, he was spending his winters on the stormy waters of Cabot Strait, fishing from small schooners in the worst of the winter weather. In summer he had gone down the Labrador in larger vessels to fish among the icebergs there. Now that the schooner days were finished, he fished with his son Ralph close to home – Hermitage Bay in winter and Long Reach in summer.

"'Tisn't the best, you understands. But 'tis all we got left."

He and Ralph had a venerable three-horsepower engine in their dory and fished with the latest in nylon nets.

"We gits out to the grounds quicker now than in old times and catches fish easier than ever we could fishing cross-handed. Our gear's better than ever it were . . . but the fish is fewer and far between. Nowadays we got to find four or five dollar for every dollar us needed when I were a youngster, but the merchants hardly pays no more for fish than in olden times. 'Tis all a wonder to me."

Most autumns when Phil "settled up" at Garland's store (the principal merchant at Gaultois) it was to find himself in debt.

"I got no learning so's I can't rightly argue with what the merchant's got wrote down. But I knows he sells our salt fish to the Portuguese for forty dollars a quintal and pays we five. I knows he buys molasses, butter, and other stuff in St. John's for a few pennies a pound, and we pays dollars. They's not much as I can do to keep out of the hole, but I hopes my boys'll get enough learning to come out in the clear."

Phil Dominie did not speak of such matters with bitterness, or try to excuse his lack of financial success. He was proud of never having taken the dole or any other government assistance, and of having always managed to provide for his family, as well as assisting his neighbours when they were in difficulty.

"Us al'ays gives the other fellow a hand," he told us earnestly, leaning forward to tap my knee for emphasis. "Us *has* to do that, you understands. 'Twas the way she al'ays been upon this coast."

Perhaps partly because Claire and I were so very much in love, Raymonds Point seemed an enchanted place. For several days we explored it and its neighbouring coves, sometimes by ourselves, sometimes accompanied by the boys and their dog. We daydreamed (and talked to the Dominies) about the possibility of buying the little school, converting it to a home, and settling here.

They welcomed the idea.

"Yiss, bye!" Phil said. "Suppose you and the maid drops anchor here, you can have the school and welcome. Never be short nothing you need. Stone Valley'll see to that, be it grub, or firewood, or company."

Although the odds were that we would not be taking him up on the offer, we hesitated to say so even to ourselves. I temporized by telling the Dominies we had to return to Milltown for our mail then visit Hermitage and perhaps St. Pierre. After that, we would see.

"Good enough, skipper," Phil replied, "but promise we you'll not go clear without you puts in to Stone Valley."

We made sail for Milltown and, not long after, raised the Hills' boat coming our way. I hauled into the wind and the brothers came alongside. On this occasion the floating fish market provided us with two fine lobsters.

Lobsters were out of season but, as Sandy explained, "these come up hanging onto the cod net and we never had the heart to heave they overboard for fear they'd be drownded."

Late that afternoon we moored at the Milltown wharf, where I went ashore to collect the mail. Jack had written to tell me the Seamen's International Union wanted me to come to New York to discuss writing a book about the S.I.U. and suggesting a possible fee of forty thousand dollars – a colossal sum for a freelance writer in those times. Jack had added a caveat: "Take the money if you must . . . and if you want to risk ending up in a cement overcoat at the bottom of New York harbour. But get yourself another publisher."

Although the temptation was strong, the thought of giving up Bay Despair for New York appalled me. When I broached the idea with Claire, she resolutely turned it down.

"I've been so happy to be away from life in a big city, Farley. Please don't drag me back into one again."

I never loved her more than at that moment.

Next day we sailed from Milltown, through Little Passage and across Hermitage Bay to Hermitage Cove. A short-lived but ferocious storm that broke over the cove that night did not dampen the "time" we had been promised. Enlivened by fiddles, harmonicas, and a quart or two of the white stuff, the party at Sandy Hill's lasted until dawn.

I went on deck about ten next morning to check our mooring lines (we were lying at the dock) and was appalled to see coils of black smoke pouring out the cabin windows of the *Teressa G.*, a big motor launch from Gaultois belonging to Garland's stores. She too was lying alongside the wooden wharf, a scant fifty feet ahead of us. Instinct told me to let go our lines and get out of there, but I delayed in order to raise an alarm by sounding our fog horn.

Hastily roused, the crews of two big herring seiners from Nova Scotia that had come in to shelter from the storm and were moored well astern of us and the *Teressa G.* now saw the smoke and ran to let go their lines. Although well equipped with fire-fighting gear, they clearly had no intention of trying to save the burning vessel. I started our engine and was about to cast off when a dishevelled Claire emerged from the cabin.

The frightening pillar of smoke from the burning boat, and two lesser plumes belching from the exhaust stacks of the seiners, apprised her of what was happening. All she said was, "What can I do?"

I don't know what was going through her mind but I could see she wasn't going to panic so I changed *my* mind.

"Stand by to take *Itchy* to the other side of the harbour! You might have to do it on your own. I'm going to see what I can do for the *Teressa*."

She nodded and I trotted off down the wharf. Jumping aboard the *Teressa G.*, I cautiously opened her cabin door, but could not enter. Choking billows of smoke repulsed me. I hoped there was nobody down below.

Now the elderly skipper of the doctor's boat limped onto the wharf dragging a large CO_2 fire extinguisher. Taking it from him, I unleashed a gush of foam through a cabin window of the burning vessel. This had some effect in slowing the flames, which were now visible within. Then *Teressa G.*'s mate, half-dressed and very groggy, appeared and with the help of several others we got a bucket brigade going until a hose could be rigged from shore and the fire was finally doused.

Then, and only then, did the seiners return to the wharf. When nobody would take their lines it seemed to dawn on them that they were no longer welcome. As they departed, one of their skippers bawled to the other in a voice that could be heard all across the harbour: "Fuckin' Newfies!"

Herbert Kendal, skipper of the doctor's boat, was a fount of information about whaling on the coast, something in which I was much interested. His great-grandfather had been brought out from Bristol about 1815 to be a whaler at Gaultois, where the Jersey firm of Newman's had built the first English whale "factory" on the Sou'west Coast. Herbert's grandfather and father had both whaled for Newman's and he himself had also done so until just after the turn of the twentieth century, when steam-driven Norwegian whale catchers arrived to sweep the local seas clean of leviathans.

"Afore them Norwegian killer boats with their cannons, their exploding harpoons, and their bomb guns come on the coast, we whaled from longboats. There was eight men to a boat: boat steerer, six men to row, and the harpooner. Them times whales was so plenty in Hermitage Bay you had to look out not to run into they. When I were a lad, one time I counted ninety spouts in sight at the one time off of Fox Island, and all big fellows too.

"Me old father and me was jiggin' squid one time and a pod of finners was fishin' 'em too. They was so fixed on the squid one breached right under the dory. Never seen it, I supposes. Dory and all went into the air and we into the sea. Father got back to the dory somehow – neither him nor me could swim a stroke – and hauled me into it with the gaff as was floating alongside. We was all right then but I don't doubt that finner found his back right sore.

"Biggest whale ever I see was a sulphur bottom [blue whale] as Father and his crew got fast to off Pink Bottom. They put the harpoon into she just after dawn, and she towed them like a kite all the rest of the day. Took they away out to sea, then back down to the bottom of Hermitage Bay afore they could get nigh enough to lance her to death.

"She were too big for the whale boat to tow back to the factory so Newman's sent their steamer *Greyhound*. That whale measured out at ninety-seven and a half feet, with a calf inside was near twenty feet long, and it not yet born!"

Hermitage Cove turned out to be as far to the eastward as we would get. Summer was running out, and we had not found the place to settle for the winter. We decided to forgo St. Pierre and look to the west by visiting Stone Valley.

A big sea gave us a rough farewell crossing of Hermitage Bay until we sailed into the shelter of the steep-walled little fiord called Little Bay, where we found Stone Valley's thirty or so trim and ship-shape-looking houses stacked so tightly in a rocky gorge that they were practically standing on one another's shoulders. Though painted in a variety of colours, all were much alike in size and shape. The dozen or so smart-looking motorboats in the harbour were also remarkably similar to each other as, we would soon discover, were the cats, the hens, and indeed the people. Walking about in Stone Valley gave one the rather unsettling sensation of being in a house of mirrors.

Because the shore cliff was so steep there was no proper wharf and I could see no place to moor until a young lad came rowing out in a dory and piloted us to Garfield Strickland's stage. Here we tied up with our mainmast spreaders practically poking a hole in Garfield's kitchen window. A dozen or more people crowded onto the rickety stage to welcome us, Cecil Dominie prominent among them.

"Some glad to see your leetle boat come down the bay," he told us as he led the way to his and Clara's snug house clinging to the steep slope like the nest of a cliff swallow.

"See, skipper, Phil were here yestiday so all hands knowed you was thinking to light at the Point. We hopes you does and calls Stone Valley home."

Clara Dominie took us on a walkabout. Climb-about would be more accurate. Perched on shores – stilts made of peeled logs – the houses crowded as close together as a flock of seafowl poised for flight. Handrails on the narrow paths more or less secured us from plunging into the harbour below. As Clara explained with a grin, "They's nary a bit of flat ground here, me dears, less'n it be made of wood."

The reference was to the floors of the houses.

In fact wood, not stone, was the true *leitmotif* of the place. Although the men were expert fishermen, catching herring, mackerel, salmon, lobster, and cod, most had concluded the inshore fishery was doomed and were making or trying to make their livings using other skills. One of their specialties was building boats – mostly skiffs, but some as large as a forty-foot Cape Islander they had launched the previous year.

They were marvellous carpenters. During the heyday of the herring fishery, they had produced barrels in such quantity that in one year they sold seven thousand dollars' worth – an astronomical sum for the time and place. They could and did build almost anything that could be made of wood, literally from cradles to coffins. Their coffins were famous for lightness, durability, and tightness. Ches Strickland of Milltown had told me, "A Stone Valley coffin won't leak nary a drop was you to sail it out to the Grand Banks."

They also made household furniture of all kinds: not the rough-and-ready stuff any outport man could fashion, but tables, chairs, daybeds, and ornamental items with the craftsmanship of cabinet makers.

They did everything from scratch – from felling logs far inland, floating them down the rivers to salt water, then rafting them behind their boats to Stone Valley, to milling them into lumber with machinery they mostly made themselves.

Garfield Strickland, to whose stage we were moored, had just completed a beautifully built twenty-eight-foot trap skiff. The day after our arrival we helped launch it then moor it alongside *Happy Adventure* to await the arrival of the coastal steamer that would deliver it to a customer in Placentia Bay.

Greatly impressed by the quality of his work, I wondered if Garfield would be interested in repairing Harold's old schooner, *Fort Amadjuak*, for me. When he said he might, I found myself in a bit of a quandary. The fact was that Claire and I were beset with uncertainties about where we should settle. Although enormously attracted to Bay Despair, we felt it might be too difficult of access, especially while I was researching my history of the island and would need to get in and out quickly and often. We had begun considering "dropping the hook" in Cape Breton, or perhaps some place in the southwestern corner of Newfoundland. In any event we had pretty well concluded we should sail to the westward and see what offered. If nothing suited, we could always come back to Bay Despair.

Meantime, we decided to enjoy a few days exploring the Little Harbour fiord so we set off for Sam Hicks Harbour, which lay a few miles farther into the land. We did this despite (or perhaps because of) the fact that Cecil had warned us against the place, saying vaguely that "Sam Hicks were a hard place for luck."

It turned out to be the visual antithesis of Stone Valley for it boasted several acres of green and level land, a vigorous stand of birch and spruce, and a stream full of brook trout. Sam Hicks Harbour seemed almost to beg for human occupancy, yet was uninhabited and appeared at first glance always to have been so.

However, as we rowed around it in our dinghy we came upon a massive platform about forty feet wide made of flat, carefully fitted stones and extended from somewhere below low-tide line to well above high-tide mark. Its purpose puzzled me, until I recalled that the ancient Basque whalers had built similar structures to serve as slipways up which whales could be hauled for flensing.

Peering over the side of our dinghy we could see a tangle of large, greenish-white objects on the bottom of the harbour somewhat resembling the tangles of dead-fall logs in a blasted forest. These were the bones of long-dead leviathans. When we walked the landwash, we came upon many water-worn bone discs, oval in shape, an inch in thickness, and the size of dinner plates – spacers from between the vertebrae of very large whales.

Back at Stone Valley I questioned Garfield about our finds. He was evasive, muttering that "they mought have been some quare fellows there one time, no doubt." When I pressed him, Garfield admitted that around the middle of the previous century an Englishman named Sam Hicks ("me woman's great-granddad"), together with a few other families, had tried to settle the harbour that bears Sam's name but, after a few years, gave it up and moved to the hard scrabble of Stone Valley.

Persistent questioning brought out some reluctant explanations for the move. After three houses had been built, so Garfield said, it proved impossible to build another at Sam Hicks Harbour. Every attempt to do so collapsed, or the structures "was pushed over at night and broke up like lobster pots hit after a horrycane." But, Garfield insisted, storms could not be blamed for the damage because it had taken place even on windless nights.

"Dey was other t'ings . . . strangers wearing clergymen's clothes seen walking along the shore." Then two settlers going to the stream one night for water found "a dark-skinned babe" lying dead at the watering place. Hesitant to touch it, they went for assistance, and when they returned the body had vanished.

Sam Hicks's own house had apparently (and unwittingly) been built across an unseen path. Unknown people were seen walking toward the house and passing through a wall, to emerge on the far side of the structure. Yet people inside the house neither saw nor heard anything unusual.

Even more disturbing was the fact that the settlers' boats would not stay on their moorings. They inexplicably went adrift even in calm weather, and some disappeared altogether.

As a consequence of these and other strange occurrences, the settlement was abandoned and people avoided the place thereafter.

There were exceptions. A sometime Stone Valley schoolteacher, Levi Dominie, told me that in the 1880s, when he was "still a suck-ling," his mother and his aunt, both of whom were strong-willed women, took him with them in a dory to Sam Hicks Harbour on a berry-picking expedition.

The women pulled the dory's bow up on shore there and, leaving the baby aboard sleeping in his cradle, began gathering raspberries along the landwash. Levi's mother, who had been glancing back every few minutes to assure herself the child was content, was appalled to see a naked man, his head hidden by long black hair, rise out of the water beside the dory to stand waist-deep, staring down at the infant.

Though terrified, the women "screeched at he" and began pelting him with stones; whereupon he dived and swam away, surfacing only to breathe. Emerging at the mouth of Dory Brook he ran up the bed of the stream and disappeared into the woods.

"Arter that," Levi concluded his account, "Stone Valley folk give that place a wide berth. My mother told me the berries there was some good, but not good enough to take *her* back. No, nor nobody else as has so much sense as a crackie dog . . . if you'll pardon me for saying it, skipper."

· 13 ·

Queen of the Coast

Parting from Stone Valley was not easy, nor were we allowed to leave empty-handed. Garfield Strickland filled our fuel tank then refused payment. Cyril Dominie topped up our supply of alcohol, also gratis. Someone contributed a quintal (about a bushel) of salt cod. Ladies piled our cabin with fresh bread, pies, cakes, bottled mackerel, and jars of berry jam and gave us cushions artfully embroidered with local scenes.

"Don't be forgettin' we!" people shouted as *Happy Adventure* drew slowly away from Garfield's stage.

So we began the long outside run toward the distant Canadian mainland. The coastal cliffs mounted ever higher as we slipped past Pushthrough and then the naked capes of the great inlet of Facheux Bay. We might have put in to Muddy Hole had not Cecil Dominie warned me, "Folks there is right cross-grained," adding that a few years earlier during a sou'east gale, seas bursting *inside* the cove had smashed three of its houses and all of its dories.

Concluding that discretion was the better part of valour, we pressed on and, as dusk fell, rounded Pinchgut Point to enter one of the most spectacular harbours in Newfoundland.

Called Francois on the chart (but Fransway by those who live on the coast), the settlement consisted of sixty or so houses ringing the narrow shore of what looked like the crater of an extinct volcano that had been flooded by the sea. One entered the harbour through a narrow, crooked slit in a massive basalt barricade a thousand feet high; crater walls soared high above the skim of human habitation, forever threatening it with destruction from falling ice in winter and rocks all the year round. It was definitely an up-and-down sort of a place. As one of its inhabitants would tell us, "You needs claws on your elbows to keep a holt in Fransway."

Its people were imbued with the kind of vigour that characterized the residents of Stone Valley, though at first they seemed somewhat cool to strangers. When we eased alongside one of Fransway's three small wharves, nobody showed any interest in us except for one small boy and the inevitable black dog. Both eyed us cautiously but neither would take our lines. Then, as I jumped ashore to make the vessel fast, a strongly built middle-aged woman came out of a large store attached to the wharf. This was the widow Durnford (pronounced Dunford), owner of both wharf and store. She acknowledged my introduction with a nod before informing me in forthright style that she had no "fresh stuff" for sale and did not accept "furrin money" for what stock she had. Furthermore, I would have to move my boat because her own small coaster, the *Mayflower*, was due in that evening.

Claire and I were down below eating supper and rather lugubriously contemplating the coolness of our reception when there was a rapping on the cabin trunk. At my invitation, a wisp of a man with

Wharf at Francois.

an endearing smile eased down the companionway to present us with a steaming pot of boiled dinner.

Leslie Fudge, his wife, Carol, and their three children lived in a little house perched precariously over the landwash not far from Durnford's wharf. They had seen our reception by the widow and Leslie had come to make amends. It was the beginning of a friendship that would endure for many years.

Bad weather kept us tied up to one or other of the three wharves for the next several days during which Leslie, Carol, and their children became our hosts, guides, mentors, and providers. Accompanied by the older Fudge children, Claire and I ambled around the gravelled paths that served as roads, among close-packed houses that elbowed one another for space upon the narrow fringe of shore. Massive crags loomed all around. One of these, an enormous semi-detached pillar called The Friar, seemed poised to come crashing down at any moment and annihilate half the settlement.

There were no gardens because there was neither space nor soil. Few dogs were to be seen, but there were any number of lean, short-tailed felines that looked as if a bobcat had been one of their ancestors. A brook and waterfall in the middle of the village provided clear, cold water for all; a tidy little Anglican church offered the grace of God to those who required it. The harbour was dotted with dories coming or going or nodding at their moorings. Several larger vessels lay at Durnford's; at the adjacent government dock; and at a wharf and store owned by John Penney and Sons, of Ramea, a group of islands twenty-five miles farther west.

There were almost 400 people in the settlement, with 113 children in the four-room school. Except for a few men who went off to the woods to work as loggers, and the shopkeepers, lighthouse keepers, and Leslie Fudge (who could not go to sea because he was subject to chronic seasickness), almost all the able-bodied men and older boys were inshore fishermen.

They fished year-round from their big dories, to such good effect that Penneys kept a small power schooner in Fransway to carry the catch to the company's filleting plant at Ramea. Fransway men fished even when the weather was foul enough to keep the coastal steamer tied up.

"She's a hard coast, me son," the skipper of the *Mayflower* told me. "Open to every blow from east through south to west. T'ick a fog, oftentimes. Wintertime the dories gets iced so bad you got to beat it off with an axe. Some got engines now, though most still goes at it cross-handed with the oars, and maybe a scrap of canvas to steady her in a blow. I don't say as but they's the bestest seamen in this old island."

A storm that came on while we were there brought some draggers in for shelter. These big steel vessels bullied everyone else away from the government wharf and tried to do the same at Durnford's, but changed their minds when widow Mae Durnford came out on her dock with a shotgun cradled in her arm. Canadian draggers ("fish killers from away") were not loved by inshore fisherfolk.

Discovering that Leslie was an expert carpenter, I got him to fix a broken gaff and a cracked boom and make some other repairs on *Happy Adventure* that were beyond my own rough-and-ready skills. His talents were extraordinary but he was so self-effacing they were only accidentally revealed. Shyly he offered to help me deal with a fuel problem in the engine. This he did by gently disassembling, fixing, and reassembling the entire fuel system, which was of British origin and unlike any he had ever before encountered.

The storm was succeeded by a fog so dense as to be almost palpable. I would never have dared venture out into it even had *Happy Adventure* been equipped with radar or other modern aids to navigation. The *Mayflower* possessed none of these but her skipper thought little of choosing this impenetrable morning to set off on a voyage.

Six hours later Leslie shouted to me from the window of his house.

"Best show a leg, skipper. Beer truck's comin' in."

I could hear the drumbeat of the *Mayflower's* engine approaching through the fog, but not until she was alongside Durnford's wharf and had begun unloading the first of some sixty cases of beer did I realize *she* was *it*.

Mae Durnford had political friends in faraway St. John's. A few years earlier, when she learned that a few carefully selected outports were to be permitted to open beer stores, she had applied for a licence. Alas, Fransway's church was presided over by a temperance-minded minister who was able to scuttle the widow's plan. Undaunted, she applied for a beer store in Rencontre West, a nearby settlement of about a dozen families guarded by the fourteen-hundred-foot mountain bastions of Blow-Me-Down and Iron Skull. The place was considered almost inaccessible even on the

Sou'west Coast and perhaps because of this it had no church. Never mind. It now found itself with a beer store – the *only* beer store for seventy miles along the coast. And Mae became a wealthy woman.

When we left Fransway, a fair breeze sent us westward on a broad reach past the superb palisade of cliffs and headlands guarding Nick Powers Cove, Aviron Bay, Cul-de-Sac, and La Hune Bay. Holding close to the coastal rampart, we could plainly see the high-water mark of breakers on the cliffs, below which no vegetation could maintain a hold against the sea's assaults. This boundary stood about eighty feet above normal high-tide line. I concluded I never wanted to be on this coast in a small vessel during a southerly gale.

Passing Cape Island, we were tempted to run into La Hune Bay to see how the members of the bridal party we had met in Milltown were faring but I was reluctant to waste a fair wind so we sailed on.

I am sorry now. Two years later Cape la Hune was "closed out." By 1966, when Claire and I did visit it, all that remained was a small Masonic Hall, a few collapsing sheds, and the usual debris of an abandoned settlement. A large lithograph of King George V and Queen Mary still hung on the wall of the hall as a token of times past.

When I walked along the cape's sandy shore, I found several flint points fashioned by Beothuk hunters who had made the cape their departure point for canoe expeditions to offshore islets to hunt nesting seabirds and collect eggs. I also found flints of the so-called Dorset culture, an Eskimo-like people who lived on this coast long before the start of the Christian era. On a later visit, Claire and I would examine a cave near the mouth of La Hune Bay where the Beothuks had buried their dead. Local fishermen had carried off the skulls, fixing them to the mast tops of their dories, perhaps as gestures of bravado.

Sailing past Cape la Hune, we held well off shore to avoid two nests of reefs, sunkers, and breakers known as Cape Rocks and Gulch Cove Sunkers. We saw little of them, for which I was properly thankful, but did see plunging flights of gannets, wheeling multitudes of terns and kittiwakes, and bullet-swift companies of puffins and guillemots (called turrs in Newfoundland). These all testified to the presence of good fishing grounds and added a living element to a waterscape undisturbed by any other vessel. *Itchy* sailed alone on a coast that had once swarmed with fishing boats.

By dusk we were approaching the Ramea Islands, a handful of barren rocks some seven miles off the mainland shore where there was a good harbour, a store, and a fish plant owned by a woman who was even more redoubtable and remarkable than the widow Mae Durnford.

Ramea harbour was a busy place. Fifteen or twenty large dories were coming or going, or lay hauled up on the hard in St. Pierre fashion. Several longliners tugged at their moorings. Two power schooners shared John Penney and Sons' dock with two large steel draggers whose crews were busily unloading fish.

We tied up to a vacant corner of the Penney wharf, and I went to the fish plant office to ask permission to lie there overnight. A cheerful young man ushered me to the inner sanctum: a large, second-floor room overlooking the harbour, furnished with padded chairs, a lounge, an old and well-polished mahogany desk, and, on one wall, a pair of large and primitive oil paintings of fishing schooners. Behind the desk sat not the male titan of industry one might have expected, but a woman who could have modelled for a sentimental Hallmark grandma card. Crinkly grey hair crowned a round, rather homely but jovial face. Blue eyes peered at me sharply through glittering, rimless spectacles.

"I am Marie Penney," she announced firmly. "Please sit down and tell me what we can do for you."

This, of course, meant: tell me who you are and what you are doing in my kingdom.

Ramea – Penneyworth *in foreground.*

For that is what Ramea was. As the owner of John Penney and Sons, Marie Penney was central to the operations of two fishing companies, three fish plants, and several retail stores that, together, dominated the coast from Bay Despair almost as far west as Port aux Basques. Though the plants at Gaultois and at Burgeo were nominally owned by Marie's daughter, Margaret, and her husband, Spencer Lake, Marie Penney had a hand in both.

Not for nothing was she known as the Queen of the Coast.

Born at Notre Dame Bay in the north of Newfoundland, she had married John Penney, the easy-going inheritor of a long-established family business that was then following the salt-cod business into decline. Marie changed the company's course. Although John continued to issue the orders and sign the cheques, Marie really ran the company. Recognizing that freezing plants were the wave of the future, she saw to it that Ramea was in the forefront of changing ways.

While John drank more than was good for him, Marie made such a success of the family business that in 1948 she could afford to make a "gift" of $25,000 to the federal Liberal Party to ensure John a senatorship in Canada's Parliament. His induction was one of the two highlights of her life. The second was when she was invited by the governor general to dine with the Queen of England at Rideau Hall.

Thereafter Marie's world began to come unstuck. The first blow was John's death, brought about, so it appears, largely from apathy and alcohol. The second was when their only child, Margaret, who was as vivacious and wilful as her mother, ran off with Spencer Lake, a married man from St. John's. Equally shattering: Spencer was a Protestant and the Penneys were formidably Roman Catholic.

I knew none of this when, scruffy and unkempt, I introduced myself to Marie Penney.

"The author of *People of the Deer*!" she said, to my surprise. "I have read your book. I do not agree with your opinion of the missionaries. Nevertheless, I am happy to meet you. . . . And what brings you here? Another book perhaps? Well, you and your wife must come to Four Winds – that's my home – for dinner tonight."

When I brought this invitation back to Claire, together with a description of our hostess, she was shaken. As she would later write:

> *Farley and I had been living for six weeks in the cramped quarters of our rather grubby little schooner, dressed in sturdy pants and sweaters. I had only one summer dress with me in case of special occasions, and it was a bit mildewed and rolled up in a plastic bag. Well, it would have to do, but I was certainly not overdressed for what followed.*
>
> *Four Winds was by far the largest house in Ramea, if not on the Sou'west Coast. It stood on a hill raised well above the other houses on a small and treeless island. A square, solidly built frame structure, it was exposed to every wind that blew.*

Its broad front door opened into a welcoming centre hall with hardwood floors, an upright piano, and a flight of broad, polished stairs. To one side was a formal living room filled with Victorian furniture. On the other side was a spacious dining room with a grand table and matching chairs. Mrs. Penney's favourite room, to which she graciously led us, was at the back of the house. It was lined with books and framed family photographs, and furnished with cosy armchairs. This was where she entertained guests before dinner, with sherry brought from Spain in her own ships, served in crystal goblets by her Portuguese houseman.

We dined at the huge mahogany table set with a white damask tablecloth, sterling silver cutlery, bone china from England, and monogrammed linen napkins. The effect of finding all this in an isolated little village in the middle of an ocean was a culture shock. Why, I wondered, would Marie Penney live in this remote place? Most of Newfoundland's merchant class lived in St. John's, far from the smell of fish. We would learn that Marie, despite her elite lifestyle, felt a strong connection with and responsibility for "her people," as she called them. Her attitude may have been colonial, or even medieval, yet I didn't sense any undercurrent of resentment from the other islanders. It seemed that most Ramea people were proud to have this worldly but kindly woman living among them.

At the end of the evening I explained to our hostess that we would have to sail on next morning. She refused to hear of it.

"You are not to take your little schooner out of Ramea until I tell you to! There is so much here for you to see. Kevin, my nephew, will be your guide. Whatever you wish to do, please tell him and he will arrange it for you. Just don't forget – if the weather's fit there'll be croquet on the lawn tomorrow. I shall expect you two to be there."

Kevin Smart, a lean and intense young man, was learning the fisheries business from his aunt. When I told him I'd long wanted to see what life aboard a dragger was like, he arranged it for me.

The *Penneyworth*, smallest and oldest vessel in the company fleet, no longer fished far from home. I boarded her at four next morning and was welcomed by Skipper Max MacDonald, Mate John Symes, Engineer John Harvey, and a young deckhand named Rodney. The sixty-foot wooden vessel's Kelvin diesel thumped to life, the lines were let go, and, huffing black smoke from her exhaust, *Penneyworth* put to sea.

We steamed toward the mouth of White Bear Bay (Wiper Bay, it was called locally) and just as dawn was breaking shot the net over the starboard side to begin the first trawl of the day. *Penneyworth* towed slowly over a very rocky bottom while Skipper Max kept a sharp eye on his depth finder for warnings of snags that could "hang us up." When I asked why we were fishing such rough bottom, he explained that our quarry – redfish or brim as most fishermen called it – had been "pretty well fished out on the good grounds," by which he meant the level, sandy, or muddy underwater banks.

Until the recent catastrophic overfishing of haddock and the steep decline in cod stocks, redfish had been considered "trash fish." Now they were being rapaciously pursued, to be marketed as ocean perch. At first, catches of redfish had been enormous, and draggers twice the size of the *Penneyworth* had been able to fill their holds while within sight of their home ports.

"Them days they only kept brim fourteen, sixteen inches long. Smaller stuff was shovelled over the side. Nowadays we keeps anything ten inches long, and *they's* getting scarce. No use to keep anything smaller than that. The fillets offen them is too small to feed a cat."

"Well," said I, "at least the small fry you pitch overboard stand a chance to grow to a useable size. Maybe you'll catch them another day."

Max looked at me as if in sorrow at such ignorance.

"No, sorr. They's gone for good." And he explained how the rapid decrease in pressure as the trawl is hauled to the surface dooms the fish it contains.

"They blows up like balloons and their eyes pops out. They never gits down below again. The gulls and dogfish gets they and that's the end of it. Likely in a few more years us'll see the end of the brim altogether."

We shot our first trawl at 0530 and hauled back at 0630. As the two "doors" that keep the mouth of the net open underwater came aboard, the bag (or cod end) came to the surface a hundred yards astern – a rosy mound of dying fishes gleaming in the light of the rising sun. The cod end was hauled aboard to spill about fifteen hundred pounds of brim onto the deck. Almost all the fish were too small to be worth keeping.

The rough ground off White Bear Bay had torn the net, so now all hands including the skipper turned to, mending it with heavy twine from wooden shuttles that served as needles.

We shot again at 0900 and half an hour later got hung up on a rock or a wreck. Max freed the trawl by slowly steaming in circles while the mate worked the tow wire back and forth with the big deck winch. This haul turned out to be a bumper one – enough to fill the wooden pounds set up on deck for sorting. The brilliant crimson colouring of the fish quickly faded as Rodney and the mate tossed the keepers into the hold, where the engineer stowed them, mixed with crushed ice, in wooden bins, and as the rest of us shovelled the bulk of the catch overboard.

Max told me that a few years earlier the use of ice had not been necessary because fish had been "so plenty" the ship could be filled in a day. Now it might take a week to do that.

"'Tis old fish, surely, time we unloads it. Ice helps some but I wouldn't eat it meself. The plant fillets and freezes it anyhow; then off it goes to the mainland, where I dare say they don't hardly know the difference."

The bulk of the catch from the first two hauls had been redfish, with some small cod and a few such exotics as lumpfish, wolffish, dogfish, and sculpins. Perhaps half the catch had been stowed in the hold – the rest had gone overboard to form a glittering wake stretching a mile astern of the ship, a magnet for thousands of gulls.

Having shot the trawl three times in ninety fathoms with only meagre success, Skipper Max now took us out to a depth of a hundred and fifty fathoms, where we made two two-hour drags that took us almost to the Burgeo Islands and back. We were lucky to happen on a patch of good ground and ended the day with nearly nine thousand pounds worth about $250 penned below decks.

Max told me he and his crew had to average at least six thousand pounds a day in order to make a bare living. They fished on shares. As owners, John Penney and Sons took 67 per cent and was responsible for operating costs, though not for the crew's food. The *Penneyworth* had been designed to be fished by a crew of six, but could no longer provide a living for that many so now she fished with four. They fished every day that was "fitting" all year long, Sundays and holidays included. And each day stretched from four in the morning to whenever the last fish was unloaded at the dock, usually not before nine at night. The only time off they got was when they were too sick to go to sea or the weather was too foul for the *Penneyworth* to sail.

The weather had been moderate all morning but by mid-afternoon a hard sou'easter was kicking up a big sea and making the little *Penneyworth* execute such wild gyrations that I could not endure the cramped and smelly forecastle where I had gone to get warm. Retreating to the cramped wheelhouse, I jammed myself in beside Skipper Max, who was at the wheel.

By six in the evening it was blowing a gale with driving rain and occasional flails of sleet. Visibility was almost zero when Max finally ordered the gear hauled aboard, and we headed home. Despite the storm, Max belted the little vessel along at full throttle, making her buck and leap while solid green water roared over our decks and smashed against the wheelhouse windows.

"Best to hurry in afore the night shift comes on at the plant," Max bellowed apologetically. "They's some slow to handle fish."

We were then making a full nine knots through the seething mass of reefs and sunkers surrounding the Ramea isles. There was a dim and jumpy old radar set, but Max paid it no heed. He *knew* where he was and where he was going. At 8:45 he laid *Penneyworth* alongside the plant's now all-but-invisible wharf in a screeching wind and almost total blackness. As the hatch covers came off and the crew began winching out the fish, the skipper invited me home with him for a scoff, but I declined. What I wanted was a stiff drink in the cosy dimness of *Happy Adventure's* tiny cabin. Of one thing I was now absolutely certain. I did *not* want to fish for my living on the Sou'west Coast of Newfoundland.

I visited the plant next morning. It was a low-ceilinged wooden building crowded with zinc-topped tables that formed a *disassembly* line for whatever species of fish happened to be "on the go." On one side of the shed a "cutting line" of boys and men was filleting the fish we had caught, while on the other side women and girls standing shoulder to shoulder packed the fillets into cartons ready for freezing. All hands wore heavy rubber boots to protect their feet from the stinking swirl of icy salt water mixed with blood and slime that coated the concrete floor. There was too much racket from the engine house to permit conversation with the workers but I later learned that the women were paid sixty cents an hour, the men seventy. They did not work regular hours but were perpetually on call, hurrying to work whenever a dragger arrived and the plant whistle summoned them, and remaining at the cutting and packing tables until the current lot of fish had been cleared away. In addition to wages, they also received unemployment stamps issued by the federal government according to the number of hours they put in "on the line." Under certain conditions these stamps might later be converted into cash – *if* one had enough of them.

"With the fish gettin' so scarce," one man told me, "you has to have the stamps to keep bread on the table. 'Tis a hard go, old man."

That afternoon Claire and I dressed in our best and climbed the hill to Four Winds to play the delayed round of croquet before again dining with Mrs. Penney.

The croquet ground was a patch of rich green lawn (the only lawn of any kind on the Ramea Islands) lovingly created from soil brought by ship from the Canadian mainland. The players included our hostess; Gladys Stewart, a Scots nurse employed by the provincial government to care for the islanders' health who also served ex-officio as Mrs. Penney's lady-in-waiting; Kevin Smart, and his parents visiting from Montreal – she in heavy tweeds and he in golfing garb; and a real, live Colonel Blimp with a white moustache and ruddy complexion (he was actually only a "majah, in the Injun Ahmy") and his sprightly wife, who, before her marriage, had been a Clement – one of the Jersey merchants who through the nineteenth century and well into the twentieth had dominated the Sou'west Coast, returning to Britain to retire and to enjoy the rewards of having served in the distant colony of Newfoundland.

Amiably we batted croquet balls around until the fog rolled in and Scotty, the nurse, clapped her hands and dourly directed us to the dining room, where we enjoyed another excellent meal accompanied by good wines served by Julio. Julio had arrived in Ramea in 1931 as a stowaway aboard one of the company's transatlantic schooners, and Marie had trained him to be Four Winds' major-domo.

Dinner over, Julio served port and coffee in the living room before a crackling fire, and Marie Penney put us through our paces.

"You must earn your dinner, you know," she said as she directed us in games such as Twenty Questions and charades. When these began to pall, she sat herself down at her big, old-fashioned piano and belted out Victorian-era and traditional Newfoundland songs, while Scotty hectored us into singing along.

It may have been a bit ridiculous but it was fun, bringing back vivid memories of childhood celebrations at my grandparents' home in Ontario before the arrival of television and home-entertainment centres. There is magic in remembering childhood, and Marie Penney knew how to lead one back to it.

By the time Claire and I made our way down the hill to *Happy Adventure*, the fog had once again become impenetrable. The plant was silent, awaiting the arrival of the company's newest and largest vessel – the 150-ton *Senator Penney*, which had been fishing on the Grand Banks for ten days and was now log-loaded and homeward bound.

As we climbed aboard our little vessel, we could neither see nor hear any signs of life about us. There was only the pervasive stench of rotting fish offal to remind us of the enormous distance we had travelled from the mansion on the hill back into the world of fisherfolk.

· 14 ·

Seduction

Wednesday morning, August 22, dawned clear and bright as we took our departure from Ramea on a course intended to bring us to La Poille, fifty miles to the westward. We had some involuntary passengers aboard. Late the previous night, Skipper Max had given us four enormous spider crabs (the snow crabs of commerce) stuffed into a burlap sack. He explained he had made a special haul for us over "crab bottom" because "the old skippers t'ought as spider crabs aboard brought a vessel fair winds and full sails. I hopes these does the same for you."

His crabs must have got their signals crossed. No sooner had we cleared the harbour than a brisk westerly sprang up and was soon blowing a dead-muzzler right on *Happy Adventure*'s nose. We had to beat against it, and that meant tacking four or five miles to the south then north again almost to the coast in order to gain a mile or two of westering.

Growing impatient, I started the engine and we slogged along until we were abeam of the fifty or so little islands constituting the Burgeo archipelago clustered up against the coast.

Somewhere among these islands lay the settlement of Burgeo, home to the Caribou Fisheries owned by Marie Penney's daughter and son-in-law, Margaret and Spencer Lake. Marie had given me strict orders to put in here but I was determined to hold on for La Poille.

Then the gods intervened. Maybe Marie had better access to them than I. Just then, the oil pressure gauge blew out, spraying hot oil in all directions. Cursing, I dived below and shut down the engine. Since I had no means of repairing it at sea, I decided to put in to Burgeo and see what the fish plant's machine shop could do for us.

Passing a small lighthouse, we entered a channel that ran north a mile or two between barren shores dotted with houses to the Caribou Fisheries wharf. We came alongside, to be greeted by a big and floridly handsome man about my age. This was Spencer Lake.

"Mrs. Penney called Margaret on the radio to tell us you'd be dropping in. Good to see you! Let's have your lines."

I explained our problem, and Spencer invited Claire and me to have lunch with him and his family at what he called the Staff House while the plant's mechanics looked at my engine. This gracious, white-painted clapboard house had been built more than a century earlier as the residence of one of the Jersey merchants. Now it belonged to Caribou Fisheries, on whose books it was listed (for tax purposes) as a hostel for transient officials and business visitors. In fact, it was the Lakes' home, housing them, three of their four children, seven purebred dogs, and two maids. As a mark of status it was surrounded on its landward sides by a stalwart chain-link fence, the first and only such we were to encounter during all our travels in Newfoundland.

In anticipation of our arrival Margaret, a slim, dark-eyed beauty, had prepared a four-course luncheon complete with vintage wines, and we were received as if we were illustrious guests rather than the nondescript drifters we were.

After the leisurely lunch, and despite Margaret's insistence that we linger for coffee and liqueurs and, preferably, overnight, we headed back to the dock, determined to resume our voyage. Spencer accompanied us and did not seem at all surprised to find *three* men from the plant's machine shop refurbishing *Itchy's* engine.

"Needed a good overhaul," he told us, smiling. "Long trip ahead of you. So leave the lads to it and you two come back to the Staff House for dinner. Then, if you've a mind, you might enjoy a good soak in Margaret's new bathtub from Boston, of which she's very proud."

No greater temptation can be offered to wandering mariners in small boats than a hot bath. Bringing along the bag of spider crabs as the only hostess gift we had to offer, we meekly followed Spencer back to the Staff House. After luxuriating in the promised soak, we were entertained in a wide living room through whose array of picture windows one could look out upon a world of rock, water, and ships, with the feeling of being monarch of all one surveyed. As we nibbled snacks of steamed crab legs, smoked salmon, and red salmon caviar, Spencer and Margaret asked cogent questions about the writing and painting life and our personal histories. The martinis Spencer lavished on us were very, very dry and we were in a jolly mood by the time we went in to dine on fillets of sole and roast caribou served on exquisite china by a uniformed maid, while our host and hostess extolled the virtues and delights of life in Burgeo.

"Finest kind of people here. Salt of the earth. Do anything for you. Give you everything they've got," Spencer testified as he poured more wine.

"And so *honest*! So *loyal*!" Margaret interjected, bestowing a fond smile on the shy young maid who was serving our dessert.

"The stories they've got to tell!" Spencer added. "My God, if *I* could only write . . . there's a dozen books right here in Burgeo. Now, who's for some Napoleon brandy?"

By the time dinner was over, Claire and I were so nearly comatose as to be easily persuaded to spend the night ashore – in a king-sized bed with scented linens.

Such were the beginnings of the Fall.

Breakfast was a late and lingering affair during which Margaret and Spencer queried us about our plans. When we confessed that these centred on finding a small coastal community, perhaps in Cape Breton, where we could winter the vessel and ourselves, Margaret pounced.

"Why on earth look any farther? Why not stay here? You'd be as welcome as the day is long. Burgeo's made to order for a writer and his artist wife! You really ought to stay!"

"At least take time to look around," Spencer insisted. "Give us a day or two to show you the sights. We'll take you on a tour of the islands tomorrow. Show you a little bit of paradise."

Burgeo was at its best the following fine, late-summer's day as we cruised the tickles and runs between the islands in the Lakes' luxurious launch, the *Turr*. Spencer explained that most of Burgeo's sixteen hundred residents now lived on the largest island, where they were handy to the plant.

Operating four big draggers, the fish plant was the economic mainstay of the community, employing up to two hundred people. Some fifty or sixty families still lived on the smaller, or "offer" islands, where the majority of Burgeo's people had lived dispersed before the plant was built. The offer islanders still took their livelihoods from the small boat (or inshore) fishery as their forebears had always done.

Burgeo's elite consisted of the Lakes, followed at some considerable distance by a husband-and-wife team of British doctors stationed at the cottage hospital that served the region. The minuscule "middle class" included an Anglican clergyman, an RCMP constable, five or six teachers, a provincial welfare officer, and four independent merchants (the plant owned the largest store).

Although the Lakes admired the sterling qualities of the inhabitants, they felt a dearth of what Margaret delicately called "interesting people." The phrase rang a bell for me.

"Listen," I told Claire when we were alone together. "I think *they* think we're interesting people. You know, the kind who might liven things up for them during the long winters here. Playmates to keep them from getting bored." My suspicions did not sit well with Claire, who tends to think the best of everyone and never looks for ulterior motives.

"*I* think they like us just for ourselves," she replied, "and I like *them*. I think they're very nice."

We did not sail on the next day. Or the next.

Happy Adventure remained in the hands of workers from the plant, who seemed to find endless problems to resolve. Claire and I remained as guests of the Lakes, who never ceased their efforts to enchant us with Burgeo.

Unaware of my aversion to the "hook-and-bullet crowd" who hunt and fish primarily to satisfy their blood lust, Spencer extolled the "sporting" possibilities of the region.

"There's all the moose, caribou, ptarmigan, rabbits, turrs, and ducks you can shoot, any time you've a mind to do it. No reason to worry about closed seasons or bag limits here."

"And the fishing," added Margaret. "We've some of the best trout and salmon rivers in the world. And the least fished. Spencer and I have permanent fishing camps – comfortable cabins, really – on three of the best rivers. You're welcome to use any of them for as long as you want."

One sunny morning they took us in the *Turr* to the Big Barasway, a vast salt-water lagoon bordered by miles of white sand beaches lying just west of the islands. Although the water was too cold for swimming, we sported on miles of pristine beaches, played games, dug clams, and sunned ourselves while an attentive staff grilled salmon and served it accompanied by goblets of chilled white wine. As the afternoon waned, they revived our flagging appetites with steamed clams in cognac and butter sauce.

After several days of *la dolce vita* in beautiful weather, my conscience was pricking me. When I told our hosts we really *must* be getting on, they only intensified their efforts to persuade us to remain. The plant owned a small house that they now offered to rent to us for a nominal sum. It had no plumbing, but Spencer grandly offered to install running water and all the amenities, including a bathtub, if we would take it for the winter.

"Why not?" demanded Margaret. "You won't be trapped here, you know. You can travel to the mainland on the coast boat any time you want."

"Indeed," Spencer added, "or aboard one of our vessels. The *Swivel* – she's our refrigerated freighter – often sails to Boston and Halifax. She'll be sailing to Montreal in a couple of weeks. You're welcome to go along in the owner's stateroom. She could take your car too. The coast boat could bring it here from Fortune and we'd swing it aboard."

The temptations being offered were having their effect upon both of us, especially Claire, who, faced with too many uncertainties, very much needed to settle somewhere, if only temporarily. And now the weather became the Lakes' ally. On August 28 a hurricane warning was issued for all of southern Newfoundland. Small craft ran for shelter. Soon scores of fishing boats lay triple-moored to the plant's wharves with *Happy Adventure* in their midst.

As it happened, the eye of the hurricane passed well to the south of Burgeo, but we were hit by a fierce sou'easter. Hardly had it finished battering the coast than there came another hurricane warning. The season for small-boat sailing was clearly over. Reluctantly I concluded we must leave *Happy Adventure* in Burgeo for the winter.

The question of what Claire and I would do remained unresolved. I felt I needed to discuss future plans with Jack McClelland but the storms had disabled Burgeo's radio/telegraph link to the outer world, and the nearest functioning telephone was at Port aux Basques. Leaving Claire with the Lakes, I took the next coast boat west, phoned Jack, then found myself marooned in Port aux Basques for two days waiting for the eastbound boat to sail while yet another gale blew itself out.

With little else to occupy me I went walking. On a rocky, windswept stretch of shore I came upon two middle-aged brothers, Tom and Mark Anderson, who, together with their father, Gabriel, were defying modern times by building themselves a hundred-and-fifty-ton schooner.

The three men had spent many years together in the coastal trade, mostly freighting coal from Cape Breton and potatoes from Prince Edward Island to the outports of Newfoundland in an old Grand Banks fishing schooner. When, in 1960, this vessel caught fire and was condemned, the brothers and their eighty-year-old father and skipper immediately set about building a replacement.

Tom and Mark and a team of horses spent the best part of the next two winters in the woods, felling and hauling out the logs from which to cut twelve-by-fourteen-inch keel and keelson pieces, naturally curved timbers and knees, and three-inch-thick hull planking. The keel had been laid the autumn before my visit. The hull was now fully framed and partly planked but, as Tom apologetically explained, it would be another year before the vessel was ready for launching.

"Takes a power of time, me son. Everything got to fit tight as your skin so's when 'tis done she'll be stanch and dry."

She would certainly be staunch. Her planks and framing looked heavy enough for an icebreaker. Every piece of her was cut and fitted (using only hand tools) with a precision that had to be seen to be believed. Clambering aboard the partly completed vessel was a little like going inside the skeleton of a leviathan. Her ribs thrust high above the rocky shore like those of some antediluvian monster.

She still had no name and when I wondered why Skipper Gabe glanced uneasily at me. Mark cleared his throat and answered, "Might jink a vessel to name her afore she was launched off."

One evening after a boiled dinner shared with Mark's family, he told me that he, his brother, and his father had already "used up" twenty-six axes, five adzes, and several ten-pound mauls building this vessel. And of their savings there was little left.

"What odds, bye, we still got tea and lassy and they's plenty fish in the sea and meat in the country. Us'll finish her off come summer, then we'll be on the go again."

I lacked the courage to speak of something painfully evident to me. I knew the day of the tramp coasters was virtually over, and the vessel taking form on the hard below Mark's house belonged to another time. All I could do was wish her builders well.

Happy Adventure may have found a home for the winter, but Claire and I were still adrift. We accepted Spencer's offer of passage to Montreal aboard the *Swivel*, planning to drive on to Ontario and then, after consulting friends and family, decide what to do next. I wired the wharfinger at Fortune asking him to ship the Morris to us on the next westbound coast boat.

Since the *Swivel* would not depart for another week, Spencer suggested he and I sail *Happy Adventure* to White Bear Bay for some partridge (ptarmigan) hunting. We took with us one of the Lakes' pedigreed English pointers, Sport by name, and their "gillie," Dolph Warren, a lean and vital little man with a good admixture of Mi'kmaq blood in him. We had barely cleared the Burgeo Islands when we spotted a distant vessel passing to the south at a speed suggestive of a naval vessel. As she slipped out of sight, we speculated about who and what she might be.

An easy four-hour sail along the austere coast took us to "Wiper" Bay. We entered under power and steamed some seven miles into the land until we were astounded to behold a gleaming white ship lying at anchor. She was the distant vessel we had seen earlier. As large as one of the coastal steamers, she had the flaring bows and cruiser stern of a warship . . . but she flew no nation's flag.

Whoever she was, as far as Spencer was concerned she had no business to be in White Bear Bay. He considered these waters his own private hunting and fishing preserve.

"What the hell's that bloody thing doing here?" he demanded of wind and water. He did not add, "without my permission," but might as well have done. "Bastard better not be fishing salmon! Let's find out."

As we closed with the stranger, she grew more and more imposing – and ominous. She carried no name on her bows. Not a soul was visible on her bridge or on the great sweep of her decks. She appeared to be ignoring us the way a liner in harbour ignores the local bumboats.

Spencer was becoming more and more agitated.

"Take us alongside!" he ordered. "I command the Canadian Ranger detachment on this coast. We'll damn well find out who she is and why she's here."

Although by no means sure this was a good idea, I slowed the engine and we approached the towering stranger very cautiously – so cautiously that Spencer could not contain himself. Leaping up on the cabin top he cupped his hands and bellowed, "Ahoy there! What ship are you? What's your port of registry? Why aren't you flying an ensign? Identify yourself!"

While I knew Spencer was a lieutenant in the Rangers (a civilian militia charged with keeping watch and ward on Canada's coasts), I also knew his "command" consisted of fourteen fishermen volunteers armed with antiquated .303 rifles, scattered along a hundred miles of coast. I was not convinced we were a force to be reckoned with. An officer in a white uniform who now appeared on the stranger's bridge may have felt the same.

"Who the hell are *you*?" he replied, looking down on us with unconcealed contempt.

Spencer told him. At length. With vigour. By the time he had finished, the officer was no longer alone. About a dozen sailors in uniform had materialized on the main deck, ranging themselves along the railing to stare down at us unsmilingly.

The officer spoke again. This time it was an order. "Come alongside my landing stage! We will discuss the matter."

It was at this point that Dolph panicked and scuttled into the shelter of the cabin, muttering, "Oh me soul! 'Tis the Red Chinee!"

This was 1962, and the Cold War was heating up as the United States intensified its crusade against godless Communism. The consequent hysteria was making otherwise sensible people believe that if there wasn't a Communist under every bed, there probably was one around the next corner. Dolph's reaction was understandable.

So was mine. I jammed the throttle forward and *Happy Adventure* sheered away from the ominous stranger. Then, as we scuttled under her stern, we were at last able to see her name – DANGINN – written across her transom in foot-high letters of gold. Under it was her port of registry: MONROVIA. The vessel's name sounded vaguely Chinese, or maybe Japanese. And Spencer and I both knew Monrovia was a registry-of-convenience widely used by shipping that wished to conceal its real origins.

I did not slow down until we rounded the headland and were out of sight of the *Danginn*. There we drifted and had a drink or two while discussing what ought to be done. Dolph and I were for returning to Burgeo, but Spencer would have none of that.

"Can't let that foreign bastard get away with whatever it is he's up to. You see those launches hanging from his davits? He could be charting the bay. Could be a Commie spy."

The rum was taking effect and my courage was returning.

"Yeah, I suppose we should put up a bit of a show. I've got my old army battledress jacket aboard with captain's insignia still on it. Could put it on. Could promote you to colonel, Spencer. Say you're in civvy clothes. With me as your adjutant we could board the bugger and demand to see his papers. Tell him he's in a prohibited zone and there's a NATO exercise about to begin," I concluded, getting into the swing of the thing.

"Yes, by God!" Spencer agreed. "And whatever else he's doing, the fucker's probably after our salmon. We'll run him off!"

Although Dolph was not supportive, we turned *Happy Adventure* about and headed into action.

Gingerly I brought her alongside *Danginn's* landing stage, which had been lowered on the port quarter. A squad of sailors watched intently as Spencer and I climbed the stairs, then surrounded and escorted us along the main deck. We passed a rack of salmon rods, which made Spencer growl, and were able to peer through the broad windows of a glittering dining saloon occupied by a single diner. Whoever he was, he did not deign to give us a glance as we were shepherded past.

Instead of being taken up to the bridge as we had anticipated, we found ourselves being herded down into the bowels of the ship, ending up in a room without windows or portholes. There, behind a steel desk, sat a slim, dark-complexioned man wearing a captain's gilt-encrusted hat. He offered no greeting. I was acutely aware of four crewmen close behind as I waited for my "Colonel" to take the lead. When it seemed that the cat had got Spencer's tongue, I broke the silence by nervously introducing him as my commanding officer, adding that the *Danginn* was anchored in a restricted area where a military exercise was about to take place.

Spencer now entered the fray with a peremptory demand to see *Danginn's* papers, including the cruising permit without which she, as a foreign vessel, had no right to be in Canadian waters.

Her captain leaned back in his chair and grinned.

"You want my papers? So. First I will see *your* papers proving you are not pirates, yes?"

A dreadful moment ensued when all we were able to produce was Spencer's driving licence.

It cut no ice.

"So. You drive an auto. What is that to me? I think you are dead-beats. Now get off my ship. Go quick!"

The sailors hurried us back on deck and jostled us down the companion ladder to where Dolph was waiting in *Happy Adventure's* cockpit – with a shotgun in his hands.

"Oh me son," he said fervently to Spencer, ignoring the gap between lord and master, "I t'ought you was took!"

We wasted no time pushing off and heading down the bay, with Spencer waving his fist at the *Danginn* while muttering dire imprecations. We retreated a good four miles to shelter behind Grip Point while we put our ruffled feathers back in order, a process that involved opening another bottle. Then Dolph rowed Sport ashore for a much-needed run while Spencer and I planned our revenge.

That night the two of us set off in inky darkness in our little bathtub of a dinghy for the head of White Bear Bay, where there was a cabin occupied by Garfield Hann, a Burgeo man who worked as a part-time fisheries warden during the salmon spawning run. We left Dolph behind to look after Sport. Or maybe it was the other way about.

Garfield also worked at the plant and so could be counted on to do what Spencer required. He had a big trap skiff in which, weather permitting, he could make the run from the warden's cabin to Burgeo in three hours. We despatched him bearing a telegram I had pecked out on my portable typewriter. It was addressed to NOIC (Naval Officer in Command), Coastal Defences, Halifax. It read:

FOREIGN VESSEL APPROX 200 FEET OVERALL EQUIPPED WITH COMPLEX ELECTRONIC GEAR AND ASIAN CREW DISCOVERED WHITE BEAR BAY STOP WHEN BOARDED CAPTAIN REFUSED DIVULGE ANY INFORMATION STOP CONSIDER PRESENCE AND ACTIONS HIGHLY SUSPICIOUS AND URGENTLY RECOMMEND INTERCEPTION
SPENCER G LAKE OFFICER COMMANDING
CDN RANGER DETACHMENT BURGEO

Spencer and I rowed back to *Happy Adventure*. Sometime well before dawn we heard the sound of Garfield's engine thumping past, but did not really wake up until the morning was half gone. We were a heavy-lidded lot as we partook of what Spencer called a "whore's breakfast" – cigarettes and coffee. Although Dolph was still mumbling about an invasion by Chinese Communists, Spencer and I were having a reality check.

"Who do you think that floating gin palace really does belong to?" I asked.

"God only knows. Somebody with money enough to make his own rules, anyway."

"The Prince of Monaco, maybe? Or some Arab potentate? How about the Aga Khan?"

These suggestions did not comfort Spencer, who, instead of answering, added a shot of grog to his coffee and sloshed it down. Eventually he felt well enough to go partridge hunting with Dolph so I rowed the nimrods and Sport ashore. Leaving them to comb the surrounding hills, I started back to *Itchy*. From midstream I could open the whole length of White Bear Bay but could see nothing of the *Danginn*. I boarded my own vessel and went back to sleep.

Around noon I was jolted out of my bunk, to bang my head on the cabin trunk as the world seemed to explode around me.

Staggering on deck, I was in time to see and feel a four-engined bomber thunder over at masthead height in what must have been the second of two very close passes. Even as I ducked, comprehension dawned.

"Oh shit! That telegram . . . Garfield must have delivered it! Oh *double* shit!"

As the big Royal Canadian Air Force plane climbed steeply and swung out to seaward, three shots rang out from shore – the agreed-upon signal that the hunters wished to come back aboard.

Although Sport seemed unperturbed, Spencer and Dolph were in a state by the time I reached them. Dolph was convinced the plane had been full of game wardens come to arrest us for hunting partridge out of season. Spencer understood the real implications behind the bomber's appearance and was feeling his neck.

"Jesus H. Christ, Mowat," he said accusingly once he was back aboard *Happy Adventure*. "Now you've done it! You and your fucking telegram! Start up your goddamn engine! Dolph! Help me get the anchor up! We're getting the hell out of here!"

Running out of the bay we saw nothing of the *Danginn* –
nothing to indicate she had ever existed. Oh, how we wished that
this would prove to be the case. All the way back to Burgeo, Spencer
was preoccupied with visions of military courts of inquiry into who
had been responsible for putting Atlantic Command on alert. I was
afraid the incident would end our comfortable relationship with the
Lakes. Instead, its consequences were such that for years to come
Spencer would hold me in high regard.

Garfield Hann had set off for Burgeo with the dedication of a
Paul Revere. Shortly before dawn he had come in sight of a spectral
monster anchored in the bay and was so startled that he squeezed
an extra knot out of his old engine, managing to reach Burgeo as the
telegraph operator was finishing breakfast. Within minutes our
message was on its way again.

Canada's defence command rose to the challenge with admirable
efficiency. An Orion reconnaissance bomber based on Prince Edward
Island thundered off the runway bound for the Sou'west Coast. As it
closed with White Bear Bay, the radar operator and visual observers
searched for the intruder.

Their quarry was no longer there. It appears that shortly after
Garfield's boat passed by, *Danginn* upped her anchor and departed for
parts unknown. The bomber arrived to find *Happy Adventure* in sole
possession of the fiord. Having assured themselves that my little
bummer could not be the target they were seeking, the bomber's crew
flew out to sea and instead of heading back to base, flew eastward.
Some years later I met one of them who finished the tale for me.

"We hadn't had a mission in weeks and it was a nice, clear day
so the skipper decided to put in some air time and show a new radio
operator some of the Newfie sights. We flew close over St. Pierre,
then just as we were getting set to head for home, we spotted a big,
white boat tearing along to the south leaving a wake a mile long. We

made a couple of passes over her and got her name. She was still in territorial waters so we tried to make radio contact but she ignored us and kept going like a bat out of hell. There being nothing more we could do – we reported what had happened and went home."

Halifax immediately put out a general alarm and requested the U.S. naval base at Argentia, Newfoundland, to lend a hand.

A U.S. reconnaissance plane found the "target" still speeding south. When this aircraft, too, was unable to get any response to radio calls, the U.S. command dispatched a destroyer at flank speed with orders to intercept the fleeing vessel and escort it into Argentia.

The pursuit on the high seas took several hours, and then the *Danginn*, for such the vessel was, refused to comply until the destroyer brought her guns to bear. Reluctantly, the fugitive turned back and was escorted to the Argentia naval base, where she was boarded and examined. And her identity was revealed.

Far from being the Chinese Communist spy ship of fevered imagination, *Danginn* proved to be a flag carrier for rampant capital-ism – the private yacht of one David Keith Ludwig, who, according to *Time* magazine, owned one of the world's largest commercial fleets as well as a vast array of mines, oil fields, refineries, cattle ranches, and incidental possessions, all of which made him one of the planet's richest men.

And one of the most private. As *Time* reported: "About the only place that Ludwig's wealth shows through is aboard his $2,000,000 yacht *Danginn* on which he occasionally likes to entertain movie stars and other celebrities. . . ."

Ludwig's wealth also showed through in his arrogance. Coming north for a little salmon fishing in Newfoundland, he had not both-ered to obtain the requisite Canadian permits to cruise, or to fish, in Canadian waters. And, when challenged, he had ignored (in order of their importance) the local commander of the Canadian Rangers, the Canadian Armed Forces, and the United States Navy.

Did he get away with it? Of course he did. When the U.S. naval commandant at Argentia realized who it was he had arrested, the *Danginn* was hurriedly released, presumably with appropriate apologies. And this despite a request from Canadian authorities that she be held at Argentia until charges against her could be investigated.

I do not know if Washington punished anyone in the U.S. Navy for their lèse-majesté in arresting one of the monarchs of American capitalism, but I do know how Ottawa dealt with the commander of the Burgeo detachment of the Canadian Rangers.

A month after the *Danginn* incident, Spencer Lake received a letter of commendation – and promotion to the rank of captain.

Dolph and Sport and I could only bask in the reflected light of Spencer's glory. It was enough.

Dorothy Spencer at Messers Cove.

· 15 ·

Dropping the Hook

On the morning of September 12 I went to the government wharf to meet the coastal boat that was bringing us the Morris Minor. By the time I reached the dock, some forty or fifty men, women, children, and dogs had assembled to greet the first automobile to reach Burgeo and the first many of them had ever seen.

They watched intently as *Baccalieu's* derrick-man adroitly hoisted the car off the foredeck and swung it onto the wharf. Children yelled triumphantly. A group of young men and women from the fish plant raised a ragged cheer when I got in and, surrounded by a surge of dogs and people, cautiously eased the little vehicle up the wharf and onto the stony track leading into the village.

"'Twon't be no time 'fore dey's a road from Burgeo to all de other places!" crowed one young man. "Be clear sailing ashore after that!"

Not everyone was as ecstatic about the prospects for overland transport, or as ready to renounce the age-old allegiance to sea travel. The Bishop of Newfoundland, who was touring the southern portion of his diocese, happened then to be in Burgeo, staying at the Staff House. He was not overly enthusiastic about the new arrival.

"Indeed. The automobile has reached Burgeo. A mixed blessing perhaps? I wonder, will it carry these good people to the top of the surrounding hills . . . or might it take them over the edge of a cliff? Whatever. I don't say as it will make them one whit the happier."

Spencer came in just then, anxious to tell us about a not-quite-completed house at Messers Cove that might be for sale. He suggested we drive out there in the Morris and take a look.

Margaret and Claire squeezed into the back seat. I drove, while Spencer piloted us along rocky tracks that threatened to shake the guts out of the car and us. As we came abeam of the school, several teachers and forty or fifty students rushed to the doors and windows for a glimpse of the automotive age. Had the Queen been coming by in a gilded coach, I doubt she would have attracted much more attention than did our salt-stained little puddle-jumper. Margaret Lake bestowed a regal smile and a wave upon the enthralled audience.

The house we sought turned out to be a white-painted frame bungalow perched, somewhat precariously, I thought, on a bald granite dome commanding an unparalleled view of the outer islands and the rolling ocean beyond. The house's owner, Harvey Ingram, was at work completing the afterdeck (rear porch). Spencer introduced him to us then inquired if he might be interested in selling.

Hesitantly the young man admitted that his wife of less than a month was not happy with her new home. She felt that it and Messers Cove were too far from the centre of Burgeo where, presumably, the action was.

"She has her eye on a bit o' land right handy to the plant we might build onto, could we sell this one."

How much was he asking?

After some thought, he opined that $4,500 would enable him to rebuild in the new location.

To Claire and me this seemed like a give-away price for the snug little house with its large, airy kitchen; cosy parlour; and three small but adequate bedrooms, all on one floor. There was even a bathroom that, though devoid of fixtures, was something few outport homes possessed.

Claire was enchanted by this "cottage by the sea." I was delighted with its location on the shore of a sheltered cove shared by only four other houses, and far from the bustle and stench of the fish plant.

"Hell of a bargain!" Spencer enthused as we bounced back toward the Staff House. "And Ingram'd likely be willing to take the money spread out over a year or two with no interest asked. We could let you use the plant's carpenters, electricians, and plumbers to finish it up. Most anything you needed we could either find here or ship in for you on one of our boats. . . . What do you say?"

"Say *yes!*" Margaret chimed in, seizing Claire's arm affectionately. "Oh, *do* say yes!"

Claire and I lay long awake that night. Did we *really* want to anchor ourselves in this or any outport on a year-round basis?

At breakfast we had not made up our minds. Nor had we done so two days later when, having signed on as crew members of the *Swivel* – a manoeuvre designed to avoid the problem that the ship was not licensed to carry passengers – we stood on her bridge as she drew slowly away from the dock and out into the stream, bound for Montreal with our Morris firmly lashed atop the after-hatch.

Swivel was a strange bird – almost as strange as her name. Built in 1942 for the U.S. Navy as a deep-sea salvage vessel, constructed of softwood "on the cheap," she had been laid up by the Navy in 1947, then sold as war surplus to a civilian company, which used her as a small coastal freighter. In 1958 Caribou Fisheries had bought and converted her into a "reefer" – a refrigerated carrier. Since then she had been hauling frozen fish from Newfoundland to Gloucester, Massachusetts, with occasional voyages to Halifax and Montreal. Near the end of her working life and receiving only the minimum maintenance and repair, she was kept going mainly by the extraordinary competence and ingenuity of her crew.

Our cabin on the upper deck, once the quarters of a naval salvage master, had been turned into the owner's cabin. Claire was delighted with it, particularly the private bathroom Margaret Lake had had installed. This was such a far cry from the "facilities" *Happy Adventure* had to offer that I felt constrained to promise Claire something similar (if less ornate) when we reclaimed the *Fort Amadjuak* – still languishing at a dock in St. John's – and refitted her.

By dawn next day the *Swivel* was lumbering westward across the Gulf of St. Lawrence. The top-heavy old tub rolled like the proverbial drunken sailor, but we did not care for we had our sea legs. After a hearty breakfast of eggs and potatoes fried in pork fat, we made our way to the afterdeck and climbed into the Morris, which then became a private observation car from which to enjoy the aerial acrobatics of phalanxes of gannets from the Bird Rocks of the Magdalen Islands as these eagle-sized birds flung themselves like black-and-white javelins into schools of herring.

During the leisurely days of the passage west, we spent much time on the bridge, where, under the tolerant eye of Captain Moffat, I stood my trick at the wheel, managing to acquit myself well enough to gain acceptance as a quondam member of the crew.

One evening they threw a party for us. It was held in *Swivel's* cramped little dining saloon. The cocktails were Nuns' Delight – a queasy mixture of cherry wine and grain alcohol from St. Pierre. The hors d'oeuvres featured smoked salmon canapés (a travel gift from Margaret Lake) and pickled cod tongues (the cook's contribution).

All hands except for the wheelsman and a lookout were in

attendance. First Mate William Moulton, a dishevelled, almost toothless man in his late sixties, officiated. He was seconded by Obie, the hatched-faced, pop-eyed chief engineer. The bosun and one of the deckhands provided raucous music from an accordion and a harmonica. When the cocktails ran out, the steward produced a gallon jug of aromatic Martinique rhum.

We docked at Montreal on the eighteenth. While the Morris was being swung ashore, Claire and I accompanied Captain Moffat to the harbour master's office to "sign off" from the vessel's crew. Here we encountered a shipping-news reporter who wanted an account of our voyage. Claire obliged.

"We've had a smashing trip," declared Claire Mowat as she and her husband disembarked at Montreal from the trim Caribou Line flagship Swivel. "It's Caribou Line for us from now on," added her husband, Farley, firmly.

Seen off on their voyage by the Bishop of Newfoundland, the Mowats occupied the bridal suite, and were feted by Captain Moffat at a cocktail party given in their honour.

"Sparkling conversation, brilliant company, incomparable cuisine," said Farley. "It's difficult to know which we admired most."

"And don't forget the impeccable service," added Claire, formerly a Toronto artist, who also commented on the ship's decor:

"The most authentic reproduction of Newfoundland provincial I've ever seen!"

Commenting on the food, Mr. Mowat added:

"No detail has been spared to capture the age-old tradition of Newfoundland cuisine. The seal flippers, prepared in the immaculate and gleaming galleys, were extraordinary."

The Mowats say they have cancelled their season's tickets with Cunard Line and plan to travel exclusively with Caribou Line from now on.

Returning to Toronto, I was immediately enmeshed in the writer's world, playing a performer's role in what seemed to be an endless round of publicity for my recently published book *The Black Joke*, while engaging in preparations for the upcoming publication of *Never Cry Wolf*.

Meanwhile Claire was finding life in Toronto more demanding than she remembered or expected. One morning near the end of September, after a particularly gruelling round of parties and entertainments, she raised the image of the little house by the shores of Messers Cove. We discussed it with mounting enthusiasm until we realized with some considerable surprise that a decision had finally been made. I sent off a telegram to Spencer Lake, asking him to buy the house on our behalf and telling him we hoped to take possession before the end of November.

His reply came next day: "HOUSE IS YOURS LETTER FOLLOWS WELCOME HOME."

Jack McClelland, who was sincerely appalled by our decision, nevertheless did everything he could to smooth our way, including making a generous advance on royalties for my next book, whatever it might be, and introducing us to a friend who was an executive at Simpsons-Sears department stores. This kindly fellow arranged for us to acquire on credit the essential furniture and household equipment we would need, and to expedite its shipment to Burgeo.

He was astonished to discover that the goods would take at least a month to reach us there.

"We could send them to Alaska a lot quicker. You folks surely *are* going off to the back of beyond."

In mid-November we boarded the Ocean Limited train to North Sydney, crossed Cabot Strait by ferry, then steamed eastward in the *Bar Haven*. Because the Sou'west Coast chose to welcome us back with a spell of fine weather, the journey took only five days.

Our house at Messers.

Claire's account best describes the warmth of our welcome.

Our new home stood off by itself, its clapboard walls painted a pristine white in contrast to the turquoise, yellow, and green of the other houses in the cove. The back door was ajar and I stepped warily inside, to find the kitchen warm and welcoming. Sim Spencer, our nearest neighbour, had fired up the range. A mob of children poured in behind us, hauling our suitcases. One little girl of seven or eight held out a paper bag to us. In it was a loaf of homemade bread – a gift more welcome than roses for it was Sunday and the shops were closed, and there wasn't a morsel of food in our new home.

The house was far from finished. Farley and I and Leslie Fudge, a handyman we had met in Francois, went to work on it. I painted while Les and Farley built walls and cupboards. They also installed a set of bathroom fixtures. To get running water they ran an intake pipe to a shallow well they dug in a patch of muskeg behind the house. The well was only six feet deep before it hit rock bottom, but the rain kept it full most of the time. The water looked like tea but was pure enough and we soon got used to the colour, though a bathtub full of it did look odd.

The men also dug a ditch amongst the rocks and installed a pipe leading downhill to the sea a hundred yards away. No one objected to this simple sewage system, either on sanitary or ecological grounds. In a land too rocky or too marshy for septic tanks, it was standard practice to empty the night bucket over the end of the wharf every morning. We were just being a bit more modern. We had a pipe to do that for us.

At first we did feel a little isolated from the world. But every Monday, weather permitting, of course, the eastbound steamer brought mail to Burgeo. This was our main umbilical cord to the "outside." There was no television and the only standard radio station we could get was the CBC from Sydney. Anyway, our receiver was usually tuned to the shortwave so we could hear what the men on the fishing boats off the coast were talking about.

The weather was rough. Almost every week a gale blew up. Winds of seventy and eighty miles an hour were commonplace and gusts frequently reached a hundred. Fortunately they seldom came without warning. We would watch the southern sky turn from pale grey to the smeared and gloomy colour of school blackboards and know a "blow" was coming. Then the chimney would begin whistling, and the waves would pound the shore until our little house vibrated on its rocky foundation and tiny waves actually appeared in the toilet bowl.

The first time this happened I expected scenes of damage and destruction to follow. But no one's roof blew off. The power line from Burgeo's diesel generator stayed in place atop poles planted deep in rock-filled cribs. Boats, large and small, survived at their moorings with extra lines ashore. Small children were kept home from school. The coast boat anchored in the refuge of some cove. And I learned the lesson that people didn't flaunt man-made schedules on the Newfoundland coast in winter time.

A mummer in our kitchen.

During our early months at Messers, we were preoccupied with homemaking, leaving us little time to engage with the neighbours; nevertheless they found ways and means to involve us in their lives. Every kitchen in Burgeo, including ours, was common ground. Visitors were so frequent that we sometimes felt overwhelmed. Usually I was able to retreat behind the barrier of my typewriter, leaving Claire to hold the fort, but outside the house I found myself inducted, willy-nilly, into the male life of an outport tribe.

I was taken handlining for cod, netting for herring, trawling for flatfish, and jigging for squid. I was carried off gunning for ducks and ptarmigan and for surreptitious ventures deep "into the country" from which three or four of us might return in the dark of night hauling slides laden with moose or caribou meat.

As 1962 neared its end, we found ourselves engulfed in the greatest festival of the outport year – the Twelve Days of Christmas. From Old Christmas Day, December 25, until New Christmas Day on January 6, despite snow, sleet, or hail, every ambient soul in

Burgeo seemed to be on the go in the guise of masked mummers re-enacting ancient rites rooted in early Christian or, more likely, in pagan times.

This brush with the enigmatic past sharpened my urge to delve into the history of Newfoundland. I had already begun investigating the probability that Norsemen from Iceland and Greenland had made extensive explorations of Newfoundland and Labrador as early as the end of the first millennium. I thought if this indeed proved to be the case there would be a book in it. However, when I broached the idea with Jack McClelland, he was less than enthusiastic.

"Newfie screech [the rawest kind of cheap rum] has addled your brains, Farley. I've *told* you, Canadian readers don't give a damn about Newfoundland and they sure as hell won't be lining up to buy a book about a bunch of Norskies stupid enough to cross an ocean to raid that barren, bloody pile of rocks!"

Nonetheless I went ahead with my plans, which still included restoring the *Fort Amadjuak* to service. Since she had been built for the Arctic, I thought that – properly repaired and refitted – she ought to be just the ticket for the Norse project.

In mid-December I arranged with two Burgeo fishermen, Ephram Cook and a cousin of his, who were bound for St. John's on personal business, to bring the *Fort Amadjuak* back to Burgeo to be overhauled and refitted.

Making a snuggery for themselves in the vessel's wheelhouse (the rest of her interior was a shambles), the two men set out from St. John's on December 21. By midnight of the twenty-third, *Fort Amadjuak* was steaming through a snowstorm some fifteen miles off Cape St. Mary's at the southeasterly tip of the Avalon Peninsula when the fuel line to her three-hundred-horsepower truck engine apparently broke, flooding the tightly enclosed space with gasoline.

The consequent explosion might have blown the wheelhouse

and its occupants sky-high. Instead, it blew *Fort Amadjuak's* stern clean out of her.

She went down like the proverbial stone. Her crew – one of whom had been sleeping while the other steered – barely had time to fling themselves out of the wheelhouse, cut the lashings of a dory on the foredeck, and leap into it before *Fort Amadjuak* slid out from under them and took the long plunge. Virtually in their shirtsleeves, they abandoned everything, including their life jackets, only finding time enough to snatch a packet of Purity biscuits, a carton of cigarettes, and a hand-held boat compass.

As Ephram later told me, "'Twere blowing half a gale from nor'ard, you understands, and the nearest land to sud'ard were Bermuda, twelve hunnert mile away. If that were the way us had to go, I t'ought us'd need a compass. . . ."

Fortunately the north wind fell out. Nevertheless, with only one set of oars between them, it took the castaways eight hours alternating at hard pulling against sea and current to reach Newfoundland. Which they did at Distress Cove – an uninhabited bolthole in Placentia Bay's hard coast. It took another day to row to Placentia itself, where there was a telegraph station.

Late on Christmas Eve Claire and I were at the Staff House, having dined with the Lakes and other guests. Outside it was bitter cold and snowing. Inside, all was aglow with the warmth of good food and drink. There a handwritten telegraph found me. In elegant capital letters on a yellow form, it read:

COLLECT TO CAPTAIN MOWAT BURGEO
PLACENTIA HARBOUR 24 DECEMBER
YOUR BOAT SUNK DORY SAVED HOMEWARD BOUND HAPPY
CHRISTMAS
EPHRAM

Ephram Cook had kept his message to within the ten-word limit permitted before an additional fee per word would have been charged. A few days later (after he had turned over to me the dory, the compass, and the pair of oars), he apologized for having sent me a collect telegram. He would not have done so except that every cent he and his cousin possessed had gone down with the ship.

The dory turned out to be the most memorable Christmas present I have ever received. She served Claire and me throughout the years we lived in Burgeo as our principal means of transport within the settlement and for exploring the outer islands and nearby coasts.

We spent a wonderful winter in Burgeo, managing to accomplish a lot of work at typewriter and drawing board despite the distractions and attractions of exploring a new world. Then, in March, a letter came from my U.S. publisher inviting us to Boston for a week. When Spencer Lake offered us passage on the *Swivel* to Gloucester (only a few miles from Boston), we decided to take a break.

Meanwhile an immense tongue of arctic pack ice had thrust far south, reaching the northeastern coasts of Nova Scotia. Consisting mostly of old polar ice almost as hard as concrete, it posed a grave danger to ships not specially strengthened for ice navigation.

The *Swivel* was not ice strengthened, nevertheless on April 4 we sailed aboard her. Two days later she lay helplessly embedded in the pack a few miles to the north of ill-omened Sable Island. We knew that if the wind came westerly, the ice would drift clear of Sable's engulfing sands, but if it blew from the east we would be in serious trouble. We also knew there would be no help from three icebreakers then stationed on Canada's Atlantic seaboard. The most powerful of these was out of action due to engine trouble. A second was unsuccessfully trying to free a freighter jammed in the pack in Cabot Strait. The third was immobilized in heavily rafted ice off Louisbourg.

Farley – winter work.

It was some comfort to find we had company. The floating continent of ice was inhabited by companies of harp seals, whose females had given birth to white-coated pups on the floes only a few weeks earlier. Hundreds of sleek pelagic seals of all ages and sizes were to be seen from *Swivel's* deck. Utterly beguiled, Claire and I watched as they porpoised through narrow leads or hauled themselves out on the floes to bask in the spring sunshine. They were totally at ease in what looked to be a fearsomely inimical environment. For them this icy world was no frozen desolation – it was a glittering paradise. Our admiration for them was tinged with envy.

They were viewed quite differently by some of the ship's crew. Although Sou'west Coast men were not and never had been sealers, two of our deckhands had brought rifles aboard with which they began blazing away at the seals. Magenta-coloured swirls in the green waters and crimson splashes on white ice marked the hits. Most of the seals shot on the floes were mortally stricken yet a good many of the wounded managed to slide off the pans to disappear – doubtless forever – into the black depths.

When I demanded of one of the gunners why he was shooting seals he replied with some asperity, "Because dey's dere!"

To which his companion added, "'Tis for the sport, ye see. And what odds? Dey's t'ousands and t'ousands o' dose fish-eating buggers. Rats of the sea, we calls 'em."

Claire was distraught and sickened by this butchery. I was furious. It cast a shadow over us – one that would spread and darken in the decades ahead during which I would make several journeys "to the ice" with sealers from the Magdalen Islands in the Gulf of St. Lawrence, with others from the northern coasts of Newfoundland, and with Norwegian sealers at the great sea-bight to the north of Newfoundland.

I went on these bloody expeditions to record and to bear witness against a holocaust that was consuming as many as a million seals a year, a massacre committed with the full support of Canada's federal government and of the legislatures of the several Atlantic provinces, a slaughter of wild creatures on an almost inconceivable scale actively or implicitly sanctioned by most of the Canadian media and by all-too-many citizens of my country.

An atrocity that is being continued to this day, I hold it to be a heinous crime against life on earth.

· 16 ·

The Petit Nord

Summer that year was the foggiest in memory on the Sou'west Coast. Most of the time we might as well have been living at the bottom of a barrel filled with grey cotton wool. We hardly glimpsed the sun until late July when we travelled by coast boat to Port aux Basques to try to trace the tenth-century explorations of northern Newfoundland by an Icelander named Thorfinn Karlsefni.

We needed a car but none was available in Port aux Basques so we rode the Bullet 130 miles north to see if we could rent a vehicle in Cornerbrook. Although the largest town in western Newfoundland, all it had to offer was a three-ton truck or a Vauxhall – a British-made sedan suitable for elderly ladies to drive on English country lanes. Dubiously we chose the Vauxhall.

The sun blazed down as we drove north through forests ravaged by pulp-and-paper companies. Despite this desecration, the Bonne

Bay valley – an enormous chasm carved by glaciers – turned out to be one of the most magnificent spectacles either of us had ever seen. We would like to have lingered in it but we had a rendezvous to keep at Port au Choix, a hundred miles farther north, with archaeologist Elmer Harp.

We ferried the Vauxhall across Bonne Bay to the beginning of a not-quite-completed road that skirted the western shore of Newfoundland all the way north to the Strait of Belle Isle. It was gravel-surfaced, strewn with fist-sized rocks, and deeply pitted with thank-you-ma'ams.

The Vauxhall skittered and bounced along through billowing clouds of dust at a reckless forty miles an hour. On our left the glittering Gulf of St. Lawrence rolled to a distant horizon, a mighty sea in its own right. The Long Range Mountains reared to starboard, forming the spine of Newfoundland's Great Northern Peninsula, the Petit Nord as it was more familiarly known.

An hour beyond Bonne Bay we came to Cow Head, where we stopped to give the Vauxhall and ourselves a rest. Originally Seacow Head, this small peninsula jutting into the gulf derived its name from herds of walrus that used to haul out upon its sandy inner beach. Although they are now almost exclusively arctic animals, the great tusked creatures were, prior to the sixteenth century, enormously abundant in the Gulf of St. Lawrence. European entrepreneurs put an end to that. They slaughtered the seacows by the hundreds of thousands for oil, ivory, and leather until, by early in the twentieth century, the last of the gulf walrus had been destroyed.

Claire and I went for a walk along the isthmus behind the head, whose high sand dunes had been carved away by westerly gales, exposing an ancient beach studded with whale and walrus bones and several large boulders that, we discovered, had once served as anvils for the shaping of stone tools and weapons. Each of these was surrounded by a litter of flint flakes and discarded cores from which points and blades had been struck off.

A hammer stone of dense, black basalt rested atop one of the boulders. Laboriously shaped by grinding and pecking, and polished by generations of use, it perfectly fitted the human hand. It fitted mine so well I felt compelled to strike a few flakes from one of the many discarded cores nearby.

"Who do you suppose used these things?" Claire wondered.

"Beothuk Indians, maybe. More likely some of their distant ancestors, but God only knows how many thousands of years ago. Perhaps Elmer will be able to tell us."

Elmer Harp and his student crews had spent several summers excavating prehistoric habitations at Port au Choix, an almost-island peninsula jutting out into the gulf. He was especially interested in sites once occupied by a mysterious people who were neither Eskimo nor Indian. Eskimo legends refer to them as Tunit. Modern archaeologists labelled them Dorset people because our first material knowledge of them came from excavations at Cape Dorset on Baffin Island.

For several hundred years they dominated the west coast of Newfoundland, from which they inexplicably disappeared some time between AD 500 and 1000. My studies of early Norse voyages to Newfoundland suggested that Thorfinn Karlsefni's expedition had made disastrous contact with the Tunit somewhere on the west coast of the Petit Nord. So Claire and I had come to Port au Choix to see what Elmer could show us.

The Tunit site Elmer was studying lay just behind a crescent of sloping beach facing the gulf at Philip's Garden, named after an early settler who had discovered that potatoes prospered especially well there. The garden had not been cultivated for twenty or thirty years and was ablaze with wildflowers. The splendour of wild iris, buttercups, daisies, and a score of others was due to the garden's remarkably rich soil, which, Elmer explained, was composed mainly of organic detritus resulting from the occupancy of the site by *fifty or more* generations of people of the Dorset culture.

Elmer and his students had uncovered the remains of two score Tunit houses within a space barely two hundred yards long and a hundred wide. Although reduced by time to shallow pits about fifteen feet square, these had once been semi-subterranean winter houses, turf-walled and roofed with poles covered by caribou or seal skins. At least during its final occupancy, Philip's Garden had been the more or less permanent residence of a goodly number of people, not simply a campsite of transient nomads.

"The last time it was inhabited – probably about nine hundred years ago if the carbon-14 dates we've been getting are reliable – there could have been a hundred and fifty people, though some would likely have been away catching salmon in the mainland rivers, hunting caribou in the mountains, or collecting seabirds and eggs from the offshore islands," Elmer explained.

Unlike post-Columbian Europeans at Port au Choix who made their livelihoods from codfish, these early settlers relied on pelagic seals. In the spring they ventured far out onto the ice, returning to land towing sleds laden with skins, fat, and meat from both young and adult seals. Unlike modern seal hunters who slaughter seal pups for their pelts alone, the Tunit wasted nothing.

The importance of their centuries-long dependence on seals can be gauged by Elmer's calculation that he could fill a couple of freight cars with bones his crews had already unearthed at Philip's Garden. Small wonder the soil was so miraculously fertile.

Claire and I spent a few days as volunteer diggers, concluding it might have been no bad thing to have lived at Philip's Garden a thousand years earlier. Although Elmer could not tell us why or when the

Tunit disappeared from Newfoundland, I believe the answer lies in the singularly close relationship between them and the pelagic seals.

By the middle of the tenth century the climate of the north-western Atlantic region had warmed significantly. Winters became so mild that what little ice formed in the Gulf of St. Lawrence could no longer have provided safe nurseries. In consequence, the seals would have been forced to abandon the gulf and seek safer ice off the coast of Labrador. As they retreated northward, so did the Tunit.

Two or three centuries later, when the warm cycle ended and the return of cold winter weather made it possible for the seals to re-occupy their old breeding grounds, the Tunit could not follow for they had been overwhelmed by a new adversity. Their world had been invaded by a belligerent new people who called themselves Inuit and for whom the Tunit were no match. The harp and hood seals reclaimed the Gulf of St. Lawrence, but the Tunit never did for they had vanished from the earth.

Although Port au Choix taught us something about the lives of the vanished Tunit, it had nothing to tell us about the Norsemen we were seeking, so we pushed on. The Vauxhall shuddered and juddered northward to Plum Point, where we turned east off the coastal road on a trail bulldozed over the Long Range Mountains by a lumber company. The road, such as it was, descended through what had once been heavily wooded valleys to the head of a great inlet called Canada Bay. We were bound for the outport of Englee at the mouth of this bay. We tried to reach it by road but, when the Vauxhall sank to her belly in a mud wallow that might have given pause to a water buffalo, we abandoned her and completed the last fifteen miles of the journey by boat.

Perched on a rocky peninsula, Englee was dominated by three families who among them seemed to own everything of value, including a lumber mill, a salt-fish operation, the one and only general store, and a fish-filleting plant. The latter was under lease to Spencer Lake's Caribou Fisheries, which each spring despatched Arthur Moulton from Burgeo to run the Englee plant and process fish caught by two deep-sea draggers on the banks off Labrador.

Englee was first occupied by English speakers around 1850, when intrepid fishermen from Notre Dame Bay began rowing and sailing their open bullyboats to the Petit Nord looking for new cod grounds. For a century prior to that, the peninsula had been French territory, with Normans and Bretons sailing to it every spring, fishing from its harbours until late in the autumn, then returning to France. The English, however, came to stay.

At first the French tolerated these squatters but, as their numbers increased, there was conflict and bloodshed. In the end the English seized possession and sent the foreigners packing, but victory did not ensure a peaceful future. Fractious internal struggles – mainly religious – continued to make life lively. By the time of our visit to Englee, six denominations – Pentecostal, Apostolic, Salvation Army, Church of England, United Church, and Roman Catholic – were competing for its fewer than two hundred souls, each sect maintaining its own place of worship and running its own school.

The United Church, which had been dominant for years, was faring badly. A previous minister had fathered so many illegitimate children within and without his flock that a large part of his congregation had defected and become Pentecostals. Then one of his successors had been forced to quit after being discovered in bed with *both* his landlord's daughters simultaneously. He too then formed his own church of the apostolic breed. The temptation to investigate these aspects of life in Englee was strong but I had other fish to fry.

Arthur Moulton had passed the word around that I was looking for objects and sites from earlier times. One day an elderly fisherman, Fred Fillier, invited me to look at his garden, of which he was exceedingly proud because of the enormous cabbages and turnips he grew in it.

"'Tis the finest kind of dirt," he told me, "but full of old Indian stuff."

He let me poke around for myself and within half an hour I had culled a tobacco tin full of flint scrapers, points, and blades from the same sort of rich black soil that characterized Philip's Garden. Evidently the Tunit had lived along all the coasts of the Petit Nord, strengthening my belief that the *skraelings* referred to in the Karlsefni sagas had been Tunit.

Finding evidence of a Norse presence was another matter. I was hopeful when one of the plant workers, who was building a house on the edge of the settlement, told me he had come upon a "skiliton" – a very old one with a smashed-in skull but no traces of clothing or other possessions. When the local ministers and the priest concluded this was the relic of a "pagan" from the dark and distant past and so could not be buried in sanctified ground, the plant worker bundled the bones into a soap-flakes carton and abandoned them under a bush on a nearby hill.

I asked to see the remains and was taken to the spot. The carton had disintegrated, allowing the mahogany-coloured bones to spill down the slope with the skull resting against a clump of moss. Covered in black mould, it could tell me nothing until it had been cleaned. Since the only source of running water in Englee was the fish plant, I took it there and as surreptitiously as possible began washing it in a basin provided for the employees.

Unluckily, a woman filleter saw what I was about and panicked. She was a big woman with a powerful voice, and if Arthur Moulton had not appeared from his office I expect there would have been a mass exodus from the plant that morning. Assuring the anxious workers that the "head bone" I was washing came from a bear, Arthur hustled me out of the place. Nor would he let me take my find into his home. I had to promise to put it back where I found it. Instead, I now confess, I hid it at the bottom of my kit bag wrapped in a sweater, where it remained until we returned to Burgeo.

The skull found a resting place in the provincial museum at St. John's, where it was identified as "female, probably native and possibly Dorset [Tunit], though conceivably early European." Death had apparently been due to a crushing blow to the side of the head.

Next morning Arthur seemed anxious to send me on a voyage to the northward aboard the plant's collector smack delivering salt to summer fishing stations along the otherwise unoccupied coast between Canada Bay and Hare Bay. Claire elected to remain at Englee but I seized the opportunity to examine nearly fifty miles of coast that might well have been visited by the Norse.

Skipper Alf Pollard welcomed me aboard the twenty-ton *Hedley J. Davis.* An elderly vessel, she was nearing the end of her time but Skipper Alf – "sixty years old and fifty of they in the fishery" – proudly insisted "she were still good for it."

He might have been speaking of himself as well. One of twelve children raised at Hooping Harbour on "oatmeal, venison, herring, berries, and salt fish," he and his wife had managed to produce only ten offspring, a deficiency about which he was somewhat apologetic.

"'Twere me own fault, certainly, being as I were at sea most of me time. Me woman were good for half a dozen more youngsters. A girt strong woman, she kept busy on the stages and the flakes making salt fish until an hour or so before her time would come and a child be born. T'ought nothing at all of it."

The *Davis* was heavy laden with several tons of salt in wooden barrels. Her crew consisted of the skipper and two fourteen-year-old boys, one of whom was Alf's son. They were a smart pair of hands and in their father's generation would likely have become skipper-men themselves. But now they had only the summer months to learn the seaman's trade. In winter they went to high school in Roddickton and saw their home, and the sea, only on weekends.

We steamed northward on a lovely summer morning past low, sloping cliffs that were still wooded to the storm-tide line. Twenty miles offshore to the east the Grey Islands loomed out of a calm sea like a pair of monstrous battleships. They had until recently been inhabited by a few fishing families, as almost every little crack and cranny along the entire five-thousand-mile coast of Newfoundland had at one time harboured its cluster of human beings for whom fishing had been not just a livelihood but an entire way of life.

Our first port of call was Hilliers Harbour, now occupied only in summer by families from Halls Bay, Green Bay, and the town of Springdale, 125 miles south. Most of the men worked during the winters in lumber camps in the interior of the island but come spring they migrated north, seemingly driven like birds to follow the patterns established by their ancestors.

In June seven or eight "crowds" (extended families) would set out from Notre Dame Bay in a flotilla of eighteen-foot open skiffs driven by make-and-break engines, laden to the gunwales with women, children, old folk, dogs, fishing gear – and high hopes and expectations for a bumper catch. This grand excursion was mostly coast-wise, entailing only one open-water run of eight to ten hours' duration if the weather was good, but at least twice as long if a storm blew up.

These modern water gypsies bore the surnames of people who had been making the voyage for a hundred years. One of the men at Hilliers Harbour would tell me: "Me poor old father, and *his* father, made the voyage every year with a leg-o'-mutton sail and hauling on sweeps, and never give it a thought. These times, when 'tis all ingines, 'tis hard to know how the old fellows done it. Some was lost, of course, but all hands looked to it as the finest holiday of the year."

The Hilliers Harbour men fished with cod traps, hand trawls, and jiggers – the nylon gill net not having yet arrived upon the scene.

Theirs was a salt-bulk fishery in which gutted and headed cod were preserved wet in heavy brine. Periodically the smack would pick up the salt-bulk and carry it to Englee.

Our appearance was the signal for every human and dog to come crowding onto the fragile stage head that served as a wharf. As we slid gingerly alongside, men and boys swarmed aboard to help unload twenty-six hogsheads of salt. While this heavy work was underway, I went ashore to look around and to chat with the children, women, and old folk. They were an outgoing, friendly, and particularly good-looking lot, and I was struck by how many of them were blond and blue-eyed.

As the unloading proceeded, a heavily laden skiff came in from hauling one of the traps. Among the catch was an absolute giant of a cod. It was as long as I was tall, and I have a photograph of the two of us to prove it. Weighing perhaps a hundred pounds, it must have been one of the last of the great codfish that were once so abundant in Newfoundland waters.

Although exposed to northeasterly weather, Hilliers Harbour was a beautiful place. It had a carefree, almost festive air about it. Everyone lived in tilts made of spruce poles and tarpaper, roofed with old canvas sails. When there were no fish to be cut and salted, women and youngsters meandered into the country to pick berries, gather firewood, and catch salmon and trout in the many brooks. At night when the work was done, or during heavy weather, people gathered in one of the larger tilts lit by kerosene lanterns to listen to battery radios, or to sing, tell stories, play cards, and have a scoff.

I asked a group of older girls if they wouldn't rather be in Springdale.

"Yiss, sorr. Sometime I does," one sixteen-year-old replied. "I misses the cars and the stores, but sometimes when we sits around a shore fire of an evening, I don't mind living here 'cause it's like we was just one family. They don't have that no more in Springdale. Nor Cornerbrook. Nor St. John's neither."

Wandering among the scattered tilts I came upon a cage made of driftwood and old fish netting, containing half a dozen young but almost fully fledged herring gulls. I thought they might be pets, but it was not so. Taken as nestlings, they were being fattened on a diet of cod livers, to become the centrepieces of celebratory birthday scoffs.

"Some good eating, me son!" Skipper Alf told me. Well, why not? *Pâté de foie gras* is an epicurean delight.

Living for several months of the year this far from sources of manufactured goods, the summer people of Hilliers Harbour did as their ancestors had once done. They made what they needed. Because the terrain was so rough, there were no wheels in Hilliers Harbour. Hand barrows made of saplings or driftwood served instead. There were no iron trap anchors to be had so the men made killocks – wooden anchors weighted with stones – of a pattern virtually identical to some recently dug from peat bogs in Denmark and carbon dated to about 2500 BC. Almost anything people required that *could* be made of wood *was* made of wood, and nobody I spoke to counted this a difficulty or a hardship. I suspect that one of the more powerful attractions bringing people back to this place year after year was the prideful knowledge that not only could they survive in what was virtually a state of nature, but they could also contrive a good life for themselves from what came to hand.

Although the people pressed us to stay overnight, Skipper Alf prudently decided to push on while the good weather held. At his invitation I took the wheel, steering a course close under a forbiddingly cliffy coast toward the outthrust Conche Peninsula fifteen miles to the northward. The boys sprawled on deck in the warm sunshine while Alf went into the forecastle, lit the old Shipmate stove, and cooked up a big cod from Hilliers Harbour that had been two days in salt pickle. Lightly boiled then drenched in smoking-hot salt-pork fat, it was delicious.

The Conche Peninsula was a stunning composition of layered red sandstone slabs pierced every few hundred yards by huge sea caves, some of them big enough to have swallowed a full-rigged ship. Its sheer, eastern face ranged from flame red through glittering gold to molten orange and was made even more impressive by the presence of a cathedral of an iceberg grounded in thirty fathoms off the cape.

We delivered salt to the several families at Conche, Crouse, and finally Croque – all summer stations like Hilliers. Nobody in them seemed to know what the place names meant or who had bestowed them. I thought they might be corruptions of the Basque language, for the Basques had fished this coast before the French.

At dusk we cleared for home with one of the lads at the wheel while Skipper Alf and I repaired to the forepeak for a noggin of my rum and a feed of his dried capelin toasted on the hot stove top. Afterwards all four of us crowded into the small wheelhouse where the skipper played his accordion. We sang Newfoundland songs and old sea shanties while our wake spread astern like phosphorescent milk spilled from the rising moon.

I took the wheel for the last two hours of that calm and lovely night. It had been a voyage into the living past, for the summer fishery would soon be gone, and with its passing the memories of a truly ancient way of life would disappear.

Extricating ourselves from Englee was no easier than getting to it. The smack wasn't available and a big run of cod was keeping the fishermen and their boats occupied. Eventually I persuaded a patriarch to unlimber his retired trap boat and take us to the foot of Bide Arm, where we had left our chariot.

The Vauxhall may have been relieved to see us again. At any rate she carried us at a sprightly pace back up and over the Long Range. But as we descended into a black fog on the gulf side, she seemed to lose heart – and blew two tires in quick succession.

We eased our way northward from Plum Point through a string of tiny hamlets, including Bird Cove, Blue Cove, Seal Cove, Black Duck Cove, Deadmans Cove, and Bear Cove, to Flower's Cove, from where, on some days, it was possible to take a ferry of sorts across the Strait of Belle Isle to Labrador.

Not on this day. The strait had vanished under a pall of fog rolling in over the coast road. In consequence we saw almost nothing of the few people scattered like flotsam along the shore – people who made their livings partly by fishing the fierce waters of the strait and partly by "furring" in the mountainous interior. We did see quite a lot of the scraggy little horses that provided most of the land transport. In summertime, when they were not much needed, these creatures were given the freedom to come and go as they pleased. On this day it seemed to please a lot of them to materialize out of the fog directly into our path.

For twenty miles beyond Eddies Cove, the road was little more than a trail bulldozed along an ancient beach composed of water-rounded stones mixed with the bones of thousands of great whales that had been butchered in the strait by fifteenth-century Basques and on into the twentieth century by Norwegian whalers. Uncountable carcasses stripped of their blubber had driven ashore on the northwest coast of the Petit Nord to form a boneyard of awesome dimensions.

At Lower Cove we turned away from this cemetery of giants and headed for St. Anthony, the only town on the Petit Nord. I hoped to travel from it by boat to the remote community of L'Anse aux Meadows (Lancy Meadows to its inhabitants), where the excavation of a recognizable Viking settlement was underway.

St. Anthony had celebrated the completion of the overland umbilicus connecting it to the outer world by erecting Loon Lodge, the first and only motel on the entire peninsula. We thought to find a room in it, but this was not to be. The spanking-new structure was already filled – not with transients but with citizens of St. Anthony, who had never before been able to enjoy the dubious pleasures of staying at a motel.

We found an alternative at Mrs. Decker's Boarding House. Although her house was full of travelling salesmen recently arrived by car and truck, eager to exploit a virgin market for aluminum cookware, "New York" women's fashions, and encyclopaedias, Mrs. Decker, a robust and motherly woman, kindly offered us her daughter's bedroom. This turned out to be a boudoir draped in pastel fabrics, garnished with garish dolls, and crowded with gifts for a mother-to-be, including a bassinet. We gratefully accepted, for Claire was coming down with a bad cold and needed to get her head down.

Leaving her to settle in, I went to see the manager of the local fish plant, seeking some way to get to Lancy Meadows. He offered me passage down the coast as far as Quirpon aboard the plant's fish collector, the hundred-ton schooner *Gull Pond*, departing early next morning.

I boarded the *Gull Pond* just after dawn. Built in Nova Scotia nearly forty years earlier, she was still in moderately good shape though stripped of all her sail and dependent on a diesel engine. Skippered for the past twenty years by Captain Hedley Hillier, her crew had been reduced from fifteen or twenty fishermen to the skipper's two teenaged sons.

Our first port of call was St. Lunaire, two hours' steaming to the northward where – with much ado – we landed a truck we had been carrying as deck cargo. This, the first motor vehicle to reach the little outport, had nowhere to go except back and forth along a rocky path to Griquet (pronounced Cricket), a scant three miles away.

Griquet was the skipper's home port and he had planned to spend the night there, sending me on to Quirpon by motorboat. However, his weather sense told him a nor'easter was in the offing so he decided to take me on in the *Gull Pond*.

Wind and waves gave us a rough passage to Quirpon Island at the northern tip of the Petit Nord. The island thrusts into the flank of the North Atlantic the way the weapon called *arpoi* by its ancient Basque inventors, *arpon* by their Spanish imitators, *quirpon* by the French, and *harpoon* by the English had thrust into the flesh of the great whales that once frequented these waters.

Cocking an eye at the grey spume streaming in over Quirpon Island, Skipper Hillier recommended I stay at the nearby village until the weather was fit for a boat to take me on to Lancy Meadows. But, afraid a nor'easter might pin me down in Quirpon for several days, I was determined to travel on at once if I could find the means. Eventually I persuaded the owner of a trap boat to attempt the ten-mile run to Lancy Meadows.

Just off Noddy Head our engine failed. By the time its owner managed to get it going again, we were almost in the surf. This decided him to set me ashore in uninhabited Hay Cove and beat a retreat to Quirpon. By now it was blowing like the devil, and a hard, cold rain was pelting down. I slogged across bleak and sodden barrens for several miles to an outthrust point upon which clung a forlorn little cluster of houses that proved to be Lancy Meadows. Not far beyond it some tents and fragile-looking plywood sheds streamed with rain and rattled in the rising wind. These sheltered the Norwegian adventurer Helge Ingstad and his crew of archaeologists, who were excavating what Ingstad claimed was the camp where the Greenlander Leif Erikson and his companions had spent the winter of 995–996.

Ingstad and the crew were sheltering from the storm in a crowded wall tent. Squeezing through a flapping canvas door, I introduced myself as a fellow seeker after early Norwegian venturers to North America. This roused no comradely enthusiasm from the Scandinavians. In truth, they were about as welcoming as if I had identified myself as one of the abominable *skraelings* who, the sagas tell us, made the New World too hot even for belligerent Vikings.

In retrospect I do not blame them. If Lancy Meadows did indeed turn out to be Leif Erikson's Vinland, their niche in history would be assured. And Ingstad had suffered his share of rebuffs in a life-long pursuit of this goal. These included a failed attempt to annex east Greenland to the Norwegian Crown and some dubious enter-prises with the German occupiers of Norway during the Second World War. As he and I talked (or, rather, as I talked and he grunted occasional, reluctant replies), it became painfully apparent I was trespassing on his turf, both literally and figuratively, and that the sooner I departed the happier he would be.

Night was falling and I was wet, cold, and hungry. When no offer of hospitality was forthcoming, I went back out into the gath-ering storm to see what I could find for myself. What I found was George Decker of Lancy Meadows, the man who had originally led Ingstad to the grassy mounds and hummocks that local people had thought might be an old Indian burying ground.

George and his family welcomed me in proper Newfoundland style. They shared a steaming pot of turrs with me, dried my wet clothing beside the kitchen stove, and provided a feather bed to sleep in. They also told me a good deal about what had been taking place at the archaeological site. Since many of them were, or had been, employed at the excavation, they knew more about it than Ingstad perhaps realized.

The gist of what they had to tell me, combined with my own researches, would persuade me that L'Anse aux Meadows was indeed the site of a failed Norwegian attempt to establish a foothold in Newfoundland. However, the expedition was not Leif Erikson's but was most probably that of the Icelandic Norseman Thorfinn Karlsefni.

I examined the site next day, then, with little more I could accomplish on this visit, asked George Decker to find me a boat for the trip back to Quirpon. He offered to take me in his own trap skiff but before we could depart a large motor yacht entered the harbour and anchored off. A stoutish man wearing a gilt-encrusted captain's cap came ashore in a launch and introduced himself as Chesley Dawes from St. John's, owner of the gleaming *Hemmer Jane*. He seemed pleased to meet me.

"Heard in St. John's you were interested in the Vikings. Well, so am I."

He told me his construction company had a government contract to erect protective buildings over Ingstad's excavations and that he was here to inspect the work.

"My men has done some digging of their own, you know – putting in foundations and such like stuff. They've found some right peculiar things. Things you might like to know about. I'll be through here in a couple of hours so why don't you come aboard and I'll run you back to St. Anthony if that's what you've a mind to."

So it was that I concluded this, my first visit to Lancy Meadows, in *Hemmer Jane's* teak-panelled saloon drinking cocktails mixed by Ches Dawes's charming female companion while he elaborated on the wiliness of Norwegians in general, and of Helge Ingstad in particular. It was a far cry from the wheelhouse of the *Gull Pond*.

Back at Mrs. Decker's Boarding House, I found Claire much improved and ready to hit the road again so we spent the next several days working our way southward, trying to equate the saga descriptions of Karlsefni's voyage with the west coast of the Petit Nord.

This took us into a score of coves and harbours where we met many fishermen, housewives, children, dogs, and inquisitive horses. Eventually we concluded that St. Paul's Inlet, only a few miles to the south of Seacow Head, was most likely Hop – the harbour where Karlsefni had tried to plant the first European settlement of which we have any certain record in North America.

Summer was drawing on, and since we wanted to spend some of it sailing *Happy Adventure* in Bay Despair, we pressed the Vauxhall hard. On August 8 she delivered us to Cornerbrook, where we bade her a fond farewell and made our apologies for ever having doubted her staunch English heart.

Two days later we nosed into Burgeo aboard the coastal steamer *Taverner*.

Joan and Arthur, *last of the big schooners, in Bay of Spirits.*

· 17 ·

Back to the Bay

We had worked hard all spring on *Happy Adventure*. She had been in poor shape – the result of three years of inadequate attention culminating in a winter of being shoved about by wind and ice while moored at the head of the reach. We had had to scrape her to the wood, inside and out, and repaint her, black above the waterline and copper below; dark red decks and cabin trunk; cream and white inside the cabin. All the rigging had been overhauled and much of it renewed.

Some of this had been completed before we left on the trip to L'Anse aux Meadows. Immediately upon our return, we frantically undertook the rest. Because the weather was uncooperative – gales, rain, and fog – we moved aboard to take advantage of every fleeting opportunity to complete the work and be ready to set sail at once if the weather turned fair.

This it did on August 17. Waking to a clear morning and a south-westerly breeze, we dropped our mooring and cleared from Burgeo, bound east. Our plan was to spend some time in Bay Despair then sail on to St. Pierre, where we would rendezvous with Jack McClelland. Jack and I would then bring the vessel back to Burgeo while Claire returned aboard the coastal steamer.

Crowding on all sail, we went belting down the coast. Before long we overtook the *Penneyworth* dragging for redfish. Skipper Max wished us a good voyage by sounding three long blasts on his siren.

A heavy swell – legacy of the gales of the past several weeks – was running, but *Happy Adventure* rode the grey-beards at a good seven knots, sending spray over her bows and attracting a pod of about thirty pothead whales. They seemed to think we were invit-ing them to join in a game. Porpoising in the breaking seas, they spouted so close aboard that we could smell their fishy breath.

It was a magnificent day and a magnificent sail with perfect visibility. The granite wall of the Sou'west Coast stretched to the horizon ahead and astern. Swells booming in from the south were bursting fifty feet high against the cliffs. A few small and cottony clouds floated high above; otherwise the sky was a translucent sap-phire bowl.

As we passed the red ochre mass of Cape la Hune, the wind freshened right out of the west, allowing me to steer a course for Richards Harbour "wung out" with the mainsail to port and the mizzen to starboard and every sail drawing full and hard. This was as close to flying as our little vessel was ever likely to get.

Dusk was falling, and we were going at such a clip we sailed right past the crack in the wall that gave access to Richards Harbour. Only a quick glimpse of a house alerted me. We hove to, doused sail, started the engine, and headed into the cleft through a combination of heavy swells and rising seas. We shot through it to find ourselves in the tranquility of the hidden harbour.

The old-fashioned brass patent log we had been towing astern showed we had sailed fifty-two nautical miles in just under nine hours – something of a record run – but then I botched it by hitting the small wharf so hard the impact shook several empty herring barrels into the harbour. However, Richards Harbour was running true to form and only one person, a youngish man, was on hand to witness my disgrace, although plenty of others probably saw it from behind curtained windows.

Ephraim Sims, just returned home after a year spent in St. John's, took our lines and helped me make fast. I inveigled him aboard for a drink then asked him about the origin of the harbour's name. He told us the place had been settled around 1840 by a deserter from a British naval vessel whose first name was Richard but who never did reveal his surname. When I began asking further questions about the history of the place and its people, Ephraim politely excused himself and went ashore.

Although the next day was Sunday, no service was held in the little church. It had been without a resident minister for ten years and the schoolteacher – who acted as lay reader – was away for the summer. We walked along the paths in a watery sunshine that imparted a strange sense of unreality to the scene. People dressed in their Sunday best stood or wandered about aimlessly. They spoke when spoken to, but volunteered nothing of themselves even when we admired their tiny gardens, the earth for which had been labori-ously collected far in the country in baskets and pails, and which grew little but turnips and cabbages.

The gloomy atmosphere becoming more than we could endure, we decided, despite a bad forecast and the thunder of great seas bursting into the narrow entrance, to make a run for Pushthrough, perhaps stopping en route for a look at McCallum, another settlement with a reputation all its own.

Once outside, we found the wind had fallen light. A huge swell was still running and fog was thickening. I set a compass course to clear Whale Rock, at the mouth of Bonne Bay, but either I erred or the current took us astray for we found ourselves enmeshed in a maze of sunkers and reefs and had to run hastily out to sea. Eventually we did find Whale Rock and steamed gratefully past it into McCallum's harbour.

In earlier times when it had been called Bonne Bay Harbour, the settlement had been renowned along the coast for its vigour and independent nature. However, around 1920 it fell under the baleful influence of a stranger who tried with some success to turn it into a kind of feudal barony.

At the time of our visit, McCallum was ruled by a man named Riggs (no relation to Captain Ernie Riggs, skipper of the *Baccalieu*) whose rule was absolute. Ches Strickland, the Milltown merchant, had warned me about "the King of McCallum."

"Never cross him, me son. He's the law on that part of the coast. Even the Mounties don't go in there. Best steer clear of him."

Riggs discouraged the use of cash in his bailiwick. All internal business was conducted on the debt-and-credit system. Imported goods had to be bought through his store (it was the only one in McCallum) and all local produce sold to him. The de facto banker for a community of about 150 people, he was also the postmaster, receiving their welfare, unemployment, and pension cheques. Instead of cashing these, Riggs had the nominal recipients endorse the cheques over to him, then entered the sum, or a portion thereof, as a credit in the debt record he maintained for every adult in the community. So did he maintain the traditional way of doing business that had afflicted Newfoundland for centuries.

We moored alongside a fine new wharf built by the federal government at Riggs's behest and found it mostly occupied by Riggs's store, *his* warehouse, *his* fish flakes, and *his* 150-ton schooner.

He himself was not in residence, which may have been as well for he treated strangers with suspicion. So did his subjects. Those we met were distinctly, even truculently, unfriendly.

We did not remain long. That night I wrote in my journal: "Except for Riggs's house, which is by way of being an outport mansion, McCallum has the worst collection of hovels I've seen in Newfoundland. They are small, pinched, and decrepit, and the people seem slovenly and dour. Perhaps it's just as well it had its name changed. Bonne Bay doesn't suit it at all."

From McCallum we worked our way through an inside passage until we were abeam of Pushthrough, but decided to give it a miss in favour of Raymonds Point. As we entered Long Reach the fog dissipated, the skies cleared, and a warm westerly breeze allowed us to shut down the engine (which had been stifling us with diesel smog) and enjoy a lovely sail. We peered into the little coves and harbours along the way, promising ourselves to visit all of them someday.

Another storm was forecast so I moored at the remains of Raymonds Point wharf with a web of warps and hawsers that could have held the *Queen Mary* in a hurricane. Safe again in the arms of what we privately called Bay Desire, we went happily to bed.

Next morning we found ourselves floating in a soup of little shrimp about an inch in length, transparent except for black eyes and pink blood systems. These were the legendary krill that once sustained countless species, from great baleen whales to wandering albatross. At Raymonds Point that morning the krill were being pursued by multitudes of mackerel and young cod engaging in a feeding orgy that churned the water. We watched, fascinated, as the krill flipped themselves into the air in their efforts to escape, forming little iridescent clouds through which silver-and-blue mackerel shot like javelins.

No Dominies were in residence so a day or two later we left a message in their tilt and sailed for Gaultois to buy kerosene for the lamps. As we entered Little Passage, we disturbed hundreds of black-backed and herring gulls gorging themselves on krill. Several bald eagles looked on hungrily from nearby cliffs.

A rising headwind and lowering skies warned of weather coming so we put our lines ashore at the Gaultois fish plant wharf, where we could feel secure, if half stifled by the pungent stink. We were moored alongside *Teressa G.*, whose life I had helped save the previous year at Hermitage.

The gathering storm brought in several other vessels, including two of the last of the big bay schooners, *Shirley Blanche* and *Joan and Arthur*, who loomed over *Happy Adventure* like a pair of mallards over a duckling. The *Castaway* appeared from Burgeo with Spencer Lake aboard and, shortly afterwards, the *Swivel*, skippered by Jim Moffat, arrived to load frozen fillets for transport to Gloucester. These vessels and their people created a festive scene and mood. So much visiting, drinking, yarning, and eating was going on that Gaultois could almost have been re-enacting what had once been the most important event of the year on the Sou'west Coast – Settling-Up Day.

From its inception in the seventeenth or eighteenth century, Settling-Up Day in Newfoundland was always September 7. On that day the clerks of Newman's in Gaultois would roll puncheons of rum out on the wharf and knock out the bungs so all comers could help themselves. What followed was an uninhibited celebration that lasted until September 10, by which time almost everyone who dealt with Newman's at Gaultois would have arrived. Then the free booze was cut off and settling up began in earnest. One by one the fishermen were allowed into the merchant's office to be told how much they owed the firm, and what credit remained to pay for their purchases for the ongoing year. It was very seldom that a fisherman came out ahead at settling up.

While Newman's (which also had branches at Cape la Hune and Pass Island) remained the main merchant on the coast, the people certainly did not become rich, but then they did not starve either. However, at the end of the nineteenth century, Newman's sold out to Job Brothers, a St. John's firm that was singularly avaricious even by Newfoundland mercantile standards. Thereafter, instead of being a celebratory festival, settling up became a torment. The prices Jobs demanded for most goods rose steadily. The prices paid the fishermen for their produce fell steeply. Job Brothers made enormous profits, which attracted other and equally rapacious merchants until the bubble burst worldwide and the Great Depression of the late twenties and early thirties set in. Those years, which continued until the Second World War, were the darkest that outport Newfoundlanders ever knew.

When the weather (and my head) had cleared sufficiently, we sailed across to Hermitage Cove where, to our great surprise, we found that Sandy and Kent Hill had stopped fishing for a living. Instead, they were casting concrete blocks that could be easily mortared together to make fireproof chimneys. Since the chimneys of most outport houses were only sheet-metal stovepipes that had a dismaying tendency to overheat and set the buildings on fire, the Hills' version proved an instant success.

It was a sobering glimpse into the future for, if the Hills had given up fishing, it meant the game was drawing to a close, with all that this implied for the people of the Sou'west Coast.

Sandy was unapologetic.

"Got to do something, skipper. Not enough fish still on the go to feed a cat. Can't feed we at the two and a half cents a pound Spencer Lake and the other fish plants pays. Seems Joey Smallwood's going to have his way. Fishermen'll have to get out of it or starve."

Now we tried to make a run for St. Pierre. When easterly weather slowed our progress, I started the engine to help us along. All went well until we were off Pass Island, where the bedding bolts holding the engine in place let go. I noted bitterly in the log: "Those goddamn St. Pierrais installed it with black-iron lag screws instead of bronze bolts, and they've corroded away to nothing!"

The wind stayed easterly, preventing us from making headway under sail alone so reluctantly we turned back to Gaultois, the nearest place repairs could be effected. Before we could set off again a full gale blew up, putting an end to any hopes of reaching the French Isles this season. Though Claire was desolated, I was secretly relieved. *My* love affair with St. Pierre was over.

We waited out the gale with *Happy Adventure* nuzzled up against the wharf while rain thrummed on her decks and the wind whined in her rigging. I lit our miniature coal stove and stoked it to a red glow. Claire busied herself with watercolours while I pecked away at my portable typewriter. For variety, we read, or listened to the thin voice of a distant CBC station in Nova Scotia.

On the third day the wind fell light and we decided to run back into the bay. As Claire was letting go our lines in the misty morning, a white-haired man wearing an old-fashioned seaman's jersey appeared in a dory alongside. Without a word he placed several freshly caught mackerel on the deck, smiled at Claire, and rowed away. We had no idea who he was. He seemed like a visitor from an earlier time.

We lunched on his mackerel as we made our way through Little Passage to moor again at Raymonds Point. None of the Dominies had yet returned so I helped myself to a salt fish from Cecil's tilt and brought it back for Claire to cook for supper. As the afternoon waned, the sun came out, revealing a dory being rowed toward us by the elderly fellow who had given us the mackerel in the morning. He came alongside and this time introduced himself.

Although crippled by rheumatism, seventy-year-old Wilson Northcote had rowed the eight miles from Gaultois to pick berries at Raymonds Point! Disappointed at not finding the Dominies, he was happy to see us. When we invited him to share our supper, he accepted with shy grace. A big, soft-spoken, sheepdog sort of a man, Wilson had been born at Little Passage, where his mother died when he was ten. When he was thirteen his father drowned, and Wilson became head of a family of two brothers and a sister. Through the rest of his teen years, he supported them all by going to sea as a deckhand aboard a Gaultois schooner fishing the Grand Banks. At nineteen he became mate of the vessel then went on to become skipper of her and later of several others. During the succeeding fifty years, he captained twenty-three transatlantic passages under sail. When engines replaced sail, he came ashore. By then his wife had been twenty years dead. Now he was living with his daughter, who was married to "a fellow with ulsters" who had not worked for decades past.

Wilson Northcote was not that sort.

"I'se the kind of fellow has to keep underway. 'Twould be the end of I and I stayed to home. I jigs cod from me dory most of the winter and sells it to Lake's plant at Gaultois, though you might better say I has to *give* it away. Summertime I sets lobster pots, jigs squid, sets a net for salmon, and when I feels like it picks berries at all them old places that's gone out now."

Among the stories he told us of his time at sea was one about a voyage he made as a young hand in a schooner homeward bound from Oporto after delivering a cargo of salt fish.

"Our Old Man liked a drop, you understand. He were dead drunk in Oporto and stayed that way the first nine days at sea. Might have stayed that way till the last trump hadn't we rushed his cabin and took away his drink.

"We never done it just for badness, you understand. He were the only one aboard could navigate deep-sea. Without he, we never would have knowed where we was to.

"When the Old Man sobered up enough to come on deck and take a sight, it come out we was south of the Azores and nigh a thousand miles off course.

"Well, me dears, that were a pickle! The skipper were all for putting in to the Azores for more supplies, but we knowed what he were up to. We kept the schooner full-and-by and told the skipper he'd have his drink the day and hour we raised Cape Race. He swore pretty bad, but done his part and when we got home we was but two weeks overdue."

Leaving Wilson to his berry picking, we sailed for Head of the Bay to telegraph Jack, telling him of the change in plan. I instructed him to fly to Gander, rent a float plane there, and join us in Milltown. He replied that he would arrive in mid-September.

We expected to remain a few days at the Milltown wharf, but soon had reason to think otherwise. At midnight the *Bar Haven* arrived under command of a new skipper, who overshot the wharf. *Bar Haven's* steel prow came within a foot of cutting off the bowsprit, where I was standing clad only in underwear, desperately trying to fend off the steamer with a boathook.

That was bad enough. Worse was to follow an hour or two later when I was awakened by a great scurrying on deck. I shone a flashlight through the nearest porthole into the red-eyed face of a very large rat who seemed determined to come in. Charging out through the companionway, I found half a dozen rats skittering about the deck. They retreated to the wharf, but reluctantly. It was clear to me that, like General de Gaulle, they planned to return.

I manned the fort against them until morning, when I discovered they were from the old and decrepit coaster *Glimshire*, which had put in to Milltown wharf a few days earlier leaking so badly extra pumps had to be put aboard to keep her afloat. Her rats, being nobody's fools, abandoned her for the temporary security of the wharf. However, they were seafaring rats and anxious to find another vessel. Determined it would not be *Happy Adventure*, we departed to visit St. Alban's, in Ship Cove, four miles to the southwestward.

By far the largest settlement in the Bay, St. Alban's was an anomaly in that most of its hundred and sixty families were Roman Catholics. They were also among the poorest folk in the region. According to the welfare officer, three-quarters of them depended on the dole, and some families had been on it for two generations.

The first settler here had been one of Newman's indentured workers named Collier who, about 1840, fled into the bay to escape economic serfdom and religious harassment. One or two other Catholics joined him, hoping to scratch out a living with the help of the nearby Conne River Mi'kmaq, the only other Roman Catholics in the region. In 1857 a British naval vessel charting the bay found four families in Ship Cove – three Colliers and one Organ. Word of the existence of this little Catholic enclave spread, and a trickle of families began arriving from Placentia Bay. Children were born apace, and the settlement grew rapidly.

Avoiding the sea because its waters and shores were dominated by Protestant fishermen, St. Alban's people turned to the land for their support. They had a hard time of it. Until the later years of the nineteenth century, they lived in low-ceilinged, windowless log cabins barely heated by open fires or clay fireplaces; burning cod liver oil in their lamps; making their own clothing from a rough material called twincey; and baking their bread (when they had flour or meal) in iron pots heaped over with embers. For the most part they subsisted on country meat and fish with what little flour, cornmeal, and oatmeal they could trade for the few saleable products they produced, chiefly birch and spruce bark for lining the holds of ships carrying salt bulk fish to foreign ports.

Michael Johns of Conne River once told me, "Our people was right sorry for them poor folk. We give them what we could, for they was always needy."

Living conditions at St. Alban's started to improve early in the twentieth century as exploitation of the rich timber resources of the bay and the adjacent interior began. There had long been some lumbering at Head of the Bay, providing wood for local use, especially for ship building. Now lumbering burgeoned into an industrial operation. Job Brothers and Perlins, both from St. John's, built lumber mills in the bay, and a boom began. Initially St. Alban's supplied most of the labour for log cutting and gathering but when the operators began selling massive quantities of logs for pulp and for pit props in British coal mines, more men were needed and a migration into the bay from fishing outports on the coast began.

Yet although St. Alban's grew, it never seemed to prosper. Because of the inflow from coastal settlements there was generally a surplus of labour and this enabled employers to hold wages down to a pittance. Even as late as 1963 St. Alban's two lumber mills were paying wages of only fifty cents an hour, while requiring that employees buy all their goods at company stores, where the markup was double that of independent shopkeepers.

Conditions improved during the war. In 1940 Bowater, the British pulp and paper empire controlling most of Newfoundland's forests, moved into Bay Despair and launched a huge operation cutting logs for pulp and for timber. Every available man, both from inland and from the coastal settlements, was hired. By 1942 twenty to thirty thousand cords of pulp a year were being shipped out of the bay to Bowater's paper mill in Cornerbrook on giant barges towed by ocean-going tugs. In the mid-1950s, the bottom fell out. Although Bowater was still able to sell twenty-two thousand cords of pulp logs each year for export abroad, it found the profit margins insufficient so it closed the whole operation down, throwing the entire labour force of the region out of work virtually overnight.

Conditions in St. Alban's soon verged on the desperate. Unwilling to return to scrabbling for subsistence, most people went on the dole, more or less permanently.

George Collier, onetime foreman of a Bowater camp, explained. "The company pulled out 'cause they'd cut too much wood too quick, they weren't enough left to make the kind of money they was after. We was no use to them no longer so they cut us adrift. Us'd had ten year of fair good times. Built good enough houses. Women and youngsters had clothing and gear fittin' for them for once. There weren't much us could do after that but go on the dole. Since most of the near woods has been cut and what little's left is too costly to go after, I don't says as but we has to stay on the dole. I tell ye, if Joey Smallwood was to send for we to move to someplace as they was work, us'd be off like a shot. But seems like 'tis only fishermen he wants to move. That man must surely hate the sea."

By 1963 lumbering in Bay Despair had been reduced to supplying three small mills from the wreckage of the forests Bowater had devastated to such effect that it may well take centuries before trees stand tall again in the country around the bay.

Claire and I rowed ashore to be met on St. Alban's sawdust beach by the village's newest resident, a wiry man of about my age. He introduced himself as Doctor Carlos Rodriguez, born in Peru, son of a Japanese mining engineer and an *Indios* mother.

When Carlos was seventeen, his father took him to Japan to study medicine and there, in 1941, he was conscripted into the Imperial Japanese army as a fighter pilot. He survived the war, graduated as a doctor, married a Japanese girl, and started a family. However, racial prejudice was rampant in Japan and when, because of his mixed blood, he found himself being treated as something of a pariah, he decided to take his family to Peru. There he ran foul of the local medical establishment, which found him embarrassingly overqualified. So when he heard that Newfoundland was recruiting doctors, he decided on one more move, hoping to find a place where he and his would be acceptable. Soon after the family's arrival in St. John's, the Department of Health sent them to St. Alban's.

Carlos greeted us exuberantly, insisting we come to his house, where we met his lovely wife, Teruko, and their four handsome sons, Raphael, Romeo, Hilario, and Antonio. Unable to speak more than a few words of English and very shy, Teruko was eager to make a friend of Claire. Carlos seemed equally pleased to have me to talk to. He enthused about the idyllic life he was going to create for his family, one that would be free of the problems that had bedevilled them in Japan and Peru. He showed me plans for a Japanese-style home he intended to build on a point of land across the harbour, complete with a tea house and a Japanese garden. Teruko showed us examples of her beautiful calligraphy and insisted on dressing Claire in her own bridal kimono – a gorgeous concoction of silks.

We found St. Alban's to be a motley collection of shoddily built and badly maintained houses. There was a grimy, smelly, and hopelessly ill-equipped four-room school, and two small sawmills stood mired in their own sawdust at the edge of the landwash. All of this was overshadowed by a colossal church towering stark and white above the dishevelled community. This immense structure – the second largest wooden church in all of Newfoundland – was the creation of two men: Father Hayes, long-time priest of St. Alban's, and

Sam Cox, a carpenter from Gaultois. In 1950 the priest decided to replace his rather ordinary though adequate church with something truly magnificent – something approaching the regal grandeur of one that loomed over the Quebec city of Trois-Rivières. He had seen that one in a coloured photo on a postcard and asked Sam Cox to build one like it.

Sam was only a boat builder but, finding the challenge irresistible, he set to work to raise Father Hayes's vast edifice without benefit of blueprints or plans and with only the small photo as his guide. All his figuring and planning was empirical, and he made his own sketches on wrapping paper.

Ten years after it was begun, the new church was finally completed. Only Father Hayes had any real idea of what it cost his parishioners but it was said that the carved oak pews imported from Italy were worth thirteen thousand dollars. This from a community most of whose able-bodied men were on the dole.

The bishop came and consecrated the new church, and then a strange thing happened. Murmurs of resentment about the cost began to reach Father Hayes, and he was so outraged he refused to hold services in what he was now sometimes referring to as "the cathedral" or even to open its doors to his parishioners.

While we were in St. Alban's, the imposing door to the new church remained closed and locked. Jack Spencer, who lived at Milltown but was welfare officer for the entire bay, told us Father Hayes intended to keep it locked until his congregation had cleansed itself of malice.

"I think," said Jack solemnly, "that won't happen soon. They're a right stubborn lot. I'll tell you what they're like. In 1955 everybody around Head of the Bay got together and raised the money and give the labour to build a doctor's house and dispensary at St. Alban's – it being the biggest place – so as to persuade the Department of Health to send in a doctor.

"The first they sent was a young Irishman, fresh out of college, I suppose, and with a pretty good opinion of himself. When he come off the steamer at St. Alban's he looked the new house over, and all hands thought he'd be right happy with it. But no. You see, it was heated with wood stoves the same as all the houses in the bay, and that weren't good enough.

"He wanted one of them new furnaces like the rich folk in St. John's, that you don't need to poke billets into every hour or two to keep it going.

"Well, skipper, people had put a lot into the place, and St. Alban's folk let him know *they* weren't planning to spend any more on any newfangled stove. Nothing much happened till winter come and heat was needed. Then, 'I needs a furnace,' this young fellow says, 'or I can't answer for what could happen.'

"When the next steamer come in from Port aux Basques there weren't no furnace aboard of it. None on the next one neither, or the one after.

"'Twas a bad winter for the flu hereabouts. When it hit St. Alban's, people came crowding into the dispensary. Here's what the new doctor told them.

"'You don't have the flu. What you've got is rheumatic fever. 'Tis pretty bad. You must get into your bed and stay there so long as I says. It could be six weeks, but you got to stay there never moving unless you must or the fever will find your heart and that could be the end of you.'

"There was near seven hundred souls in St. Alban's them times. It should have been a pretty lively place but by the time December come, she was so quiet you'd have thought 'twas a ghost town. By that time half the people was flat on their backs in bed, afraid to move a muscle for fear they'd find their hearts. And the other half was staying in to look after the sick, and deathly afeared they'd come down with the fever too.

"I don't know where it might have ended but Emmy Collier, a right devil of a woman, got suspicious. She wrote a letter to the department in St. John's and when she never got an answer, sent off a telegram. St. John's sent a telegram back to the doctor asking him what was happening.

"Next day the doctor was on the wharf at Milltown ready to catch the steamer, all his gear along with him. He sees Ches Strickland and tells Ches, 'P'raps you better send word to St. John's the folks in St. Alban's is took pretty bad. I'd send it meself but I has to fly back to Dublin to look after me poor old mother.'

"Ches called St. John's and next day a float plane with a doctor aboard shows up at St. Alban's. The doctor took one look ashore and flew right back out. Day after that, planes come in thick as flies to a dead moose and they was full of doctors and nurses and the like.

"They went right at it . . . but do you think they could get them St. Alban's folk out of their beds? Told them as they only had the flu, but nary a one believed them. Them people was taking no chances. After a while they did begin to get their legs under them and hop about, but very, very careful, and 'twas a couple of months afore the last of them left their houses."

The Rodriguez family persevered at St. Alban's for two or three years – until their dream of creating a Shangri-la could no longer be sustained. We never learned what became of them after they left the Bay of Spirits and the island of Newfoundland.

· 18 ·

Basques and Penguins

A spell of splendid autumnal weather set in so we cast off from Milltown and went rambling: first to Conne River, where as usual we anchored off and rowed ashore to visit Michael and Emilia John. Though Emilia was now almost helpless, she still retained her sparkle, pressing our hands warmly and stroking Claire's cheek as fondly as if Claire were her own daughter. Michael did not leave her side for more than a minute or two.

"Not much time left," he murmured in a quiet aside. "Not going to waste none of it."

They insisted we have a meal with them and share a grilse – a young salmon – caught that very morning by one of the younger members of the band. We would gladly have stayed several days at Conne but a sou'west breeze was making up, and when *Happy*

Adventure's anchor began to drag we hurriedly went aboard and got underway.

That night we sheltered in Jack Damps Cove and slept easy under a gigantic moon. In the morning the wind was gone so we motored the short distance to the mouth of Little River. Not to be mistaken for Little Passage, Little River paralleled the Conne. It was singular in that it drained a large and tidal salt-water lake. Ches Strickland at Milltown, who at one time ran a little mill on the river, had told us about it.

"She's a kind of a tickle, you might say, running into the heart of God's country. White pine growed so tall in there one time that navy ships used to get their masts out of it. The bestest timber ever sawed on this coast come from Little River. 'Twas a wunnerful sight . . . afore Bowaters got into it! 'Tis the only place on the Sou'west Coast a man can *sail* right into the country. In that little t'ing of your'n, skipper, you could go far enough to shoot yourself a bear or a moose right from the deck. Here now, I'll sketch you off a chart of it."

Sketch in hand, I poked *Happy Adventure's* nose into Little River. Narrow and steep-sided, it had ample depth but also a furious current from the falling tide and the river's natural flow. Our little ship had to fishtail her way upstream like a salmon. With the engine going full and the propeller churning furiously, it took us two hours to go three miles.

We emerged from the river into a big body of water. Instead of being surrounded by the formidable hills and cliffs that characterized most of Bay Despair, the lake was cradled in rolling lowlands. These had been covered by dense forest but now were mostly reduced to tangles of stumps, felled and discarded trunks, and brush piles – just awaiting a spark before bursting into a monumental conflagration. It was a depressing spectacle. Despite the fine weather, I felt as if we were heading into something akin to Joseph Conrad's *Heart of Darkness*.

Ches's sketch showed an anchorage at the eastern end of the shallow lake. Feeling our way across was tricky work, sometimes with only a foot or two of water under the keel and with the knowledge that if we went aground the falling tide would strand us there until the next high tide. *Happy Adventure* was *not* flat-bottomed so she would fall over on her side if the water ebbed from under her.

Suddenly a ramshackle skiff propelled by a rattling old outboard shot out of a hidden cove toward us. Its unshaven occupant, a shifty-eyed young man, glumly warned us that when the tide was out we would find ourselves high and dry in the middle of a swamp. He may have been trying to get rid of us; I suspected he had a still hidden in his cove. We took no chances. *Happy Adventure* came smartly about and we ran back to Little River. The tide and current soon shot us downstream to the safety of Long Reach, where we set course for Roti Bay.

We were greeted at the mouth of the bay by the big seal who seemed to be its guardian. He accompanied us right to the inner end, where we found an indifferent anchorage on sand bottom in a bowl almost surrounded by barren hills plunging steeply into the water. An ideal place for blow-me-downs. Dropping our heaviest anchor, we rowed ashore, landing on sheets of silvery-coloured slate in which millions of tiny purple garnets were embedded, giving the rocks a glittering iridescence. We were tempted to take the time for some serious prospecting in hopes of finding garnets of gemstone size but were afraid to leave *Happy Adventure* in such an exposed situation. As beautiful as the inner bay was, it wasn't safe to linger so we moved on to Clay Hole, where we went ashore to dig a bucket of clams and fill another with winkles and blue mussels. Windrows of tiny winkle shells stippled the landwash, each with a neat little hole bored into it by a carnivorous snail called the wolf whelk. These pierced and empty shells seemed to beg to be strung together as necklaces. That evening as we ate a supper of clams and mussels in which we found many minute seed pearls, Claire whimsically speculated about the prospects for a jewellery factory in Roti Bay. "Pearl, garnet, and shell necklaces for very *little* people."

After a couple of days and nights of amorous indolence we again set sail, ghosting past Raymonds Point to Harbour le Gallais, a place which had been highly recommended to us by the Dominies. This superb harbour was sheltered by a line of hills crouching like a flock of broody old hens. We anchored in a tight little inner cove separated from Long Reach by a neck of low land and went ashore to explore this grassy spit. It had once been cultivated and still boasted a gnarled old apple tree and a quantity of late but juicy raspberries. There was also a dilapidated tilt ten feet long and eight wide with log walls that stood only three feet high. Despite this, its birchbark-covered roof was so steeply pitched there was headroom inside, where, instead of a stove, was an open hearth with a hole in the roof to serve as a chimney. Two narrow pole bunks cradled mattresses of spruce boughs. There were no windows, and the slab door hung on leather hinges. Cecil Dominie would later tell me he remembered this tilt from his childhood days and that it had been rebuilt several times since then. It stood as an unintended memorial to almost-forgotten times.

Halfway along the spit we came upon three circular depressions, each about twelve feet in diameter, similar to the fire pits built under the great iron or copper cauldrons in which early Basque whalers had rendered whale blubber into oil. Morgan Roberts had found evidence of a forge on this spit, so I searched the shoreline and discovered several lumps of fused coal and ash with metal slag embedded in some of them. I also found a few fragments of bricks and roofing tiles of the sort brought from Europe by fifteenth- and sixteenth-century Basques for the construction of their tryworks.

A more enigmatic discovery was the remains of a stone-built roadway running at least two miles west from Harbour le Gallais past

Patrick Harbour to Grip Island Cove. It appeared to be five or six feet wide except where it had been washed away by the encroaching sea or obliterated by frost settling. Its construction must have demanded great labour. Large foundation stones had first been laid and bedded, then covered with smaller stones carefully fitted to make a "cobbled" surface. Where it passed through bogs and wet places, it had been ditched for drainage.

The purpose of this formidable piece of construction was a mystery. The inhabitants of the abandoned fishing villages of historic times would hardly have built it for they had no wheeled transport and, moreover, like everyone on the Sou'west Coast, travelled and moved their goods almost exclusively by water.

Many years later I was to see roads comparable to it at an excavated and partially restored Basque whaling station in Red Bay, Labrador, dating to the early sixteenth century. These roads had been used to bring cartloads of blubber from shoreside flensing platforms to centrally placed trypots. I believe that, four or five centuries ago, the fires of a Basque tryworks must have been sending pillars of black, oily smoke into the skies above Harbour le Gallais.

The place no longer had human residents, but it had others. Among them was a colony of terrestrial shrimp barely half an inch long, living in burrows along a sandy ridge a good fifteen feet above storm-tide line. Never before, and not since, have I met their like.

The harbour itself held an astonishing abundance and diversity of creatures. Through diving goggles Claire and I watched huge schools of cod minnows and other fry slipping like beams of light among wavering fronds of seaweed. The intertidal zone was home to innumerable razor and soft-shelled clams, and to weird-looking scarlet mud worms, some of them six inches long. The bottom was clustered with masses of blue and horse mussels – the latter being oyster-shaped bivalves weighing up to half a pound. Scattered among them were moon snails as big as oranges. Scores of bay scallops regarded their surroundings through tiny blue eyes dotting the rims of their partially opened shells. Rock crabs with bodies larger than my hand sidled over to me as I waded out, while, deeper down, great green lobsters prowled stealthily.

No man-made aquarium could have compared. Richly fertilized with the flesh and bones of great whales that had been flensed upon its shore, the harbour offered an excellent substitute for the Hill Brothers' Floating Fish Market. Our pram became a shopping cart into which we loaded mussels, clams, scallops, and crabs. I also baited and set an old lobster trap that had washed up on the shore.

One morning I was awakened soon after dawn by a peculiar clacking sound. When I went on deck to investigate, I found a number of scallops the size of soup bowls marooned at the edge of the landwash by the ebb tide. They were flapping upper and lower shells together, a manoeuvre that, when done beneath the surface, would have propelled them through the water as if equipped with miniature pulse-jet engines. When I flipped these stranded ones back into the water, they shot off into the depths like underwater Frisbees.

We spent several idyllic days exploring, swimming nude in the relatively warm waters of the cove, picking berries, and lying on *Happy Adventure's* sun-warmed deck sipping rum and lime while speculating about what the sea might offer for dinner. Perhaps small, delicately fleshed grey sole hooked at the harbour entrance? Or sea trout from Snooks Harbour, which (greatly daring for it lay on the other side of Long Reach) we visited one day in our little pram.

As Jack's arrival date approached, we reluctantly headed back to Milltown. Off Raymonds Point we again crossed paths with a school of white-sided dolphins, nearly colliding with one who may have been dozing on the surface. It was that kind of a day. Long Reach was experiencing that rarity of rarities on the Sou'west Coast: a perfect calm. Not a cat's-paw ruffled the molten surface of the gloriously somnolent bay. I stopped the engine while Claire made clam chowder for our lunch, and the only sound to be heard was the rustle of distant waterfalls.

We were sad to tie up to the Milltown wharf for this was the end of our summer cruise together. Soon Claire would sail for Burgeo aboard the steamer, leaving Jack and me to follow in *Happy Adventure*.

When the *Baccalieu* steamed into Milltown a day late, she had a CBC film crew aboard. The director, Jerry Richardson (unbelievably wearing jodhpurs and a beret), hustled on board *Happy Adventure* to tell me he and his team had come to shoot a film called *Men and Ships* which I was to write and host!

I was stunned to hear it, for I knew nothing about any such film. When I protested, adding that my own plans would prevent me from taking any part in the project, Richardson was not at all disconcerted.

"Well," he said brightly, "we sent you a telegram at Burgeo telling you about it. Now, when and where do we start shooting?"

"God only knows! I never got a wire because I wasn't there. CBC never had an okay from me. Sorry, Mr. Richardson, but I can't just drop everything, not even for the Holy Mother Network."

Richardson was undismayed.

"Okay, then. Guess we'll just ride along on the *Baccalieu* and shoot what we see. You can write the story later."

Captain Riggs, who had come aboard for a chat with Claire and me, listened to this exchange with bewilderment. When Richardson had left us, the skipper shook his head.

"Seems like they television fellows do things ass-backwards, wouldn't you say? A powerful quare lot!"

Although night had fallen and it was too dark for small planes to be flying over the wilderness of central Newfoundland, a little Cessna on floats came whining out of the dusk, made a no-nonsense landing, and taxied to the wharf. Out clambered Jack, suitcase in hand and a half case of rum under his arm. Within the hour, our change of crew had been effected and *Baccalieu* was carrying Claire away.

Jack really should have concealed the rum. As he tried to settle himself aboard *Happy Adventure*, we were inundated with a flow of visitors drawn to us as bees to clover. Dawn found us being nuzzled by the old schooner *Queen of Roses*, who had come bumbling up to the wharf for a load of lumber.

"I hope to God *she* doesn't drink!" was Jack's heartfelt reaction to her arrival.

Soon after first light, we got underway with a beam wind to speed us on our way through Dawson's Passage, past Flobbers Cove, and into Long Reach. By then it was blowing half a gale. *Happy Adventure* stood up to it, red sails drum tight and her rigging taut as fiddle strings. Jack was in an ecstasy and would not hear of it when I wanted to reduce sail, nor would he allow me to put in to Raymonds Point.

"*Drive* her, Farley! Drive her!" he cried, crouched over the tiller, a familiar glitter in his eyes. When we were abeam of Harbour le Gallais, labouring through quartering seas breaking clear across the cabin trunk, I mutinied, pushed Jack out of the cockpit, and ordered him to take in sail while I ran the vessel into shelter.

We snugged down for the night in Patrick Harbour, having had a magnificent sail through a majestic world of wild water and pristine lands. Jack was exultant. He would not go to bed but insisted on sitting on deck until dawn, nominally (and quite unnecessarily) keeping anchor watch, but thinking (or so I imagine) of the not-so-distant days when he had captained a motor torpedo boat in red and roaring action in the English Channel.

When we woke next morning, the gale was still howling through the rigging and huge seas were whitening the length of Long Reach. It was no day to go to sea, and I wanted to walk westward from

Patrick Harbour anyway to see how far I could trace the mysterious stone roadway. As a precaution before leaving *Happy Adventure* on her own, we dropped a second anchor.

We landed the dinghy where the inhabitants of the cove had once been used to pulling up their boats. In 1940, as a consequence of the "hard times" of the thirties, the six families then living here had moved to Head of the Bay hoping to better themselves working in the woods for Bowater. Hardly a trace of their occupancy remained. If the site of their now-vanished houses had not been marked on the 1885 chart of the bay, we might never have located it at all. After a diligent search through the long grass, we turned up a few fragments of a cast-iron stove and two slabs of native granite set on end that, we supposed, were homemade gravestones.

With difficulty, for it was heavily overgrown, we followed the old road to towering Grip Head and the snug cove lying between it and Grip Island. (Grip, an antiquated British term for eagle, is still current on the Sou'west Coast.) We explored Grip Cove's shore, finding no evidence of habitation – except that a section of the landwash within the cove had evidently been cleared of boulders and levelled to form a spacious haul-out. Significantly, the roadway ended here. Its purpose now seemed clear: Grip Head had provided an ideal place to land whale carcasses for cutting up, but Harbour le Gallais offered a much better site for a tryworks, being well protected from the weather and providing safe anchorages for the awkward wooden whaling ships to lie while their cargo was being prepared.

Jack and I continued on to Lobscouse Cove but found no further extension of the road. We built a fire by the shore of that cove and cooked a scoff of potatoes, salt pork, and onions, then sat by the coals drinking black tea and yarning about the lives we had lived during the war, and those we had hoped to lead when peace returned.

"Goddamn it, Farley," Jack said moodily, "I never wanted to spend the rest of my life in an office in Toronto. Why the hell can't you and

I just keep on sailing . . . east . . . south . . . west . . . *anywhere* the fucking wind will take us?"

I had no answer for I was doing just about what he lamented his own inability to do, and I did not want to rub it in. After we had returned to the vessel, he drank silently for a while before crawling into his bunk and going to sleep. His words had unsettled me. Only a few hours of daylight remained but the wind had dropped so I upped the anchors, hoisted sail, and got us underway.

I had it in mind to take a look at a place I'd heard about from John Foote at Pushthrough. This was a cove called Cul-de-sac, six miles north of Pushthrough. Although reputedly a well-sheltered place, it had apparently never been inhabited, not in human memory at least.

"Nobody goes nigh it," John had said.

When I asked why, he had told me told that "a long time ago" the corpse of a giant squid had been found floating at the entrance to Cul-de-sac.

"I never knowed anyone who seed it hisself, but they say 'twas some big. Arms onto it as round as a man's leg and twice as long as a skiff. Eyes the size of saucers, and a beak in its head could have tore a cow apart. 'Tis what the old folks said, and I never heard nothing different. Folks stays clear of Cul-de-sac."

This was the sort of challenge a fool cannot resist. While Jack snored in his bunk I set course for Goblin Head, then altered north across the deep, which here was a stygian abyss the chart said was at least half a mile deep. We were over the centre of the deep when Jack grumpily emerged from the cabin. He looked ahead to where a huge gash gaped between eight-hundred-foot-high cliffs. It led into Cul-de-sac. We entered the gulch under power and travelling dead slow. Warily I eyed the brooding cliffs on either side. Although Jack had scoffed at the giant squid story, I kept an eye on the black, oily-looking water around us, just in case.

The gulch became a canyon a hundred yards wide flanked by ever steeper and higher cliffs. I slowed the engine until we were barely moving while Jack stood in the bows anxiously swinging the lead. I held on until *Happy Adventure* timidly nosed into a walled basin of singularly forbidding aspect. Such was its stark desolation that I offered no argument when Jack came aft and, putting his foot on the tiller, forced it hard over. *Happy Adventure* came about and as we scurried out of Cul-de-sac he apologized.

"Sorry, Farley. I felt like a rat in a trap in there."

Happy Adventure had barely reached open water again when the wind gusted up out of the southeast, blowing hard right into the mouth of Cul-de-sac. I did not care to imagine what might have happened had we anchored in the inner basin. And I forgave Jack his mutinous behaviour.

Well, almost. Knowing full well that he had a delicate stomach, I nevertheless cooked a ripe and somewhat maggoty piece of salt cod for supper. When he turned green around the gills, I felt I had tied the score. I also felt a wee bit guilty so I tried to make amends by offering to take him to the head of Bay the East to another place I had heard about – a door-sized oval hole carved by nature through a rock buttress some hundreds of feet high, accessible only to creatures with wings.

"You'll like it, Jack. It's called Virgin's Hole."

As we motored past Old Harry Head a fitting on the engine gave way, releasing a geyser of hot oil under sixty pounds of pressure. I killed the engine and the vessel, pitching heavily in a rapidly rising sea, began to blow toward Old Harry's rocks and reefs, a hundred yards or so to leeward.

Jack immediately hoisted sail and kept *Happy Adventure* heading into the wind while I replaced the fitting, refilled the reservoir, and started the engine . . . just in time to claw out of Old Harry's grasp.

The engine room was a hellish place, dripping with black oil and so slippery underfoot I had to crawl through it on hands and knees. Regaining the deck, I found Jack holding a course that would clear Pass My Can Island and take us east of Great Jervais Island. By now, however, the wind was gusting to forty knots, and the seas rolling in from the ocean were too big for us to face so we bumbled through a maze of shoals and sunkers to take refuge in Pushthrough.

We moored at a ruined wharf on the east side of the small and crowded harbour. Though we had had a gruelling run, it had restored Jack's happy temper. After we cleaned up the shambles below decks, he went ashore to acquaint himself with a "typical" Newfoundland outport. Meanwhile I twiddled the dial of our little radio, looking for a weather forecast.

I found an "all ships warning" of a full-fledged storm with winds exceeding fifty knots. The only safe moorings in the harbour were already occupied by a dragger and the two schooners *Winnie Pearl* and *Glimshire*. The skippers of both invited me to moor *Happy Adventure* outside of them, but that would have been to court destruction if the storm hauled into the northwest as was predicted.

When Jack came back aboard, we did the only thing we could: let go our lines and skittered down into the northwestern bight of Great Jervais Bay to seek refuge in the nook called Rotten Row, a sort of elephants' graveyard in which generations of derelicts had been condemned to end their days. We felt our way past a number of wrecks but each time *Happy Adventure* eased into what looked like a safe little hole she was blown out of it again.

It was nervous work but finally we found a hole where the anchor caught and held. Hastily we ran lines ashore then rowed our second anchor out and dropped it in position to prevent *Happy Adventure* being driven onto a frothing sunker in our lee.

Williwaw gusts drove rain squalls flat across the seething surface of the bay, battering us from all directions. We did not really care for we were as secure as good anchors and good lines could make us. With the little stove glowing in the cabin and a little rum glowing in our veins, we ate pea soup and biscuits by the flickering light of oil lamps and were content.

Once the storm had passed, we motored back to Pushthrough, where Jack made use of *Glimshire's* radio to try to extend his time away from work. The gods of Business proved unrelenting. His presence back in Toronto was not just required, it was demanded. Since we were now well into the season of autumnal gales, I decided we had best take advantage of whatever good weather was granted us and run like hell for Burgeo, where Jack could catch the steamer to Port aux Basques. If we dallied, there was every likelihood of our being driven into some remote cove en route, to be trapped there for days.

Early next morning we bade a fond farewell to Bay Despair and took the inside passage across Bonne Bay to the open sea. The weather could hardly have been better: a bright, clear day bringing a lively breeze from off the land. Sailing full-and-by *Happy Adventure* slipped along the coast past Richards Harbour, then headed across the broad bight enfolding the grand fiords of Hare, Devil, Rencontre, and Chaleur, intending to close with the land again at the entrance to Aviron Bay.

Things were going so well I was tempted to take a chance with Jack's schedule and do something I had wanted to do since 1957 when I had first travelled this coast aboard the *Baccalieu*.

"We've been going great guns, Jack," I said as we looked at the chart. "The forecast is terrific. We're almost sure to make Burgeo in another day. Two at the most. What say we take a little jaunt off course and go see the Penguin Islands?"

He eyed me dubiously.

"Sun getting to you? Or have you been nipping? I happen to know there're no bloody penguins north of the equator. Penguin Islands! Are you out of your mind?"

"You're right and you're wrong, Jack. There aren't any penguins in the North Atlantic – now. But up until a hundred or so years ago there used to be millions of goose-sized, black-and-white birds that couldn't fly in air but could underwater. They were the original *penguins*. We mostly know them now, if we know them at all, as the great auk."

"Aren't they extinct?"

"Yiss, me son. Slaughtered for oil, meat, eggs, and feathers until by 1860 or 70 there wasn't a damn one left alive. After that the name got transferred to much the same sort of bird in the Antarctic – your modern penguins. But fifteen miles off our port bow is a handful of barren little rocks and islets once a major breeding ground for the great auk, and where it's possible some of the very last of the real penguins lived. I've only seen it from a distance. I'd like to go ashore there. With this breeze we could make it in less than three hours. What say?"

As always, Jack was game.

All went well for a while, but when we were still two or three miles short of our objective the wind went easterly bringing the threat of foggy weather. Already a haze was obscuring the sun and the scattering of tiny islands ahead of us. We were close enough to count and identify most of them . . . and close enough to see great gouts of white water spouting into the air from the impact of the long ocean swell on the rocks, reefs, and sunkers comprising the little archipelago.

Jack looked at me questioningly.

"All right, mate," I said. "This is no place for the likes of us. New course is nor'nor'west-half-north for Grey River. I'll take in sail."

So the Penguins fell astern and I never did get the opportunity to go ashore upon them. But I no longer want to, for they are cemetery rocks. Through the five or six centuries since their discovery by Europeans, they have witnessed some of the most atrocious massacres ever perpetrated by our kind. Although they are not now completely devoid of avian life, what remains is but a thin, sad vestige of what once was. Where millions of great auks, gannets, guillemots, puffins, cormorants, gulls, terns, and sea ducks once congregated to lay their eggs and raise their young, now only a few tens of thousands still gather in early summer to propagate. The twin Gannet Isles, Colombier (Sea Pigeon) Isle, Lord and Lady Islets (the now all but vanished eastern harlequin duck was known as the Lord and Lady Duck), Turr Rocks (Guillemot Rocks), Flat Isle, and Harbour Isle, the only one ever occupied by man, are mostly desolate now. Even the lighthouse on Harbour Isle, once kept by men from Francois, is now an automated robot.

One of the last of the light keepers was Henry Marsden, whom I met in Francois in 1966. He and his father before him, and *his* father before that, had kept the Penguin light through almost a century.

"When our people first come to Fransway they was still penwins out there. Me old granddad see them when he were a youngster. He remembered fleets of English and French fishing vessels laying off the islands on a civil day, sending their boats ashore with most of the crews for to kill birds or take their eggs. They druv the penwins into pens made out of rocks and clubbed they to death. Birds of the flying kind was so many they could kill all they had a mind to just by swinging flails into the air. To make sure the eggs they got was fresh, they'd tromp and smash all the eggs they could see, then come back a day or two after to load up with fresh eggs.

"Them old-timers used to store their ships for the whole summer season with birds and eggs put down in hogsheads filled with salt. But the biggest part of what they took off the Penguins was used for bait in the hook and line fishery. Oftentimes 'twas all the bait they ever needed.

"Vessels come all the way from the Boston States for eggs and feathers. More come across from Spain and Portugal for the ile. They brought along big coppers [cauldrons] and built fires under they, stoked with penwins or other iley birds, sometimes dead, more times still alive. They tried the ile out in the coppers, barrelled it up, and took it aboard for to light the lamps in Europe.

"In me own times fishermen from La Poille to Grey River used to come out in early summer and camp on Harbour Island and fish from there through the hatching season, with birds for bait. 'Twere wunnerful fine trawl bait, certainly. Well, bye, now they's no more birds to speak about . . . nor fish neither. 'Tis the way things goes."

Young Albert.

Shape Changer

Having helped bring *Happy Adventure* home to her mooring in Messers Cove, Jack reluctantly departed on the next westbound coast boat, leaving Claire and me to get on with life in Burgeo.

Perhaps the most momentous event that winter was our acquisition of Albert, a young water dog from La Poille. As big as a Labrador retriever, he was a sway-backed creature, black as ebony except for his white chest, and equipped with webbed feet, the tail of an otter, and the attitude of a lord of the realm. He quickly became an integral member of our little family both ashore and afloat, where he demonstrated that he was a proper seadog: sure-footed, ready for anything, and afraid of nothing.

That summer Claire and I decided to visit a place to the east of Burgeo known to early French mariners as Rivière Enragée, but called by the English settlers Little River, Grey River, or simply River, though in fact it wasn't a river at all. It would have been better described as a fiord, gulf, or bay even if it did partake of some of the qualities of all three.

It was a shape changer. There was an opacity and obscurity about it that had made it notorious on the Sou'west Coast. Everyone had a story about it: generally a derogatory one. Having heard a number of these, we wanted to investigate but it was not until late in July that we could find the time. Claire tells the story of what ensued.

We moved aboard Happy Adventure anchored in the cove below our house and waited for good weather. It came on a Sunday. At first the air was so still the pealing of the church bell sounded as if it were right alongside instead of a mile away but when we got up a little breeze came puffing out of the west.

"Fair breeze making up, skipper!" the elder Sim Spencer called from shore. "Carry you to Portugal if you've a mind to sail there."

"Not going that far," Farley shouted back, but already he was preparing to let go the mooring, while I took the gaskets off the sails.

We sailed slowly eastward under the comforting loom of majestic cliffs and headlands, alone on a vast and quiet ocean. It seemed as if the whole wide world belonged to us and I felt sorry for city friends who couldn't be here to share the wonderful freedom. For lunch we sat in the cockpit and ate bread, cheese, and sardines, and drank red wine from St. Pierre, a standard sort of meal when we were underway in good weather.

By four o'clock we were off the abandoned settlement of Bear Island in the mouth of White Bear Bay, thinking we might anchor here for the night, but there was still lots of light left so we sailed on until Farley pointed the bow toward a barely visible cleft in a wall of rock.

We lowered the sails, started the engine, and were soon steering into a grim-looking canyon, but no sooner had we entered than a wall of turbulent green water rose dead ahead, thundered toward us, and burst over us. Everything loose on deck and below rolled or was washed into the scuppers or the bilges as our ship pitched and tossed as if she were on a roller-coaster ride. Spray drenched me as I hung on with one hand and grabbed at loose objects with the other. Farley clung to the tiller, trying to keep us in the middle of the narrow run, while our dory, which we had in tow, went charging madly off in all directions.

The turbulence ended as suddenly as it had started. We had passed through the narrow entrance to a fiord and were entering a broader stretch of relatively smooth, black water. About a mile ahead I could see a little cluster of houses hemmed in by high, brooding hills reflecting the last glow of the sun.

I wondered how the people there managed to live with furious over-fall at the fiord's mouth. From everything we had heard about them, they were a puzzle. Even the name of their village was uncertain. The chart we were using called it Jerts Cove, though everyone else seemed to know it as Grey River, or just River.

Its three dozen small houses stood out as vividly as images in a child's colouring book. Bunched together at the foot of a rocky slope, they seemed to have been built on one another's shoulders. From high above them a sparkling stream plunged down to run between the houses on its hurried way to salt water.

As we drew closer, we could see a lot of people moving toward the small and rickety wharf. By the time we reached it, most of them had crowded onto it.

We knew that few strangers ever visited Grey River. It was not on the route from anywhere to anywhere. The coastal steamer could enter only when tide, fog, and wind permitted, and when it did manage to get in it seldom stayed more than a few minutes. Very few Burgeo folk had ever been there. They and most other people along the coast seemed to consider the River folk backwoods primitives who talked with a funny accent, wore shabby clothes, were a bit thick between *the ears, and couldn't fathom the worldly ways of their sophisticated cousins in places like Burgeo, Ramea, or Port aux Basques.*

Even the children in Messers Cove made fun of Grey River's reputed sloth and poverty. They told us the people there wore second-hand rags, so that was where Burgeo folk sent old and worn-out clothing. Everyone was on the dole, they said. Burgeo people sang a song about River.

> *You goes down to Grey River,*
> *the sun shinin' down.*
> *You'll see all the young folks*
> *a-layin' around,*
> *waitin' for the steamer*
> *to come down the shore*
> *and bring they their cheques*
> *from the government, sure.*

The provincial government had made several attempts to relocate the Grey River people to some larger centre such as Burgeo, but not a single family had succumbed to the inducements or the threats from St. John's. Even though months might pass without a visit from a doctor, a year might go by without a teacher, or several weeks pass without freight or postal service, River folk seemed unshakeable in their determination to "stay where they were at."

Thirty or forty people of all ages had gathered on the wharf to stare at us as if we were some peculiar creatures the sea had brought to their door. There were blond little girls in faded cotton dresses that hung to a matronly length, little boys in pants with missing knees and shirts with tattered elbows. Almost every child was wearing identical red plastic sandals that, we later discovered, were the only kind of child's footgear available in River's one poor excuse for a store.

The women wore an incongruous assortment of moiré, taffeta, rayon crepe, and faded pastel cotton clothing that had the indefinable aura of castoffs. I knew this was where many of Margaret Lake's and Marie Penney's old clothes ended up, and thought I could recognize some of them, which made me feel embarrassed for the wearers. All the women and the girls over the age of ten were crowned with the same style of home permanent – corkscrew curls as tight as those on a Persian-lamb coat. My hair – straight as a ruler – must have seemed badly out of style.

The older men stood grouped together in the middle of the crowd. Dressed in shapeless and well-worn woollen pants, heavy flannel shirts, and cloth caps, they smoked pipes, chewed tobacco, and watched us fixedly. After what seemed to me like a very long time, one of them ventured a few words to Farley.

"You got only your woman aboard, skipper?"

"That's right. There's just the two of us," Farley replied.

"He's the captain and I'm the crew," I added, hoping to get at least a smile.

Every face remained expressionless.

"Any chance to buy a salmon for supper?" Farley asked no one in particular. Grey River was famous for its salmon.

"No, sir. No fishin' Sundays. 'Tis a sin."

We went below then, resigned to making do with canned bully beef. While we cooked and ate our meal, some of the onlookers drifted away, to be replaced by new ones. Despite their silent vigil, we took our coffee up on deck, where I watched an entire village fade into the obscurity of dusk then reappear as, one by one, oil lamps were lit, bringing a gentle, golden glow to forty or fifty curtained windows. The soft and subtle light seemed to draw the watchers away from the wharf. At last we were left alone. We crawled into our sleeping bags and fell into an impatient sleep, eager as tourists for morning to come and bring the opportunity to explore this strange place.

Grey River's thirty-four houses were crowded into a space smaller than a football field. It was stony, steeply sloping land, directly below a monolithic wall of rock that looked about as accessible as Mount Everest. Apparently no one had ever climbed it. I guessed that life here was challenging enough that people did not deliberately look for ways to make it harder.

A gravelled path led up the slope from the wharf into the haphazard knot of houses and sheds. The houses were the usual square, two-storey structures of outport Newfoundland, but even more colourful than usual. Some were turquoise with canary-yellow door and window trim; some pink with blue doors; some orange with green porches.

Although several boats had been fitted with make-and-break engines, there was not one motorized vehicle on the land. In fact, the only things on wheels were a few wheelbarrows. There were not even any horses because there was no pasture and, anyway, a horse would have to have been half mountain goat to get about. There were scraggy-looking sheep wandering everywhere, foraging on meagre tufts of greenery growing from crevices in the rocks. The sheep even crowded hungrily into the cemetery, which was the one patch of level ground that hadn't been pressed into service for a house site or a garden. Every tiny patch of usable soil was surrounded by a stick fence to protect a few precious potatoes or turnips from the plague of sheep.

All of this was more or less familiar to us, except for one thing. There were no dogs. There was only our Albert, who stayed close to our heels, a little intimidated by the hordes of sheep, which, far from being afraid of him, crowded around as if about to mob him.

Grey River children were as curious as the sheep. As we wandered through the community, women cautiously drew back the curtains to peer out at us and men eyed us askance from sheds and fish stages. But the children's interest in us was so intense it overcame their shyness.

Soon a coterie of youngsters was following close behind, their numbers growing until we formed a Pied Piper procession. They were fascinated by Albert because, we would learn, most had never before seen a dog except when a fishing schooner came into the River with a dog aboard. Dogs were not welcomed and no dog had roamed around River for at least half a century until we brought Albert ashore.

The children were making the most of this novelty. Had he been a camel or a giraffe, Albert could hardly have excited them more. When one brave youth actually dared touch his back, there was such a shout from the rest of the children that Albert lost his usual bold composure and headed back for the boat.

An outport lacking a contingent of black water dogs seemed an inexplicable thing to us. We questioned several residents about it, but the River folk were evasive. It wasn't until near the end of our visit that we got a clue about this mystery, and not until some months later that we were able to unravel it.

The children seemed to accept us but the adults we encountered on our walk gave only polite nods in passing. Except for one hefty woman with an inquisitive expression who bravely accosted us at her garden gate.

"I heard they was strangers comin' round so I says I got to see 'em for myself," she proclaimed, staring expectantly at us.

"Well, it's a fine day," Farley offered.

"Yiss, me dears, fine day for the wash."

While swatting at black flies we chatted about her potato garden and about our "pretty little boat."

"Don't have no stomach for boats meself," she told us, "though when me man gits home he'll take we in the dory up to Seal Brook berry pickin'."

"Is your husband away at sea?" I asked.

"No, me dear girl; he's gone bukams. Been gone a nice while, he has. Gone bukams last year besides."

We didn't understand what she was talking about so when we were out of earshot, we asked the children what she meant.

"Means her man gone bukams, sure," one lad replied with evident surprise at our ignorance. Since he didn't seem ready to elaborate, we dropped the subject. Perhaps, we thought, the poor man was in a sanatorium or an asylum.

We came to a grey-haired, elderly fellow sitting on the deck of a canary-yellow house, whittling. A dozen hens kept him company, and perhaps gave him courage because he beckoned with his knife and called out, "Fine day to ye, skipper, and you too, missus."

"That it is," Farley replied. "What are you busy making?"

"Me brooms, is all. Come up on deck if you've a mind. You and your woman, come up now. Henry Young be my name."

We unlatched the gate and climbed up on the porch, to find him carving something that looked almost as ancient as the concept of a house itself. It was a broom made from a four-foot length of a young birch tree. Originally about two inches in diameter, it had been reduced to half that by a thousand deft knife strokes splitting paper-thin shavings from the top end toward the bottom, where they hung down like a woman washing her hair. The shavings were then bound around with a strip of willow bark to form a thickly tufted head somewhat longer than that of a store-bought straw broom. As we watched the long shavings grow magically toward the end of the stick Henry was working on, he told us he made hundreds of these brooms every year.

"Sells 'em to the fish plants up and down the coast. Finest kind for sweeping they wet cement floors. Plants pay I fifty cents a bundle for six brooms. Got ten bundles going off on the steamer tomorrow, and she comes in."

I picked up a finished broom that was leaning against the wall. It looked exactly like the kind ridden by witches in the fairy tales I had read and looked at as a child.

Grey River country.

At this point Henry's wife timidly opened the door, having nerved herself to speak to me.

"Come in, me dear. Can't bide out here with the men. Come into me kitchen, sure. I'll bile the kettle."

Her smile revealed that, like so many outport women of her generation, she had no teeth at all. I followed her in and she shoved a huge, cast-iron kettle over to the hot side of the wood range. "This old thing," she said, noticing my interest in the battered kettle, which could have been a museum piece from the Middle Ages, "belonged to me poor old grandmother, it did, and her grandmother too. Foinest kind, it be. I leaves the water into it all night and it never colours. Yiss, me dear, the foinest kind."

Now that the ice was broken she became as friendly as a puppy, keeping up a steady patter of conversation, only part of which I could understand. She used the same dialect spoken in Burgeo but with a different cadence. Though the two settlements were only about thirty miles apart as the gull flies, she herself had never been so far afield and Henry had been to Burgeo only three times in all his life.

We got back to the wharf just as a shabby workboat from the Lakes' plant in Burgeo arrived. The Lump, as the plant workers called this relic, was used for such messy chores as hauling loads of fish gurry out to sea to dump. We were surprised to see her so far from home and even more to see the Reverend Mark Genge aboard. Based in Burgeo with his young family, he had the charge of the three parishes of Burgeo, Ramea, and Grey River.

"Did you have a good voyage in that old stinkpot?" Farley asked.

"Oh yes. Thank the Lord it's a mausey day [a civil day]." He mopped his high brow with his handkerchief. "And we came in on the slack of the tide. I'm no sailor, you know, but this morning 'twas smooth as ile."

We invited him aboard for something to settle his nerves and his stomach.

Farley wanted to know why the bishop would send him to the Sou'west Coast, given that he was a poor sailor.

"Somebody had to come," Mark replied with cheerful stoicism. "And I'm enjoying it. There're so many good people and so much work to be done in the parishes – so very much."

"How often do you get to Grey River?" I wondered.

"Not often enough. I take the coast boat or a lift on anything happens to come this way. I rarely get here Sundays, but the people don't care. They don't expect miracles," he said, laughing.

"But this place has special problems."

He paused and I could see he was reluctant to describe his smallest and poorest parish in an unkind way. "They're very independent, the River people. They've had to be to survive."

"Any idea how long they've been here?" Farley asked.

"Not really. The markers in the cemetery are made of wood and only last a generation or two. My oldest parishioner, Annie Warren, *thinks she is ninety-eight and she tells me her grandmother was born here. That would go back to about 1800. We just don't know. We do know, from their surnames, that many of their ancestors must have come from England – Dorset and Devon mostly – like most English-speaking folk on this coast. Historically it has been overlooked."*

Farley nodded. *"Easy to see why. You can sail along this coast even on a clear day and never even see the entrance."*

"But isn't it surprising, once you've got in, the way it changes?" Mark added. *"All the runs and tickles full of trout and salmon. Trees in all the valleys. A land of plenty, you'd think. Have you been farther up? Into the arms?"*

"We're going this afternoon," Farley replied. *"Care to come along?"*

"I'd dearly like to," Mark said wistfully, *"but I've got so much to do before the westbound steamer comes in tomorrow. The church is falling down, and I still haven't found a teacher for the school. Nobody from outside wants to spend the winter in River."*

"Mark, why does everyone look down their noses at this place?" I asked.

He shook his head as if embarrassed. "Perhaps because most people like to feel superior to someone else. I'd rather not go into it, if you don't mind. There are many stories, and probably they are just that – stories. Thanks for the drink. I must be getting along. Aunt Fannie always has dinner for me when I arrive."

"Aunt Fannie?"

"Fannie Young. Fine woman. Very kind. She usually boards the teacher, and she runs the telegraph. Something of an unofficial leader. No one would acknowledge she has any special position but not much gets done without her instigation or approval."

"Any relation to Henry Young, the broom maker?" I asked.

He pondered the question. "I don't think so, Claire, but you have to remember about two-thirds of the people here have the surname

Young. I still haven't sorted out who is cousin or aunt or uncle to whomever else."

"One more question. Can you tell me what it means when someone here says 'gone bukams'?"

"Bukams? Oh, you must mean Buchans. That's a mining company in the middle of Newfoundland. A lot of Grey River men go there to work as guides for the prospectors because they are all first-rate countrymen. There's a saying on the coast they are more like Indians than the Indians. It's certainly true they prefer to be inland rather than at sea. One of the things that makes them different."

Not far north of the settlement the fiord branched into three arms. The longest led to the northeast, another to the east, and a shorter one to the westward. We stopped the engine and drifted while we studied the chart, trying to decide which way to go.

The chart itself was an adventure. It had been laid down in the 1760s by the celebrated Captain Cook, long before he sailed to fame and death in the South Pacific. He had been just thirty-five when he explored the Newfoundland coast for the British Admiralty, and the charts he made then were still essentially the ones we had before us now.

"God almighty, look at the depths!" said Farley, looking at our chart. "Two hundred fathoms below us and thirty fathoms right to the shore! Our anchor chain wouldn't reach the bottom till we ran our bowsprit into the cliffs. And see how many headlands he called Blow-me-down! But it looks as if there might be a safe cove we could crawl into away up in the eastern arm."

There was, and it was spectacular: a niche about the size of a small ballroom, surrounded on three sides by spruce trees clinging to almost sheer cliffs, with a weightless filigree of a tiny stream floating down. Called the Nook, it was small enough so Farley could string mooring lines ashore from bow and stern, making use of some very old mooring rings set into the rocky walls that he said were wrought iron and big enough to hold a full-rigged ship.

Next day we scrambled to the top of the cliff looming high above to look for the source of the waterfall. When we reached the crest, we found ourselves on a bald ridge separating Grey River's eastern arm from the open sea boiling into Gulch Cove, six hundred feet below. The view was spectacular. We could see south to the Penguin Islands and beyond.

Surely we weren't the first to appreciate this wonderful vantage point. A lookout here could have kept an eye open for anything coming or going to seaward for twenty miles. If it was an enemy on the horizon, you would have had lots of warning. If it was a potential prize, there would have been plenty of time to spring a trap. What a lair the Nook would have made for buccaneers!

During the days that followed – most of them sunny and warm – we explored the arms in our dory. On a flat point of gravel and sand between the western and northeast arms, we found old circular tent pits and bits of flint marking what must have been a camping place used by aboriginal peoples for a long time. Grey River – an actual river that empties into the northeast arm – is one of the longest on the island. Its headwaters almost connect it to Red Indian Lake, the Beothuks' last refuge. From there the Exploits River runs all the way to the northeast coast of Newfoundland. This was once the major north and south canoe route right across the island for the Beothuks, then for the Mi'kmaqs, then for European "furriers."

One night in our lamp-lit little cabin Farley mused about that. "Buccaneers and Red Indians. Both of them outside the law and every man's hand against them. I wouldn't wonder if they got together in more ways than one . . . and if some of them are still here in Grey River."

One day we rowed to a little brook on the north side of the eastern arm. Though Seal Brook was small enough to jump across, it was swarming with sea trout about a foot long. We caught enough for dinner, then picked blueberries to be eaten with canned milk and sugar for dessert. There was a bit of a sandy beach covered with wild peas at the mouth of the brook. The peas were so tiny it took me over an hour to gather and shell enough for a meal. I didn't mind. I was learning to appreciate the Newfoundland phrase: "Dey's lots o' toime, me dear. Lots o' toime."

Another morning I woke to the sound of something squishy flapping around in the cockpit. When we went on deck, we found there had been a run of squid into the cove during the night and a falling tide had stranded some in pools among the shore rocks. Albert was a born fish-dog. He loved to eat any kind of fish and could catch them too. As far as he was concerned, squid were fish, so he had been busy snapping them up one by one and carrying them back to drop them in the cockpit, where they squirmed about and shot black ink all over everything.

Farley cleaned several squid, which I stuffed with salt pork and wild peas and baked in our tiny folding oven. They tasted wonderful, though Albert preferred to eat his share raw.

In the evenings we read and at 8:00 p.m. would turn on our small battery radio to hear the familiar voice of Harry Brown at CBN in St. John's reading the marine forecast:

". . . And now the weather for mariners and ships at sea . . ." came the faint, static-ridden voice. ". . . moderate to strong southeast winds with visibility reduced to three miles, lowering to zero in mist and fog." Since the marine forecasts tended to err on the side of optimism, this meant that if we left the shelter of our idyllic cove, the fog would likely be so thick on the outer coast we wouldn't be able to see our hands in front of our faces, so any idea we might have had of sailing farther east was forgotten. Grey River seemed to have the best weather in Newfoundland so we happily decided to enjoy its seclusion.

For nine days we did just that, never seeing another person. We were at peace there as I have seldom been before, and rarely since.

Our time in Grey River was running out. Reluctantly Claire and I hauled the anchor and sailed back to the settlement, a gentle northerly breeze pushing us along and clear skies overhead, although there was a sou'east gale raging along the outer coast. The storm outside was fierce enough to drive the old schooner *Queen of Roses* into shelter. She was moored to the wharf so we made fast alongside, then went aboard her for a chat with her skipper.

I thought he would be incredulous when I told him what the weather was like a few minutes and a few miles inland, but he just nodded.

"Yiss, me son. River be like that. Makes her own weather. Don't like nothing from outside. Specially strangers. I'd say you and your missus was some lucky you had no trouble. Most folk gives River a wide berth. When the *Queen* has to put in here, I sees to it all hands minds they ways. Don't want no foolishness here. Don't even let me old dog go ashore. They don't abide dogs in Grey River."

"We've noticed there are no dogs. Why would that be?"

"Well, skipper, you don't hear it spoke too loud but 'tis said that in the old times River folk was so foolish they'd not put by enough grub to last the winter . . . and when they run out, they'd bile the dogs."

"But why would that turn them against dogs now?"

"P'raps to spike the tale. If they was no dogs in River, how could they have et 'em? See?"

Claire and I puzzled over the anomaly of a dogless Newfoundland outport. It made little sense. Not long after returning to Burgeo, I asked Spencer Lake if he could throw any light on the mystery. Spencer told me that the dog-eating "claptrap" had originated in the

1880s after a pair of Nova Scotian men trawling for halibut from dories belonging to a banking schooner became separated from the mother ship during a sudden snowstorm.

"It was January, and wicked weather. Those two men in their dory couldn't find their schooner, but three days later happened onto Grey River. By then one fellow was frozen to death and the other had both his hands froze solid to the oars.

"Those times houses in places like River stood empty in winter because people went away into the country to live in tilts in places where there was plenty of firewood. Luckily a few River people were wintering at Frenchman's Cove only a few miles in and they came upon the dory.

"The long and the short of it is they rescued the survivor and looked after him as best they could all the rest of the winter because he was too knocked about and sick with gangrene in his feet and hands to be taken anywhere else. Come spring he was well enough so they could sail him in an open boat to Burgeo. By then he'd lost all his fingers and most of his toes. The men who brought him to Burgeo also brought those bits of him along in a wooden box so they could be buried with him if he died here, as they thought he would.

"Instead, he got better and went on by steamer to Nova Scotia and never took his toes and fingers with him. Nobody knew what to do with the bits so they asked Sam Small, the chief merchant here, and Sam said to bury them in the churchyard, where I suppose they still are.

"The tale got around that the poor chap had spent a terrible winter at Grey River in a cabin with nothing to eat but seaweed and dog meat. Well, of course, that story went all up and down the coast and the River people couldn't shake it. So at some point they decided to be rid of dogs entirely. How they were able to make out without dogs for hunting and hauling boggles me, but that's what they did, and still do. As far as River folk are concerned, dogs don't exist."

A few months later, when Claire and I were visiting Boston, I told my editor Peter Davison about the Grey River dogs.

"Grey River wouldn't happen to be the same place as *Little River*, would it?" he asked. "If so, I might have something to add to your story."

He gave me a book recently published by his own firm. It was called *Lone Voyager*, the biography of Nova Scotian fisherman, Howard Blackburn, who, early in the twentieth century, became famous in New England for sailing small boats across the Atlantic – not once, but twice, and single-handed both times. Moreover, Blackburn had accomplished this feat despite having lost all the fingers from both his hands.

It was Blackburn's fingers that rested in Burgeo's churchyard.

The book, together with excerpts from Blackburn's own account, provided some graphic descriptions of Grey River just before the turn of the last century.

On the bitter winter's day in January of 1883 when the castaway's dory drifted ashore at Little River (as he knew the place), Blackburn was met by a crowd of "thin and tattered folk . . . children running about bare-foot despite the rind of snow and ice along the shore . . . [and] by a pack of yelping dogs."

He was carried over the ice-edge and across the frozen landwash to a little group of log cabins and taken into the home of Frank Lushman and his family. His recollections of the cabin centred on a massive stone fireplace in the middle of the dirt floor and on the absence of lamps or even candles. There were only oil-filled saucers with floating wicks to illuminate the low-ceilinged, smoke-filled principal room and the two adjacent cubbyholes that served as bedrooms for the seven members of the Lushman family.

Soon after Howard's arrival, a wooden tub filled with slush and pickling salt was brought in from outside and he was told to submerge his frozen hands and feet in this frigid brine.

"I will say no more about the agony I was compelled to undergo while the frost was slowly driven out."

The five families occupying Frenchman's Cove shared what little they had with Blackburn but their scant stocks of flour and meal were almost exhausted. The caribou had failed to come down to the coast that winter, and even salt cod was running out. By February the only source of fresh meat available was their dogs.

One by one the dogs disappeared into the black iron pot suspended over the fire. Blackburn claimed he could not bring himself to eat the meat, but said he was thankful for the broth.

Each morning Mrs. Lushman and her eighteen-year-old daughter, Nan, trimmed the rotting flesh and bone from Howard's gangrenous hands and feet, then dressed the stumps as best they could.

It was fifty-one days from the loss of my first finger until the last fell off. Helpless as an infant I lay on a straw mat by the fire. My feet would not bear my weight and there was nothing I could do for myself. My life was in these people's hands. Every morning for the first two months someone would come in and say:

"Well, Skipper Frank, how is that man this morning?"

Skipper Lushman would always tell them:

"He will never see another sun rise."

I got so used to that I did not mind it.

One morning a man came in just after they had dressed my hands and feet and said:

"How is that man this morning?"

Skipper Frank answered:

"My God, he is going to live!"

*I turned to ask him why he thought so but the other man saved
me the trouble. He asked first, and Skipper Frank said:*

*"This is the first morning since the poor man has been with us that
I have noticed any steam from his water."*

Howard Blackburn also remembered having seen sixteen dogs when
he first came to Little River. Only one remained to watch his departure when, in mid-May, he was placed in Skipper Frank's skiff and
returned to the outer world.

ᐧ 20 ᐧ

Winter of Their Times

One autumn, at Jack McClelland's urging, I decided a book about outport life might be worth doing. Jack agreed, but wanted it illustrated so I invited photographer John de Visser to come and spend some time with Claire and me.

John arrived early in February and soon afterwards we seized an opportunity to visit Grey River with Mark Genge. We were to make the voyage in the *Geraldine*, a forty-foot longliner from Ramea that had been fished hard for twenty years until, as our neighbour Sim Spencer put it, she got too long in the tooth for it. Then John Penney and Sons used her as a smack for collecting fish caught at Grey River, Fransway (or Francois), and Rencontre. When she became too decrepit even for this, the company began chartering her to government officials and other unwary strangers for trips along the coast. Now a hapless St. John's bureaucrat had hired her for a trip to Grey River to inspect the government wharf there, and Mark had begged permission for himself and us to go along.

The voyage did not begin well. Although the cold but relatively calm weather was civil enough, *Geraldine*'s old engine broke down not long after leaving Burgeo, and we had to be ignominiously towed into Ramea harbour. The ever-hospitable Marie Penney invited us to her mansion while *Geraldine* was being repaired. That evening we dined at Marie's opulent table on a baron of beef and a twenty-pound salmon, while her major-domo kept our glasses filled.

The table talk centred on the fate of two large side draggers and their thirty-six crewmen, all from the Sou'west Coast, who had vanished a few weeks earlier while fishing on the Grand Banks in frigid and gale-ridden weather. Both had reported by radio that they were experiencing severe icing, with driven spray freezing so thickly to their rigging and upper works the crews were unable to clear it off. When, later that raging night, both ships went off the air, never to be heard from again, it was presumed they had lost stability and turned turtle, going down so suddenly there had been no time to send an SOS.

Marie's distress over this disaster was sincere (Ramea alone lost nine men), yet she must have been fully aware, as were most of the rest of us, that the missing ships, bought second-hand from Britain, had not been designed or constructed to endure the horrendous conditions prevailing on the Grand Banks in winter. I knew about them from the skipper of one that had limped into Burgeo a few weeks earlier with a twenty-degree list, so heavily burdened with ice she looked almost as much like a berg as a ship.

"They's warm-water boats," her skipper had told me. "Good enough for the summer fishery, I daresays. No better'n man-traps in a winter gale when 'tis freezing hard. Aye, the plants got they cheap enough. 'Twill be us as pays the price."

Marie Penney's accountant, a St. John's man who was sitting beside me at her table that evening in Ramea, put it somewhat differently, "Unfortunately the fishery is a risky business, and we all have to share those risks. Most everyone does so willingly, I believe. Newfoundland fisherfolk wouldn't expect it to be any other way."

We made an uneventful passage from Ramea to Grey River. Closing with the snow-streaked and ice-sheathed cliffs that masked the entrance, we shot through the narrows on a rising tide to moor alongside the decrepit wharf.

This was my third visit to Grey River, and I thought I had established good relations with its residents. To my surprise and chagrin, I was met this time with overt hostility. Previously I had been friendly with Frank Young, a man of my own age who, like me, was a veteran of the recent war. He was on the wharf with a number of other men as we came alongside. When I greeted him, he shook a fist at me.

"Best you stays aboard dat t'ing and goes on wit' her, or could be the worse for ye!" he warned. "And de fellow wit' de camera too!" he added.

We were lucky to be in the minister's company. Telling us to remain aboard for the moment, Mark went ashore to see what was bothering the stony-faced men on the wharf.

It did not take him long to find out. Six months earlier I had written an article about the coast-boat service for *Maclean's* magazine. Titled by the magazine's editor "Any Old Port in a Storm," the piece had been an affectionate look at the steamers, their crews, and the outports they served so well. Unfortunately, it had been illustrated with a drawing of a mythical outport that, by pure coincidence, looked somewhat like River. Furthermore, the scene was peopled with caricatures of what the Toronto artist thought Newfoundlanders looked like. A copy of this magazine had somehow made its way to

Grey River and the inhabitants had concluded I was making mock of them. As Mark explained it, "They were fit to be tied. Only it was you they wanted to tie . . . to a stake."

Although they listened to Mark's assurances that I had meant no harm (River folk would not call a clergyman a liar), few of them, especially the Young clan, were inclined to forgive and forget. They believed they had every right to be furious with me for exposing them to contempt and ridicule if nothing worse. Mark managed to establish a truce of sorts before he went off to stay at the home of Aunt Fannie Young, widow of Tom Young, who had been in effect the king of Grey River. Aunt Fannie, a wise and witty woman in her seventies, retained some of her husband's authority. Now she exercised it with Solomonic skill by sending de Visser and me to stay at the home of Frank Young's widowed mother, Melita.

"Hospitality is as sacred here as in the tents of the Bedouin Arabs," Mark explained, "so, whether he likes it or not, that makes Frank Young your protector."

Aunt Melita gave us her best bedroom. Though not much bigger than a horse stall, it was spotlessly clean. We shared its sagging double bed whose mattress, rather loosely stuffed with seabird feathers, smelt of the ocean and long-departed fish. An ornate chamber pot under the bed posed no problems for me, though John could not bring himself to use it. Nor did he care to avail himself of the holes in the floors of the fish-splitting rooms at the seaward ends of fishing stages. He yearned for privacy, but River was so tightly encompassed by cliffs and water that such was virtually impossible to find.

We tended to keep close to Mark. One bitterly chill morning we accompanied him as he gave communion to Aunt Fannie's mother, ninety-eight-year-old Lizzy Warren. Though bedridden, Lizzy, at her own insistence, lived alone in the tiny house she had come into at her marriage, cared for by members of her extensive family. Unable to speak, she was nonetheless intensely aware. There was no doubt that she thoroughly enjoyed our visit, especially the communion wine, which she sipped with lip-smacking relish, refusing to relinquish the chalice until it had been drained.

The single downstairs room, which had originally served as kitchen, dining, and living room, was the old lady's bedroom. Long ago its earthen floor had been covered with worn sails soaked in tar then covered with sand to produce a surface not unlike linoleum. Over the years rough-sawn wooden walls had been covered by layers of painted canvas until they had acquired something of the cracked and murky patina of Old Masters' paintings. A huge and ornate cast-iron stove dominated the room, whose sparse furniture included two or three birch-framed chairs with seats woven from caribou rawhide.

The walls bore only a single decoration: a large and yellowed photographic enlargement hanging slightly askew in a frame glued together with bits of cloth. The picture was of a raffish-looking, heavily moustachioed man in a cloth cap standing on a wharf beside a worn-looking woman dressed in black. The pair stared fixedly at the camera as the man passed the woman a bottle of what might have been cassia wine from St. Pierre. Although the photo had been dimmed by decades of wood smoke seeping from the kitchen range, I could see that the couple were toothless.

"Nary a dentist on the coast, those times," Mark explained as we walked away from the house. The woman in the photo was Lizzy Warren herself, he said, but Mark did not know who the man might have been – perhaps Lizzy's husband.

"Maybe she was thinking of him and that picture when she drank the communion wine. I hope she was. Poor old thing never had much happiness in her life. Widowed by the Great War, she supported herself and several children by cutting birch logs way back in the country to sell for firewood to visiting vessels. She and her elder children had to haul the wood on little slides for they had no dogs, you know. They hauled the birch billets miles and miles over rocky barrens, then down the cliffs to the cove along a gulch so narrow it is barely passable to a man on foot. A week of cutting and hauling might have fetched Lizzy fifty cents from the cook of some fishing schooner forced into the cove by weather.

"Certainly those were hard times in Newfoundland, especially in remote little places like this. Yet they were all in the same boat, so nobody was better off than any other. It was all for one and one for all – a way of dealing with life we seem to be fast forgetting."

All but a handful of the River folk were Youngs, Lushmans (sometimes spelled Lishmans), or Warrens. Lushmans constituted the second-largest clan, and Fred Lushman, grandson of the Skipper Frank who had been instrumental in saving Howard Blackburn, was their doyen. An eighty-year-old with a failing heart, he shared his home with three "loan children," two boys and a girl.

Loan children were an integral part of the coastal communities. It was normal practice for large outport families (and most *were* large) to "loan" children to people who had none of their own, especially to older folk and those who were incapacitated. Thus it was that, by mutual agreement, Frank Young's oldest son lived with his grandmother Melita, while another and younger son made *his* home with Aunt Fannie. This custom also had the advantage of spreading the burden of feeding and clothing children throughout the community. Since everyone lived in everyone else's pocket, loan children suffered no sense of alienation or loss of familial identity. Furthermore, they acquired stature in their own eyes and in the eyes of their peers by shouldering responsibilities for their elders. They earned the affection and regard of the older people, who automatically became surrogate aunts and uncles.

Mark took me to visit Uncle Fred Lushman, with whom we drank endless cups of tea served by the shy twelve-year-old granddaughter who looked after his kitchen needs.

Fred described in loving detail the life he had led as a furrier and countryman. In July of almost every year of his adult life, when canoe travel was at its best, he had paddled a hundred miles or more inland to Bear Pond (really a lake – many Newfoundland lakes are called "ponds") to a cabin rebuilt time and again by four generations of Lushmans. Here he would spend the summers quite alone, readying his outlying camps, drying or smoking caribou meat and fish, and cutting firewood to last during the long winter months ahead, which would see him snowshoeing through the forests and across the barrens trapping martin, lynx, otter, wolves, and foxes.

Fred never harmed the bears. He regarded them almost as companions in a world where he might not encounter a fellow human being for weeks on end. Nor did the bears bother him. It was as if a pact existed between them.

Early in February Fred would close out his traplines and set out for home, dragging a slide piled with furs over the still-frozen water routes. If, as sometimes happened, he was caught by an early thaw, he would pitch camp and remain where he was until the ice was gone from rivers and lakes. He would use this time to build himself a canoe of willow or birch branches sheathed with caribou hides, in which to complete his journey to the coast.

Arriving back at the settlement, he would exchange his furs for credit at a small store owned by the Penneys of Ramea, a credit that he could only hope would be large enough to provide for his family's needs.

I noticed he wore a bear's incisor hung from a brass chain around his neck. The great tooth glowed like an opal from long and intimate contact with his skin.

"'Tis what I keeps to mind I of them times," he said softly when I admired it. "I misses them bears some bad. They never done no harm to I, nor I to they."

He had something else to show us. Twelve years earlier while gunning for turrs at the mouth of Grey River, he had shot a "pinwin." He described the bird as goose-sized "wit' stubs for wings . . . mostly black and white it were, wit' a bill onto it like a splitting knife."

His description was so evocative of a great auk that momentarily I entertained the wild hope some of the vanished birds might have survived into our times. Responding to my excitement, Uncle Fred sent a boy to fetch the bird's "head bone" from among the rubbish stored in a nearby shed. The lad brought back a skull with the spearlike mandible of a yellow-billed loon. Largest of the loons, and a rarity even in the High Arctic where I had encountered it two decades earlier, it is virtually unknown in Newfoundland. My disappointment was eased by the realization that at least the memory of the penguin still survived here, a mere dozen miles from the clutch of sea-swept islets where multitudes of great auks had lived and bred.

We were still at River when February went out like a lion and March roared in like a polar bear, bringing freezing rain, pelting sleet, and a huge sea pounding against the coastal cliffs. In the midst of this fearsome weather *Geraldine*, looking even scruffier and more dishevelled than usual, arrived to take us home. First, though, Skipper Linton told us he would divert to Fransway to deliver supplies to Penney's store there.

Heedless that there was still, in his own words, "a living starm outside," he decided to depart for Fransway forthwith. Mark wisely declined to go, preferring to wait for the long-overdue coastal steamer to pick him up and take him back to Burgeo. We *should* have followed suit but I was so anxious to take advantage of an opportunity to turn de Visser and his cameras loose on Fransway that I insisted we board the old smack, where she lay grinding and thumping against the wharf.

Built of local spruce, *Geraldine* had several times been repaired above decks but her bottom had never been replanked. In consequence she was "cheesy" below the waterline, a condition that made her especially vulnerable in heavy weather. She really should properly have been condemned, and probably would have been had Linton Oxford not been her skipper.

A short, squat, morose man of about sixty, Linton was widely reputed "not to give much of a damn" whether he lived or died. His wife was a termagant who would not allow him to enter their prim, spotless, and childless house wearing boots or working clothes, nor would she permit him to smoke, drink, or entertain his friends and shipmates there. In consequence, he had long since taken to spending more and more of his time aboard the *Geraldine* until he could hardly be persuaded to go ashore at all.

His crew for this voyage consisted of a skinny youth from Sydney who had a guitar and fancied himself a troubadour. The other crewman served as cook and sometime engineer.

Rivière Enragée was living up to its ancient name. Fuelled by a falling tide, three days of gales, and a stupendous southerly sea, it had become a chaos of the waters. One look was enough to convince me that *Geraldine* would certainly founder if she dared the narrow exit. I assumed our skipper would think so too and turn back to wait for better weather, but I did not know Linton Oxford. *Geraldine* plunged into the maelstrom at full throttle.

The cook vanished into the engine room. A terrified troubadour crawled into the forepeak to await his end. De Visser and I huddled in the narrow confines of the wheelhouse, holding on for dear life as the old vessel pitched, tossed, and corkscrewed. Her skipper seemed stitched to the wheel, except that every now and again he would pop up and down like a yo-yo. This was because he was so short he could barely see out the window. Not that it mattered much. There was precious little to see except walls of water and a dizzying vortex of swirling snow and spume.

Somehow *Geraldine* endured until Rivière Enragée spat us out into the heaving grey wastes of the open ocean. Then our skipper put the wheel down and set a course as close as he dared to the coastal cliffs. Masked as they were by curtains of spray, they were unreliable visual guides. I think he must have taken his bearings largely from the chilling sound of mighty seas bursting against unyielding rock.

Then the engine quit.

Wind and water began to drive us helplessly back to the west-ward. The cook appeared in the companionway to tell us the gas line was clogged. Brusquely ordering me to take the wheel, Linton plunged below, where he and the cook disassembled the fuel system and cleared it, spilling a gallon or so of gasoline into the bilges in the process. The fumes filled the wheelhouse, and when Linton pressed the starter button I expected us to go up in roaring flames. But no, the engine caught and we were again underway, labouring painfully eastward down the coast.

Now the skipper tried to contact Fransway on the ship-to-shore radio. His antiquated transmitter would work only if he thrust a pencil into its guts and wiggled it around until some errant and unseen wire made contact. I watched tensely, for much might depend on his success. *Geraldine* was not well equipped with survival gear. She had no life jackets and, although she did have an old dory strapped across her stern, its bottom had been stove in by some long-ago accident and never properly repaired. The radio would be our only hope if things were to go lethally wrong.

Grey River and Fransway are only twenty miles apart. Three hours of punching through the blizzard had put us about halfway between the two, yet Linton was unable to raise either on the radio. Finally he flicked the pencil away in disgust.

Through *Geraldine's* frosted windows, I could see an ominous encrustation of ice building on her foredeck. As its weight increased, her bows plunged deeper and deeper into the heaving seas. There seemed to be nothing we could do about it. Anyone venturing out on deck to try to beat off the ice would almost certainly have gone overboard. But our skipper had a trick up his sleeve. He put the wheel hard over and headed the old boat toward the cliffs, while John and I clung to the wheelhouse stanchions and eyed each other with a wild surmise. Through the starboard window I glimpsed a black loom of rocks streaming with cascades of foam. *Then we saw boiling surf close on the other side!*

I shouted a warning.

When Linton ignored me, I realized he was deliberately taking us into a foam-filled cleft studded with sunkers that lay between the roaring cliffs and a maze of reefs and islets.

Called Cape Harbour Run, this churning slot turned out to be less than a hundred feet wide and crooked into the bargain. Dories from the abandoned settlement of Cape la Hune used to pick their way through it in calm weather. Dories. *Not* forty-footers. And not in a Force 7 gale.

I do not know how our skipper managed it. He did not offer to tell me, then or later. I suspect he may have succeeded because he really did not care whether he did or not.

When *Geraldine* staggered past the lighthouse at West Point Head and crawled into Fransway, the harbour seemed more like a centrifuge filled with howling squalls and hurricane gusts than a sanctuary. Nevertheless, the wharves were lumbered with herring seiners and draggers sheltering from the storm. Their crews watched in disbelief as *Geraldine* struggled toward them, so far down by the bow she must have looked more like a submarine than a surface vessel. Interest in us was particularly acute because some of the skippers had heard Linton on the radio, and all had been dreading the prospect of having to put to sea in an attempt to rescue us.

Heedless of the weather, several local residents came out on a spray-swept wharf to take our lines. Among them was my friend Leslie Fudge. Now he led de Visser and me to his own small house, where we were warmly welcomed by plump and jovial Carol, who revived us with steaming bowls of rabbit soup.

Hot grub, a belt of rum, and the heat from the blazing wood-stove made me so drowsy I didn't notice the sound of a boat getting underway. It was *Geraldine* setting off again into the teeth of the gale. According to Les, Linton was bound for Rencontre West.

"What the hell for?" I asked incredulously.

"Well, sorr, they've some beer still to the shop there, and Skipper Linton's some t'irsty man."

Carol's eighteen-year-old brother, Calvin, was home from working on a lake boat up in "Canada" all summer. He had planned to spend a while with relatives at the other end of the village but our arrival had scotched that. If he went now it might look as if there wasn't room for us in the house, and that would reflect on the Fudges' ability to provide hospitality. A touchy point. I also learned that it would be necessary for Les to take us to visit every single one of the family connections to show he and Carol weren't trying to hoard us. Visitors had to be shared, just like everything else in an outport.

We had roast caribou for dinner. Les happily told us the deer were plentiful on the high plateau a few miles inland, but the meat we were eating was illegal for, although caribou had always been an essential part of the sustenance of the coast communities, the provincial government had now decreed they were to be "protected" so it could sell hunting licences to sports hunters from St. John's, the United States, and Canada.

My berth for the night was a mattress on the floor of one of the two small bedrooms. John got the narrow bed, which was normally shared by the Fudges' children. Calvin got the daybed in the kitchen, while the kids scrunched in with their parents. The little house was crowded to busting but it felt cosy despite, or because of, the blizzard raging outside. I fell asleep thinking of Les's brother, one of the lighthouse keepers on the Penguins, marooned there long past his relief date because no vessel could get to them.

Next morning Les told us some of the men were going to try to fish despite the foul weather. I decided John and I should go too so he could photograph this mainstay of another time.

Les borrowed a big motor dory from Chesley Pink, and we set out, bundled up to the ears against a bitter wind and freezing spray. It was a hard punch to get clear of the harbour and once at sea we could find only one dory. She was fishing about a mile south of Western Head and pretty well hidden by southerly swells and a cross sea from the nor'easter. It wasn't until we were a couple of hundred yards from her that Les was able to recognize her as his father's boat. Clad in black oilskins, sou'westers, and rubber boots, sixty-seven-year-old Sam Fudge and his partner, Joe Touching, about the same age, were hauling trawls – half-mile-long lines with baited hooks set along them at intervals of a couple of feet. They had set these a week ago and hadn't been able to get back out to them since.

How they kept themselves in the dory I'll never know. They worked standing up in a sixteen-foot cockleshell that was pitching and tossing like a wild thing. We weren't much better off. John could spare only one hand for his camera, and I had to grab his shoulders to keep him from pitching overboard. Sam's little dory kept disappearing from sight into the troughs as we slowly circled her. Each time she went down I wondered if we'd see her come up again, but of course she always did.

Heaving and hauling back on the trawl line, the men were getting an occasional two- or three-pound cod. I was appalled to realize that they were fishing bare-handed though spray was freezing to their oilskins. As their dory plunged and skipped through the breaking seas, they had to perform a weird kind of ballet in order to stay on their feet – and in the boat. It had taken them an hour and a half to row out, and they would be able to fish for only three or four hours before it was time to row in again.

They hadn't even finished hauling the first of three trawls when we'd had enough. We headed in through a wonderful silvery light produced by an unseen sun glinting through snow squalls and we were half-frozen by the time we got ashore, but Carol restored us with bowls of turnips and potatoes simmered all night on the back of the stove with slabs of salt beef and salt-pork ribs. Les called this the finest ballast in the world: "Hold you down in a hurrycane, so it will!"

On Saturday afternoon ("evening" in an outport), we scrambled along the shore path to visit Sam Fudge and Annie, his bright-eyed wife. They were entertaining Joe Touching and Ches Pink in their little square house below the granite outcrop called the Bishop's Mitre.

Uncle Sam, as everyone called him, and Joe had rowed in from the "grounds" that day with about four hundred pounds of small cod in their dory. What remained after they had headed and gutted the fish would be picked up by the collector smack from Ramea when and if she could make the trip.

Joe and Sam would see no cash for their cod. Instead they would get a credit on Penney and Sons' books of about five dollars each toward debts incurred at the company store. As Uncle Sam acknowledged, "'Tis no easy thing to stay squared up on the merchant's books and not drop back."

Sam and Joe's cod would be offloaded at the Ramea plant to be filleted, packed, and frozen mainly by women and girls earning thirty cents an hour. Then the *Caribou Reefer* would carry the frozen fillets to Gloucester to be sold on the U.S. retail market at forty cents a pound. The system never failed to infuriate me. On this occasion, fuelled by a couple of shots of Uncle Sam's white lightning, I let loose a tirade about the plight of the outport fishermen.

Sam and the others listened politely while I ranted about the inequities of the system and the rapacity of the "captains of industry," as Newfoundland fish plant owners liked to be styled. To my disappointment none of the listeners rallied to my theme. A strained silence followed my outpouring, finally broken by Uncle Sam.

"Yiss, me dear man," he said, pondering his words, "'tis hard lines sometimes. Stormy times as might make a man wonder could he do better on a different voyage."

He paused and looked slowly around the table at his relatives and friends.

"The truth on it be, me sons . . . I don't believe as he could. We shapes our course as we wants to, with them as we wants alongside."

His glance drifted back to me.

"The truth on it be, sorr . . . we be well enough satisfied in this old hole-in-the-wall. 'Tis *our place*, you understands. A hard shore betimes, but we wants for nothin'. All the dollars they fellows in St. John's got stowed away won't buy what Fransway's got. We knows where we belongs."

This assertion seemed to change the mood. Everyone, Sam's wife included, had another belt of the white stuff and everyone began having a proper time. People kept dropping in – *sidling* in through a door that was quickly opened and shut against the wheening wind and driving snow. Men, women, and children crowding into Sam's kitchen brought something edible or drinkable. They also brought news.

We heard that *Geraldine* had been driven ashore in Rencontre (which didn't surprise me) but was thought to be salvageable (about which I was dubious). In any event, it seemed certain we would not be sailing home in her. And a big longliner had just come in after having somehow threaded her way through the snakepit of shoals and sunkers surrounding the Penguins to bring off Simeon Fudge, one of the light keepers. He soon showed up at his father's house with his very pregnant wife in tow. They were followed by the crews of the rescuing longliner and of another from Grand Bank armed with bottles of black rum from St. Pierre.

An accordion appeared and things got really lively. There was no room for group dancing, so everyone was content to step-dance solo and, as Uncle Sam happily noted, "like to have stamped me house into a pile of splits [kindling]."

There was singing too – long, narrative songs sung to ancient tunes – about sealers, whalers, captains, widows, lovers, trappers, merchants, even one about a famous life-saving dog with the inexplicable name of Hairyman.

Smoke from pipes, cigarettes, and the roaring stove swirled around us, giving the whole scene a dreamlike quality and reminding me of a "time" I had experienced in an Inuit encampment in the Barrenlands. There was the same uninhibited enthusiasm, the same joyful sense of being part of a life bigger than one's own.

Around midnight Carol, Annie, and the other women served up an iron cauldron full of stewed turrs, with raisin duff and platters of fried cod tongues, cheeks, and sounds on the side. This was followed by lassy (molasses) pudding with rum sauce.

It became too much for John and me so we retreated into a bedroom and crashed. About three in the morning the moan of a steamer's horn throbbed through the tumult inside and outside the house, announcing the arrival – five days late – of the westbound steamer. John and I were galvanized into action for we knew she would pause only briefly. But as we scrabbled into our clothes, Les appeared in the doorway.

"No need to run for it, me sons!" he cried merrily. "*Nonia*'ll not get her mooring lines back 'til you two is snug aboard. Us'll see to that! Wind's in our sails tonight and we be running full and by. You'm in the best of hands!"

I never had the slightest doubt about that.

Uncle Josh Harvey and Skipper Art Baggs.

· 21 ·

The Whale

We passed a good part of the next three years living happily in Burgeo. Although we spent as much of our time as we could on the Sou'west Coast, demands on a writer's life forced us to travel to the Canadian mainland and sometimes much farther afield. During the latter part of 1966 circumstances conspired to keep us away from Burgeo for almost half a year. Not until mid-January of 1967 were we free to come home.

On the fifteenth of that month we boarded the old *Baccalieu* at Port aux Basques. Skipper Ro Penney tugged at the whistle lanyard, and *Baccalieu's* throaty voice rang deep and melancholy across the spume-whipped harbour as she backed out into the stream. Once clear of the fairway buoys, she plunged her head into a rising sea and headed east. Claire and I went below, where most of the passengers were gathered in the dining saloon for tea. As the nor'easter whined through the ship's top-hamper and her old reciprocating engine thumped its steady beat, we listened to the gossip of the coast.

"Heard the gov'mint's goin' to close out Grey River," said one young fellow.

"Hah! By the Lard Jasus!" a stubble-bearded fisherman snorted into his cup. "They fellers in St. John's goin' to need a cargo of dynamite to shift Grey River."

"Fish prices is down," grumbled someone.

"Aye," a companion replied, "but there be a wunnerful lot of deer in the country. Thicker'n flies on a fish flake."

Politely the owner of a Burgeo longliner asked where we had been.

I could not resist a little bragging. "Right across the Arctic from Baffin Island to Alaska. Then to Russia and all the way across Siberia."

No one appeared at all impressed.

"Roosia, eh? Yiss . . . well now, no doubt you and your woman'll be some glad to be back in Burgeo. They's been some wunnerful glut of herring on the go there this winter. Nothin' like it been seen for fifty year."

At dusk next evening the steamer poked her nose into the run behind Rencontre Island and soon thereafter Captain Penney laid her sweetly alongside Burgeo's snow-dusted wharf. As the lines were made fast, an agile little man separated himself from the crowd on the dock and came forward to meet us, his narrow face lit by a smile of welcome. Sim Spencer had come to ferry us home.

He ushered us aboard his dory, stowed our luggage, and cast off. It was bitterly cold and a film of rubbery cat-ice was rippling over the runs between the islands. Unexpectedly Sim shoved the rudder hard over, making the dory heel so sharply that Claire and I slid sideways on the wet thwart. Sim was pointing seaward, shouting one word over the clatter of the engine.

"Whales!"

Beyond the black and glistening Longboat Rocks something else black and glistening surged into view, then sank smoothly from sight, leaving a plume of mist. It was followed by another phantom shape, then another and another. These blurred glimpses made for a thrilling homecoming. As Sim guided the dory into Messers Cove, I asked when the whales had appeared.

"First part o' December . . . along o' the herring scull. They's five, maybe six of they . . . the biggest kind."

As we scrambled up onto Sim's icy stage, the whales were lost to mind in the excitement of our long-delayed homecoming. All the lights in our house were burning. When we stomped across the storm porch and went inside, we found both stoves roaring. Fourteen-year-old Dorothy Spencer had swept and polished every inch of the house. Old Mrs. Harvey had sent over two loaves of oven-hot bread. And bubbling fragrantly on the range was a boiled dinner: cabbage, turnips, potatoes, onions, salt beef, and moosemeat.

Our home, which had stood empty for many months, was as warm and welcoming as if we had never left it. As Sim sat himself down in front of the Franklin woodstove, nursing a glass of rum, other visitors began arriving to welcome us back. Then, with familiar uproar, Albert came dashing into the kitchen bearing a dried codfish in his mouth as a homecoming present from Josh Harvey. Uncle Josh followed close behind the dog, gnome-like, and grinning thirstily as he spied the rum bottle on the table. During our absence Albert had lived with Josh and his wife, and dog and man had spent most of their time together in acrimonious debate, for both were inveterate argufiers.

Rather reluctantly, Albert delivered the cod into my hands. He sniffed in a perfunctory manner at our luggage with its foreign smells from Irkutsk, Omsk, and Tiblisi, then climbed onto the kitchen daybed, grunted once or twice, and went to sleep.

Our homecoming was complete.

Burgeo had changed enormously during the five years we had lived there. Premier Smallwood's centralization program had resulted in the closure of several adjacent outports and the migration of their residents to Burgeo, which was a designated "growth centre." Most of the newcomers had settled on Grandy Island as near to the fish plant as possible, with the result that the eastern portion of that island had been turned into a wasteland of rusting cans, broken bottles, and building debris. The human wastes of an exploding population had combined with the offal from the plant to thoroughly befoul the adjacent shoreline and the little coves where working fishermen kept their boats.

Spencer Lake, ever anxious to bring the benefits of modern life to Burgeo, had opened a supermarket that had put many of Burgeo's small shops out of business. Electricity had spread its web through an increasingly congested maze of houses. In 1962 the first two cars (our Morris Minor and a Jeep for the doctor) had been unloaded from the coastal boat but by 1967 there were thirty-nine cars and trucks rattling themselves to pieces on the stony tracks within the village. They could go nowhere beyond Grandy Island because there were no roads, but snowmobiles had appeared and were snarling out across the barrens in pursuit of caribou.

There was also a fine new school, built to mainland standards, staffed by teachers skilled at denigrating the old ways and arousing in their students a hunger for the golden future promised by the industrial millennium. Unable to assuage that growing hunger locally, some men were now spending most of the year working away, either in lumber and mining camps in the north of Newfoundland or on the Canadian mainland.

Although much had changed – and very quickly – not many local people foresaw the inevitable consequences.

Uncle Josh Harvey did.

In the evenings Uncle Josh would sit at his kitchen table listening disdainfully to a squalling little radio as it yammered out the litany of hate and horror, suffering and disaster, offered up as news. When the tale had been told, Josh would switch off the radio, pour himself a belt of alky, and let fly.

"By the Lard livin' Jasus, dem mainland fellows is gone foolish as a cut cat! Dey got to tinker wit' *every* goddam t'ing dere is. And everyt'ing dey tinker wit' goes wrong. And dat, me darlin' man, dat's what dey calls *progress*!

"Oh yiss, me son, dey believes dey's de smartest t'ings God put on dis old eart', dem politicians and dem scientists and all dem big-moneyed fellers. But I tells ye, bye, de codfish and de caribou be ten times smarter. Dey got de sense to leave well enough be. Dey'll niver blow up de world, no, nor pizzen it to death."

He minced no words when describing what he thought about the new way of life in Burgeo.

"Dem poor bastards works at de plant, workin' for wages and t'inkin' dey's some lucky. I tells you what dey is, me son . . . dey's slaves! De worstest kind o' slaves 'cause dey's *grateful* for de chance to work for Mister Lake in dat stinkin' shithole for de rest o' dere lives so dey can buy a lot o' goddam t'ings is no more use to dey than legs on a fish. Cars, bye, and telyvision. Sewry pipes and houtboard ingines. Dem fellows don't know no end to what dey wants no more. Dey's comin' out the same as people upalong in Canada and America. Dey wants it *all*. Mark my words, sorr, and dey gets what dey wants dey's goin' to choke dereselves to deat' on dere own vomit, and likely de whole world wit' dem."

The pod of fin whales – almost the last of thousands of their kind that had lived in the waters off the Sou'west Coast – remained on our doorstep as it were, fattening on the schools of herring. We had only to look out our southern windows to see them fishing. Standing on our porch we could even hear the mighty swoosh as they surfaced to blow and to breathe.

During Christmas week their occupancy was challenged by a fleet of seiners – great steel vacuum cleaners that sucked up herring with terrifying efficiency. The whales did not take kindly to these newcomers. A few days after the arrival of the seiners, the fin family shifted a few miles eastward to an inlet called The Ha Ha, which the insatiable seiners dared not enter because it was too well guarded by sunkers.

The whales were not alone in The Ha Ha. They shared it with a number of Burgeo men, including the Hann brothers, Douglas and Kenneth, from Muddy Hole, fishing cod nets from open boats and dories. Initially they had been alarmed by the arrival of the whales.

"She's a right tight place, The Ha Ha, and we t'ought, what with near a dozen fleets of cod nets into it, they whales was bound to go foul of the gear or the boats. Well, sorr, they never fouled nothing. They'd pass under our dory close enough a man could have scratched their backs with a gaff, and never bothered us. They went about their business, so us fellows went about ours."

Set in the middle of a mile-wide tongue of rocky land separating The Ha Ha from Short Reach was Aldridge's Pond, connected to The Ha Ha and the reach by two narrow pushthroughs navigable by small boats at high tide. Fishermen used the route through the pond as a shortcut. When, on January 29, the Hann brothers left The Ha Ha heading back across Aldridge's bound for Short Reach and the fish plant, they were disconcerted and alarmed to find a whale in the pond.

"I tells you, me son," Douglas remembered, "she scared we some bad. She were big enough to swallow the dory and room to spare. We never wasted no time. We was out of the pushthrough into Short Reach like a rat out of a red-hot stove! We t'ought it wunnerful queer she'd got herself into the pond until we see Short Reach were pretty near choked up with herring. We supposed a good lot had spilled into the pond – the tide being right high – and the whale must have followed after so fast she never knowed it was too shoal until her belly dragged on the rocks. But she'd so much headway she drove right through; then she were trapped."

When the brothers reached the plant and began forking their fish up onto the wharf, an interested audience gathered to hear their story.

"Think she'll stay in the pond?" asked one of the plant workers.

"More'n likely. Don't see as how she can get clear 'til next spring tide."

"Howsomever," Kenneth Hann would tell me later, "if I'd a knowed what they fellows had in mind I'd have told they she'd gone clear of the pond already."

The Hanns wished the whale no harm. There were other men in Burgeo who did not feel that way.

Shortly after the Hanns finished unloading and departed for Muddy Hole, a big power skiff put out from the plant carrying the foreman and four others. Partway down Short Reach, this boat put in to shore, where each man hurried up to his house, returning in a few minutes with a rifle and all the ammunition he could lay hands upon.

It was almost dusk when the boat slipped through the push-through and entered Aldridge's Pond. The vast shape of a whale rose and spouted dead ahead. The foreman immediately ran the boat ashore. Its occupants leapt out, took hurried aim, and opened fire. The crash of rifle shots echoed from the surrounding hills, with the solid thunk of bullets striking home in living flesh providing an undertone.

The gunners had not brought much ammunition – perhaps a hundred rounds – which was soon exhausted. Reluctantly they returned to their boat and to Burgeo, where they spent the rest of the evening in convivial drinking as they toured from house to house around the reach describing their exploit.

Most of those who heard about the incident assumed the whale would escape from the pond during the night. But, hoping she might fail to do so, nearly a dozen gunners showed up at Aldridge's Pond at dawn on Saturday. These were mostly younger men who spent their springs, summers, and autumns crewing on Great Lakes freighters in mainland Canada, and their winters at home in Burgeo sport hunting, holidaying, and drawing unemployment insurance. However, members of Burgeo's recently formed business organization (an embryonic chamber of commerce called the Sou'westers' Club) were also among those present at the pond that day.

The gunners were not disappointed. Either because the next high tide had been well below the one that had enabled the whale to enter the pond, or because she had already been partially disabled by Friday's fusillade, she was still there. When she surfaced, the sportsmen opened rapid fire.

On Friday she had been able to stay submerged as long as an hour. By Saturday noon she was so exhausted she could scarcely manage to submerge at all. And the rifle fire continued unabated, for she made a spectacular target. As one of the Sou'westers' Club remarked: "It was like a shooting gallery in St. John's at fair time. You guessed where the whale's head would come up, then let fly for all you was worth. If you was quick about it, you could pump five or six bullets into it before it went down again."

Not everyone present that day was happy with the way things were going. One fisherman, who had brought some of his children along to see what a real live whale looked like close up, later told me, "They fellows had no cause to torment that whale. What good were it to they? Happen they kilt it, what was they goin' to get from it? Sell it to the plant for frozen fillets? No, me dear man, 'twere nothing more than a pack of foolishness they was about."

The target practice did not end that day but continued all through Sunday, though in somewhat desultory fashion because Burgeo's stores ran out of heavy-calibre ammunition. Some gunners took to peppering the whale with .22 fire, but the Sou'westers' Club had a better idea. Its members unlimbered the army-issue .303 rifles and service ammunition stored at the local Canadian Rangers head-quarters. And then, as one of the Rangers happily recounted, "All hell broke loose!"

Claire and I, who were too distant to hear the gunfire, knew nothing of what was going on. Perhaps because our aversion to the casual slaughter of other creatures was widely known, a conspiracy of silence seemed to have been invoked against us. None of our neighbours, even including Sim Spencer and Onie Strickland, breathed a word to us of what was happening. Not until Thursday did I hear a rumour that a whale of some sort was trapped in Aldridge's Pond. Supposing it to be one of the smaller cetaceans, a pothead or perhaps a porpoise, I walked over to Sim Spencer's to ask what he knew about it. Rather reluctantly Sim admitted that a "girt big whale" was trapped in Aldridge's Pond. When I asked him why he hadn't told me about it, he was embarrassed.

"Well . . ." he said, fumbling with his words, "they's been some foolishness . . . a shame what some folks does . . . didn't want for to bother you with the likes of that. But now you knows, p'raps 'tis just as well."

He took me to see the Hann brothers. As they described the whale, I realized it was probably a finner – a fin whale – which might mean a rare opportunity to observe one of the truly great whales in life at close range. The prospect was wildly exciting. I was in such a hurry to tell Claire about it that it was not until I got home that Kenneth Hann's concluding words sank in.

"Some people been shooting at it. Could be hurted."

Shooting at it? Appalled, I phoned Danny Green, skipper of the little RCMP patrol boat. Danny had become a friend whom I could rely upon. Did he know what was going on? He knew.

"'Tis one of the big ones, Farl bye. Haven't seen it meself. Might be a humpback, a finner, or a sulphur bottom [blue whale]. What's left of it. The sports has been blasting it since Friday last."

"Are they bloody well crazy? If it lives that whale could make Burgeo famous! What's the Mountie doing about the shooting? It's closed season now anyhow. Nobody's supposed to be gunning."

The answer to my question was "Nothing," but Danny undertook to goad the policeman into action. Meantime I called Curt Bungy, owner of a small longliner, to see if he could take me to Aldridge's. Twenty minutes later Claire and I were aboard and underway.

Claire's journal continues the story:

> It was blowing thirty miles an hour from the northwest and I hesitated to go along, but Farley said I would regret it all my life if I didn't. It was rough and icy cold crossing the Short Reach but we got to Aldridge's all right and sidled cautiously through the narrow channel. It was some hours to high tide so there was only a foot or two of water under us, which made Curt nervous for his boat.
>
> When we slid into the pretty little pond in a dash of watery sunshine, there was nobody and nothing to be seen except a few gulls. We

peered around for signs of a whale, half expecting one to come charging at us and send us scurrying for the exit. There was no sign of one so I concluded it must have left, and I was ready to go below and get warm when Curt shouted. There it was – like a long, black submarine breaking the surface a hundred yards from us, then sliding under again.

We stared speechless and unbelieving at this monstrous apparition. It was certainly a whale of a whale – the men estimated it was between sixty and seventy feet long. A fin whale, Farley said. We anchored in the middle of the pond and began a watch during which the hours went by like minutes as we observed the comings and goings of this huge creature. It was following a circular path around the pond and would surface every now and again to blow and breathe. At first it kept away from us but as time passed it circled nearer and nearer to the boat.

Twice its enormous head came lunging right out of the water. It seemed as big as a small house, black on top and satin-white below. Then down would go the nose and the blowhole would surface followed by a back so long it looked like the bottom of a ship. Finally the fin, at least four feet tall, would appear, then a boiling of water from the flukes and it would be gone again.

We could clearly see the marks made by bullets – white holes and slashes showing the blubber beneath the black skin. They were everywhere from the blowhole back to the fin. It was beyond me even to imagine the mentality of men who would amuse themselves filling such a majestic creature full of bullets. Why try to kill it? None of the people would eat it. But then I wondered if the motive was any different from that of the mainland sportsmen who go out to slaughter groundhogs and other "vermin." It was alive, so why not kill it! But it seemed so much more terrible to kill a whale.

We could trace its movements underwater by the twirls and eddies at the surface from its tail flukes. It came closer and closer to us until it was surfacing twenty feet from the boat. Then it passed right under us. The flippers, each as big as a dory, glowed green

beneath us and the whole unbelievable length, bigger than a boxcar,
flowed under us almost within touching distance, with the ease and
smoothness of a salmon.

As dusk fell, we reluctantly left the pond and the whale (which
we would eventually determine was female). Our time with her had
left all of us half-hypnotized. Nobody spoke until we met the RCMP
boat coming down Short Reach toward the pond, and the constable
shouted that he would not allow any more shooting. I thanked him
and, as we continued on toward Messers, knew I was more passionately committed to saving this whale than I had ever been to
anything. During the rest of the run home, my mind seethed with
possibilities, hopes, and fears. One thing was certain. If the whale
was to survive, it would need more help than I alone could give.

We needed allies, she and I. Uncertain how to proceed, I called
Jack McClelland on our unreliable telephone, and he contacted
everyone either of us could think of who might be willing and able
to help save the whale. Although most of the people he called were
sympathetic, they had no practical assistance to offer. By midnight I
concluded that the only way to muster effective aid was to go public.

I told Claire, "I'm going to call in the press. Give them the whole
story. Perhaps that'll raise enough of a fuss so someone in authority
will act. I know Burgeo won't like it and things could get unpleasant
but . . . what do you think?"

Claire was very much in love with Burgeo. Her reply came from
her heart.

"If you must. . . . Oh, Farley, I don't want that whale to die, but
you'll be hurting Burgeo. People won't understand . . . I guess . . . I
guess you have to do it."

Monday morning I sent a telegram to the Canadian Press outlin-
ing the situation. I was not sanguine enough to expect my brief
account would set the media on fire so I was astounded to realize

before the day was out that the whale's predicament was being treated as a matter of national interest. The telegraph and single wireless telephone circuit linking Burgeo to the outer world was soon choked with demands for information from newspapers and radio stations across Canada and down into the United States. It appeared I had unleashed a tornado, and Burgeo was at its roaring centre.

Some of the many stories broadcast or printed during the following days stressed the assault by gunners on the whale, making it almost seem that everyone in Burgeo had taken part in an orgy of bloodletting. To my shame I did nothing to counter these accusations, mainly because I was immersed in trying to keep the whale alive and in devising ways to free her from the pond.

The week following encompassed a kaleidoscopic confusion of events. They included not only a blizzard of media activity but also an actual hurricane that for a time shut down all communications between Burgeo and the outer world.

Within our narrow confines, we struggled to keep the whale alive but she was losing ground. By the following Saturday (eight days after she had become trapped), Onie Strickland and I found her moving sluggishly, with none of the fluid grace of earlier days. Moreover, she seemed unwilling to submerge and was blowing at distressingly frequent intervals. As she swam lethargically past our dory, we could plainly see that scores of bucket-sized swellings had erupted over most visible portions of her body. The stench of corruption wafted to us as she swam slowly past.

I was unwilling to believe what I saw and smelled. To get a closer look, we rowed the dory to intersect the circuitous path she was laboriously following. When she came abeam of us and was not much more than an oar's length distant she slowly thrust her entire head out of water until it seemed to rear over us like a living cliff. As one cyclopean eye looked directly at us I heard the voice of the fin whale – a long, low, sonorous moan.

We sat unmoving until she submerged and passed beneath us, then Onie turned to me.

"That whale," he said haltingly, "I t'inks she spoke to we."

I nodded, believing as I will always believe that she had tried to span the chasm between our species.

The gravity of her condition was no longer in doubt. Many of the innumerable bullet wounds she had received had become infected and she was honeycombed by harbingers of death. On our way back to Messers, we put in at Firby's Cove to collect the mail brought by the last coastal steamer. As I hurried down from the post office to rejoin Onie at the dory, I was confronted by a man I had known since first we arrived in Burgeo – a man who only a few days earlier had expressed sympathy for the whale and our desire to save her. Now when I greeted him, he responded by spitting at my feet.

"What's that for, Matt?" I asked in bewilderment.

"'Tis for the likes of you! Strangers from away telling lies about we people. Makin' trouble for we. You and that bloody whale! Well, bye, 'tis finished now. And you be the same. Finished in Burgeo. I tells you that without a lie!"

He turned on his heel and strode away.

I had had little sleep for several days so that evening I went early to bed . . . to be brought bolt upright soon afterwards by the jangle of the phone. When I put the receiver to my ear, I heard the mellow voice of the president of the Sou'westers' Club.

"Farley? Just back from Aldridge's. We been down there two hours and there's no sign of the whale. Must have made a run for it last night. Gone right out of it, boy. Gone for certain."

"Gone?" I echoed stupidly.

And then I knew. Knew with absolute certainty.

"She's not gone . . . she's dead."

My caller was not slow to grasp the implications.

"It *can't* be dead! It *must* have swum clear! There'll be living hell to pay if the papers and the radio get the idea it died in the pond. They'll murder us!"

I hardly heard him. "The whale is gone . . . the whale is dead . . ." The words seemed to reverberate through my mind – and to ignite a hard white flame.

"You're right about that. They'll murder the lot of you. Just like Burgeo murdered the whale. Wouldn't you say that's fair enough?"

"Can't we keep it quiet?" he pleaded. "Suppose it *is* dead, it won't float to the surface for days in this cold weather. Can't we just say we think it's gone free? Think about it, Farley. You've lived here five years. It's your town too. . . ."

"No!" I replied coldly. "Not my town any more. I guess it never was."

He was still expostulating when I hung up.

I called a newspaper man in St. John's who had become the whale's unofficial agent. I asked him to contact the media and the scientists and others who were attempting to fly in to Burgeo to aid the whale.

"Tell them it's all over. Tell them they can all go home."

Word spreads fast in an outport. Even as I replaced the receiver, the kitchen door opened and Onie Strickland came quietly in.

"I t'ought as you might be wantin' me dory," he said softly.

As the dory puttered eastward, I thought the scattered, brightly painted little houses, the snow- and ice-encrusted islands, and the glittering tickles and runs between them had never looked more beautiful. I was seeing them again as I had not seen them for several years. Through the eyes of a stranger.

As we turned into Short Reach, we passed a longliner outbound for the fishing grounds. I knew all three of the men standing in the shelter of the wheelhouse, but none of them waved to me, and I did not wave at them. We were strangers all.

The police launch carrying Danny Green and the RCMP constable was already at the pond when we arrived. In tandem we searched the still waters, which were so calm and crystalline we could scan the bottom to a depth of four or five fathoms. The deeper reaches were too dark for our eyes to penetrate.

Eventually we gave up and the two boats drifted together in the centre of the silent, empty pond.

"Any chance she might have got away?" asked the constable.

Knowing that he asked as much out of hope as out of ignorance, I held my tongue and shook my head. It was Danny who replied.

"Don't be daft. She's layin' in nine fathom right under our feet. In three, four days she'll blast and come on top again. And won't that be something for the sports to crow about? Aye, eighty tons of rotting meat and blubber to remind them what heroes they is!"

Then Danny turned to me. His lean, sardonic face was expressionless, as always.

"Don't know who was the foolishest. Them fellows and their gunning or you and your meddling. Way I sees it, you never done that whale no good. You done Burgeo no good. I don't say as you done yourself no good."

I had nothing to say.

The weather turned bad again that night and did not clear enough to allow Claire and me to pay a last visit to Aldridge's Pond until three days later.

It was a frigid morning with frost smoke rising from the tickles and cat-ice crackling under the bow of Onie's dory. A fine enough day for whale watching, but we saw none. There were no distant puffs of vapour hanging like exclamation points over the dark-skinned sea.

The Burgeo whale.

The surviving members of the fin whale family were no longer with us among the Burgeo Islands.

It was a lifeless scene except for a scattering of gulls and three eagles soaring on the updrafts over Richards Head. When I dropped my gaze, we were entering Aldridge's Pond.

The whale was there.

She had been immense in life; now she loomed twice as huge. Bloated with the gases of putrefaction, she floated on her back high out of the water, exposing the pallid mountain of her belly. From a vision of transcendental majesty and grace, she had been transformed into an abomination, grotesque, deformed, and horrible.

She stank so frightfully that we had to fight down nausea.

I cannot say what Onie felt as we drifted toward the monstrous corpse. Claire was weeping quietly. I cannot express what *I* felt.

I believe we were all grateful for the distraction when a chugging engine announced the arrival of the plant's workboat. Manned by some of the men who had shot the whale, it went directly to the corpse. Ignoring our presence, the men secured a loop of wire cable just forward of the mighty flukes. Then the workboat, diminished to insignificance by its tow, put its stern down. White water foamed under its counter as it took the strain. Slowly, ponderously the whale began to move. The bizarre cortege drew abreast of us and swung into the narrow mouth of the pushthrough on its way out to sea, where the corpse could be set adrift.

Unable to surmount the barrier rocks in the pushthrough while alive, the whale floated easily over them in death – returning, now that there was no return, to the heart of mystery whence she came.

Author's Note

Claire and I have written several other books that expand upon aspects of the Newfoundland story.

First Comers

Newfoundland and Labrador were probably the first parts of the Americas to be settled or visited by Europeans. I have written two books about these early ventures. *The Farfarers* (Key Porter Books, 1998) deals with voyages by people from the northern British Isles to Canada's eastern arctic, Newfoundland and Labrador, as early as the eighth century. *Westviking* (McClelland & Stewart, 1965) chronicles the westward voyages and attempted settlement in Newfoundland of tenth and eleventh century Norseman.

Seafarers

I have written extensively about the men and ships who, during the first half of the twentieth century, dared the unquiet waters of the northwestern Atlantic to rescue other men and ships. Many of the rescuers came from the Sou'west Coast of Newfoundland. I have described some of them and their achievements in *Grey Seas Under* (McClelland & Stewart, 1958) and *The Serpents Coil* (McClelland & Stewart, 1961).

Islanders

Wake of the Great Sealers (McClelland & Stewart, 1973) is a composite picture of the outporters of the northern bays during the late nineteenth and early-to-middle twentieth centuries, illustrated with drawings and etchings by David Blackwood. *This Rock Within the Sea* (McClelland & Stewart, 1968) describes the people of the Sou'west Coast in wintertime at home and at sea. It is illustrated with photographs by John de Visser. *Outport People* (McClelland and Stewart, 1983) by Claire Mowat is an account of our life together in Burgeo, and of the inner workings of a Newfoundland outport in the 1960s.

Other Creatures

A Whale for the Killing (McClelland & Stewart, 1972) contains a full account of the circumstances leading to the killing of the fin whale at Burgeo in 1967. *Sea of Slaughter* (McClelland & Stewart, 1984) catalogues modern man's almost inconceivable destruction of non-human life in Canada's eastern lands and seas.

BOOKS BY FARLEY MOWAT

People of the Deer (1952, revised edition 1975)
The Regiment (1955, new edition 1973, paperback edition 1989)
Lost in the Barrens (1956)
The Dog Who Wouldn't Be (1957)
Grey Seas Under (1958)
The Desperate People (1959, revised edition 1975)
Owls in the Family (1961)
The Serpent's Coil (1961)
The Black Joke (1962)
Never Cry Wolf (1963, new edition 1973)
Westviking (1965)
The Curse of the Viking Grave (1967)
Canada North (illustrated edition 1967)
Canada North Now (revised paperback edition 1967)
This Rock Within the Sea (with John de Visser)
(1968, reissued 1976)
The Boat Who Wouldn't Float (1969, illustrated edition 1974)
Sibir (1970, new edition 1973)
A Whale for the Killing (1972)
Wake of the Great Sealers (with David Blackwood) (1973)
The Snow Walker (1975)
And No Birds Sang (1979)
The World of Farley Mowat, a selection from his works
(edited by Peter Davison) (1980)
Sea of Slaughter (1984)
My Discovery of America (1985)
Virunga: The Passion of Dian Fossey (1987)
The New Founde Land (1989)
Rescue the Earth! (1990)
My Father's Son (1992)
Born Naked (1993)
Aftermath (1995)
The Farfarers (1998)
Walking on the Land (2000)
High Latitudes (2002)
No Man's River (2004)
Bay of Spirits (2006)

THE TOP OF THE WORLD TRILOGY
Ordeal by Ice (1960, revised edition 1973)
The Polar Passion (1967, revised edition 1973)
Tundra (1973)

EDITED BY FARLEY MOWAT
Coppermine Journey (1958)

Peter Bregg

Farley Mowat began writing for a living in 1949. He catapulted into our national consciousness as a passionate advocate with his debut, *People of the Deer*, in 1952. He is the bestselling author of forty books, including *Never Cry Wolf*, *Owls in the Family*, *The Dog Who Wouldn't Be*, and *The Boat Who Wouldn't Float*. With sales of more than fourteen million copies in twenty-five countries, he is one of Canada's most successful and beloved writers. He and his wife, Claire, divide their time between Port Hope, Ontario, and River Bourgeois, Nova Scotia.